Teddy:
My Autobiography

Teddy:
My Autobiography

Teddy Sheringham

with Mel Webb

WARNER BOOKS

A *Warner* Book

First published in 1998
by Little, Brown and Company
Reprinted 1998
This edition published in 1999 by Warner Books

Copyright © 1998 by Teddy Sheringham

The moral right of the author has been asserted

A CIP catalogue record for this book
is available from the British Library.

ISBN 0 7515 2844 7

Typeset by Palimpsest Book Production Limited
Polmont, Stirlingshire
Printed and bound in Great Britain by
Clays Ltd, St Ives plc

Warner Books
A Division of
Little, Brown and Company (UK)
Brettenham House
Lancaster Place
London WC2E 7EN

This book is dedicated to my family, with thanks for their help, love and the unending support they have all given me throughout my life: to my son, Charlie, who has given me great happiness and lots of love. To my mum, Shirley, and my dad, Paul; my brother, Jim, his wife, Donna, and their daughters Annie and Alice.

Also to Nicola, with whom I have shared my life and love over the past six and a half years.

And finally to everybody who has helped me throughout my career.

Contents

Contents

Acknowledgements

My thanks to Mel Webb, sportswriter with *The Times*, for listening to my story and helping me so painstakingly to put it into words. Also to Alan Samson and Caroline North at my publishers, Little, Brown, for their help.

Finally, thanks are due to Barry Nevill, my friend and agent, who has worked tirelessly with Mel and Caroline to produce the book, and who now knows my career better than I do.

Foreword

by Terry Venables

When I was asked to write the foreword to this book, I thought about the nice things I could say about my friend Teddy Sheringham, and the more I thought about it, the more I realised that nice things were all I had to say about him. He's that precious combination, an absolutely top-class player who operates on a high level as a human being, too. Talk to other footballers who have played with Ted, and they'll all tell you the same thing – he's a player who's a lot more interested in the fortunes of the team than in making himself look great for the sake of it. As his manager at Tottenham and, later, in the England set-up, I can call to mind literally dozens of situations in which Ted could have chosen to grab the headlines for himself with the spectacular strike, but chose instead to give the chance to somebody else who was better placed. Ted believes that at such moments the team is what matters, not small-minded individualism. To a manager, that sort of player is worth more than can be counted in terms of mere money.

I suppose we're a bit of a mutual appreciation society,

Ted and I. We seemed to click almost from the first moment we came together as manager and player at Tottenham in August 1992. I had been aware of him since he had formed such a potent combination with Tony Cascarino at Millwall, and when he moved on to Nottingham Forest, I kept close tabs on him during his one season there, too. I thought he was the sort of player around whom I could build a side; a thinking, intelligent player who made others look good as well as being a great individual performer himself. I was absolutely delighted when Forest agreed to sell him to Tottenham, and I know the move meant a great deal to Ted, too, because he would be coming to play for the club he had supported as a kid.

That Teddy is a player of high skill is obvious, but there is an extra element to his game in that he's a winner through and through. Not all skilful players have that approach to the game, and when you find one who does, you treat him like gold dust. Teddy doesn't enjoy losing, and he never takes it easy, either in training or in a competitive match. You know that, whatever the conditions, whatever the situation, you can count on him 100 per cent. That's just one side of him, but it's a very important part of a skilful player's personality, take it from me.

When I signed him, I felt he was the last piece I needed to put into the jigsaw at that time to make us a team which could challenge for the top honours, maybe the Premiership title itself. As everybody knows, we didn't get the chance to find out, because I had to leave Tottenham in such sad circumstances, but Ted had made such an impression on me in the year we'd had together at club level that when I got the job as England coach I firmly believed he was a player who could do great things for his country and one I wanted in my squad.

Ted had made his England debut under the managership of Graham Taylor, but I don't think I'm claiming too much in saying that it was under me that he blossomed as a world-class striker. I saw from very early on that he and Alan Shearer were a good partnership who, moreover, enjoyed playing alongside each other, and I felt they were the right pairing to lead us into Euro '96. It was a campaign that was to end sadly, but Alan and Ted – England's SAS – were an undoubted success.

That European Championship showed that England had a front two to compare with any in world football, and I've taken a great deal of pleasure from seeing Ted make the most of his England career. He's a player who makes whole teams work, and he's undoubtedly the best all-round finisher – left foot, right foot, head – I've ever worked with. He scores plenty of goals himself, but it's also significant that no matter who he has alongside him, his partner will always score goals as well. It is sometimes said that great strikers need to be greedy, but Ted proves that that isn't always the case. He's the living embodiment of the phrase 'a player's player'.

Ted has sometimes been criticised for not having the extra yard of pace, but that never bothered me. In my book, speed of thought is just as important as speed over the ground. As long as you get to the right place at the right time, it doesn't matter if you've got there by legs or brain – and more often than not, Ted gets there before anybody else because they haven't thought about it yet. Since the arrival of Michael Owen on the England scene, I have often thought that it would be interesting to see what would happen if he and Ted played together – mind you, it doesn't do any harm to have Shearer around as well. We've got an embarrassment of riches in that department; England are lucky to have three such brilliant strikers.

I regard Ted as a really good friend, which I think sometimes happens in the best manager-player relationships. I think we see in each other a willingness to listen to the other guy, even if you don't necessarily agree with what he's saying. It makes for a good, open relationship in which mutual respect plays an enormous part. I enjoyed being his manager at Tottenham, and it was great to have him in my side when I was in charge of England.

Teddy has proved over the years that he is a loyal, hard-working footballer who graces any side he plays in. He's served his four clubs well and he has done great things for his country, too. He's had a distinguished career, and I don't think for one moment that his great times are over just yet. He's come a long way since his humble beginnings with Millwall. He's a man of tremendous personal warmth and integrity who has brought dignity and honour to his profession, a proud man, if you like – and he has every right to be. I hope you enjoy the story of the life and times of Teddy Sheringham. He has my continued good wishes: he's one in a million.

Terry Venables

Chapter One

The Dream That Came True

I had come a long, long way for this. Teddy Sheringham, professional footballer, aged thirty-three, whose career had had its birth in the unfashionable environs of Cold Blow Lane in south London, was playing in one of the most fabled stadiums in world soccer, part of a team that was competing for one of the great prizes in the game. And it all looked as if it was going to end in agonising anticlimax.

It was two minutes from the end of the 1999 European Cup final against Bayern Munich in the soaring Nou Camp stadium in Barcelona. It was the warm, slightly muggy, night of Wednesday 26 May, and the crowd was broadcasting at a volume of about 5,000 decibels. And Manchester United, my club, the wonderful and inspiring team of which I was such a proud member, were 1–0 down to the arrogant Germans who confronted us. Were we going to end this season of seasons, in which we had already achieved so much, with the crushing disappointment of defeat at the last hurdle? The signs were not good.

And then it happened. We won a corner on the left, and I didn't even realise that Peter Schmeichel had gambled all by leaving the goal he had guarded so brilliantly all night to come into the penalty area. I was on the near post as David Beckham took the kick and big Peter drew three defenders as the ball passed over my head. Time stood still for a moment. The whole of my career flashed before me in a blink of an eye.

Dwight Yorke, so important, so influential in this already historic season for the club, headed the ball back into the thick of the action. One of Bayern's defenders attempted a clearance, but made a mess of it and the ball ended up at Giggs's feet. He hit it back into the danger area with another of his great right-footed shots. I realised it was going wide of the post. I'd found a yard of space; now all I had to do was help it over the line from four yards out. It didn't have to be pretty or spectacular, it just had to reach the net. If it did that, it would be the most important goal in the recent history of Manchester United, football club and football legend.

I wanted to give it a real smack, to rocket over the line like a bullet. In the event, I got just the merest of touches, but it was enough to skew it into the back of the goal. The only possible reason the referee could have had for disallowing the goal was calling me for offside. I knew I hadn't been, because I could see a Bayern defender running towards and past me as I scored, but I sneaked a precautionary look at the referee's assistant, anyway. His flag stayed resolutely by his side. In seventeen years as a professional footballer, I had never experienced a feeling quite like it. We had been virtually dead and buried; now, with a suddenness that was almost scary, we were back in it. And I, a player whose emotions and aspirations had been well and truly put through the mangle of disappointment in this, my second season at Old Trafford, had played a central role in grabbing the lifeline we thought we would never see. Little did I know it at that precise second, but the absolute best was yet to come.

As we trotted back to take up our positions for Bayern's kick-off, a couple of their players remained slumped on the deck, devastated. We had only equalised, but they looked a beaten side. Within a minute, they were.

Our thoughts as play started again were that we were the only winners now, whether the game was settled imminently, in extra time or in a penalty shoot-out. We had watched as the Germans put the trophy in their cabinet long before they had any right to. We had watched as they played to the crowd with twenty-five minutes as though they had it in the bag. We had watched as they betrayed their reputation for playing calm, coldly logical football by getting more flash than we thought any German side would ever get. We hated all that. And now we were watching a team crumbling before our eyes. The self-satisfied smirk had already left their faces; they were frightened men. After eighty-eight minutes of tension-filled play, this was the defining moment of the game, the instant when we knew we were going to win – and, I suspect, the moment they knew they weren't.

David Beckham has said since that he noticed somebody carrying the trophy down the stairs with Bayern's colours already on it, a sight that made him dig that little bit deeper. I didn't see that myself, but if I had done, it would have had the same effect on me. Not that any of us needed much more incentive to go for it now.

The remaining 100 or so seconds of that game will remain with me for the rest of my life. They seemed to be played in super-slo-mo: every move, every pass, every grimace, every tackle, caught in infinite detail. No 100 seconds have ever passed so slowly – it was as though our whole footballing lives were contained within it. Through it all, I held in my head a vision of what was to be. The European Cup was going to be ours and it had been written that I was to play a part in the taking of it. I wasn't going to let the biggest prize of them all slip away now.

And so it was. The ball was played out; Ole Gunnar Solskjaer, who, like me, had been one of United's men-in-waiting all season, picked it up, ran at them and won a corner. Becks took it from the left, I got in front of my marker, rose above him and nodded the ball down, sending it on towards the far post.

It may have gone into the net – I doubt it, but in any event that question became totally academic when Ole smuggled his way in, got his boot to it and rifled it into the roof of the goal. We had done it.

Unbelievable!

Ecstasy!

The treble – the mythical treble that everybody had said was impossible. Except for us: we had always believed in ourselves and our club. I must admit that as the seconds ticked towards ninety minutes we had experienced the first glimmerings of doubt, but now that was over and done with. Even so, there was still a minute of normal time left when Ole completed the most amazing turnaround in the history of European club football. Yet the Germans didn't seem to want to know. Again several of their players lay prone on the turf, and I remember the referee going over to one of them and literally trying to pull him to his feet, telling him that there was still a minute to play.

I couldn't believe their reaction. Had it been us, we would have been desperate to get back into the thick of it, well aware that no game is over until the final whistle is blown. We would have reasoned that if the opposition could have scored twice in a matter of seconds, it was possible for us to score once in the time left. It's a difference in attitude, I suppose, but it was one that didn't reflect too well on Bayern.

Eventually the referee played his last fanfare and it was over. We were the champions of Europe. Now for the longest and greatest celebration of the three we had enjoyed in the previous few weeks.

We would still have had a marvellous season even if we had lost in Barcelona, but defeat would, nevertheless, have been a massive letdown. To have come so far along a road no English team had ever travelled only to lose our way with our destination in sight would have been gut-wrenching. But, thank goodness, it was not, in the end, an experience we had to endure. Instead the Nou Camp was transformed from our temporary workplace to a stage where we could share our moment of glory with our fans. We must have stayed out there for more than an hour, but they wouldn't let us go. We were like the top-of-the-bill act being repeatedly called back for encores and yet another standing ovation. When we finally left the field, our own private celebration did not end until about 6.30 the next morning. Just for once, my son, Charlie – who was there with Nicola, my girlfriend, her sister Mandy, their mum and Mandy's boyfriend – was allowed to stay up and enjoy himself.

It was a great night but, not for the first time in my career, I found that my own feelings were not the same as those of the family and friends who were with me. I suppose it's all a part of being a professional footballer. The event I had been a part of that night was terrific, but there were new challenges ahead. I was wondering whether my performances over the previous few weeks would give me a chance to regain my place in the England squad, or would success be followed by another setback? I've been in this game for too long to take anything for granted. I know that one week it can give you wonderful, unforgettable moments like this, and the next turn on you and give the most colossal kick in the teeth.

After a decent lie-in we arrived back in Manchester at about four o'clock the following afternoon for the most emotional few hours of the lot. I had been looking forward to our journey through Manchester on the open-topped bus. Some of the other lads had told me that it was a great experience, but it exceeded my wildest dreams. Charlie and the other players' kids were with us, and it must have been wonderful for them to be a part of it. I know Charlie, for one, will never forget it.

We were still four miles away from the city centre when we saw the first supporters out to cheer us on. As we progressed down the A56 they steadily increased in number, until by the time we arrived at Deansgate, the main street in Manchester, they had swelled into an unrelieved sea of red and white. Those who were unable to get on to Deansgate itself crammed into the side streets, where, although they would only clap eyes on us for a couple of seconds, they were satisfied that they had seen and honoured the team they lived and died for.

It was an intensely moving experience. I had a huge lump in my throat and tears of emotion sprang to my eyes. I'm a bit prone to that at the best of times – I had to stop singing the national anthem when on international duty a while ago, because it never failed to make me cry. I'm not embarrassed to admit that things like that tug at my emotions. Indeed, I am proud of the fact that

I love my country and my club enough to be affected that way.

My personal postscript to the European Cup victory and all that went with it was an immediate recall to the England squad for our World Cup games against Sweden and Bulgaria. I was wondering whether to pack a suitcase with football gear or clothes for a holiday when England manager Kevin Keegan called me to give me the news. I was exultant. I had been out of his predecessor Glenn Hoddle's squads since the 1998 World Cup finals and the new coach had not called me up for the first few games he was in charge, but now he was proving that I had never been out of his thoughts. It was my reward for having done the business on the field in the previous few weeks.

And so ended an extraordinary season encompassing eleven months in which United pulled off a feat that may never be repeated. We had entered three competitions and had won them all, proving ourselves to be the best team in England over the long run of the Premiership, the best Cup team in the domestic game and, finally, the leading team in Europe in a competition that combined the rigours of a league system with the ability to peak at the right times in the knock-out phase. It was a brilliant finish for the club and for me personally, but there had been times when my feelings and morale suffered badly through a mixture of not being selected as regularly as I would have liked when I was fit and injuries that always seemed to happen at the worst possible time.

As I had got back into pre-season training for 1998–9 after the World Cup, I knew that a section of the Old Trafford crowd held me at least partly responsible for our failure to hold off Arsenal's challenge for the Premiership title in 1997–8. To some extent I understand why. I had been brought in to bolster the forward line with my own particular skills, but after a decent start to the season, when United needed a figurehead up front, I didn't produce. I accepted that, but I knew that fundamentally I was a good player and that I was not the only reason why we had won nothing in my first season at United. At crucial times we were also without four big names: Roy Keane, Gary Pallister, Peter Schmeichel and Ryan Giggs.

So I was looking forward to getting back to work. As well as furthering the club's cause, I wanted to prove to everybody that I could still do the business. Alex Ferguson has often said to me that playing for United is different from playing for anybody else, because other teams always seem to find that extra 10 per cent against us. A good number of Premiership clubs play us as if they were at our ground instead of their own. To them, a draw at home with Manchester United is like an away win over somebody else. I had a season under my belt now, and I had learned that lesson. Now I was itching to test myself under that constant pressure.

Another element to the challenge that faced me was a human one. Early in the season, the club bought Dwight Yorke for £12 million from Aston Villa. That signing gave me food for thought. There aren't too many players in the English game who, like myself, have a legitimate claim to be a striker and combine their goalscoring talents with the type of game I play, but I looked upon Dwight as one of them. I began to wonder whether he had been brought in to replace me. I spoke to Alex Ferguson about the situation, and he said that Dwight was much more likely to play as an out-and-out striker. OK, I thought with some relief, maybe it will be fine after all; perhaps I will be able to play off him. My spirits were boosted further when I chatted to Dwight himself. The message that came through to me was that he wanted to play further forward as the main goalscorer. That was good news for me on two counts. It would be nice to know that such a high-quality striker would be up there for me and it would perhaps enable me to continue with the foraging role I had made my trademark in the previous few years. I think all the existing strikers – me, Coley, Ole, Scholes, even – figured that with such a high price tag on his head, Dwight was likely to be the number one striker and it would be up to us to battle it out for the other position. But that was fine as far as I was concerned – I've never been afraid to play for my place, no matter where I've been.

One of the two big summer arrivals was Jaap Stam. I had the utmost respect for Jaap, although I did think the club had got rid of Gary Pallister a year too early. Those two in the heart of the defence would have handled even the best pairs of Premiership strikers. Jesper Blomqvist was the other new boy, and in my view he was another first-class acquisition. I firmly believe that if Jesper had been at the club in 1997–8, we would have won the title, because when Ryan Giggs was not in the side we didn't have a specialist left-sided attacking player. Ryan is bound to pick up the odd injury here and there, because he's such a highly tuned athlete. His physical condition when he is playing his best football is right on the edge. He's so skilful and so dangerous that he is inevitably the target of close attention. If you want to negate Ryan's threat, you let your most cynical and clinical hatchet man loose on him. Sometimes, if Ryan is really flying, the would-be assassin can't get near him, but there are always likely to be occasions when his brilliance is going to be lost to a game because of the attentions of a lesser, but tougher, footballer. So I welcomed the arrival of Jesper and, having spent a season with him, I now admire him even more.

It was a pretty short pre-season, because not only did we have the comparatively meaningless FA Charity Shield game to play with Arsenal, but we also needed to get into competitive mode quickly for the European Cup qualifiers. I came on as a substitute for the last ten minutes against Arsenal at Wembley but we were already 3–0 down and the game wasn't really going anywhere. There was time, however, for the debut performance of the chant that was to dog me through the season: 'Oh, Teddy, Teddy, he went to Man United and won **** all'. It was great to prove what complete rubbish it was by the end of the campaign, although I expect the morons who chant it will continue to do so. I can live with it, because I had the last laugh: the United fans amended the words to 'he went to Man United and he won the lot'.

I came on as a substitute in the first League game, against Leicester, when we were 2–0 down with about twenty minutes to go. I scored our first goal, and David Beckham got another to give us a 2–2 draw. I got my first start in the second leg of the European Cup qualifier at LKS Lodz and got a decent write-up in the newspapers, although we didn't really play very well, to be honest. Dwight Yorke had not yet arrived, so the manager went with Andy Cole and Paul Scholes.

There was, however, a grim time on the horizon for me. It began in a reserve game. After I scored my second goal of the game I felt a twinge in my knee. I thought little more about it, but that wretched knee was to cause me a lot of pain during the season, not all of it physical. By the time we played Charlton in September, I was out of the side. There was a place in the team to be won and it was terribly frustrating to be forced to sit there and watch while the other guys staked their claims.

For me, playing in the first team is a matter of pride, not money. If a footballer is worth his salt, he always wants to be playing. I know I do. Even if doctors and nurses were paid the kind of money I earn, and I had to live on their salaries, I would still want to be a footballer. It's what I do, what I'm good at. I still want to be the best in a good side. It's not always possible, but it's something I never stop striving for. It's the way I am able to express myself professionally: I have a talent, and what could be more natural than wanting to display that ability? Don't get me wrong – the money you are paid is lovely, and you don't turn it down, but when push comes to shove, it's definitely not at the top of my list of priorities. Achieving most certainly is.

So there I was, out of the side and champing at the bit to get back into it. I tried to use my time sensibly and positively, taking stock, reflecting on what was going on around me and planning what I could do to make things work in my favour again. It was, nonetheless, a trying time. Unfortunately, it was something I was going to have to get used to.

I had barely got myself back in full training again when the day of the Champions' League game away to Bayern Munich arrived. I went along expecting to be a substitute at best, but instead found myself starting the match alongside Dwight Yorke. You don't have to take my word for it that I had a very good game that night in Munich. You can pick up any daily newspaper from 1 October and see it for yourself. If I wasn't the Man of the Match, I know deep down that I must have been pretty close to it. Dwight and Scholes scored in a 2–2 draw, which was a really good result for us.

I flew back to Manchester with the rest of the squad that night feeling buoyant. I thought, the boss has got to pick me now. I know I've had a great game, and so must he. Surely he won't leave me out after this. But he did. He dropped me, relegated me to the subs' bench for the trip the following Saturday to Southampton. He did have the decency to talk to me, explaining that he thought I had played really well and that he was delighted with me, but that he needed to freshen things up. I accepted his judgement – our manager is right a hundred times more often than he's wrong – but it didn't mean I was happy with the situation. I am a proud man who lives to play football, not plays football to live, and all I wanted to do was to get out there. Anyway, there was nothing I could do about it, so I sat on the bench and watched as Yorke, Cole and Cruyff scored in a 3–0 win. I came on as substitute, but it wasn't the same.

I had to face up to the fact that I wasn't really fit. The left knee was still causing me problems. It gave me trouble again against the Saints, then I did it in completely in a reserve game soon afterwards. This time I was to be out of action for two months, during which I began to wonder whether I was ever again going to be fit enough to challenge for a first-team place. The joints in my knee seem to be looser than normal, a quirk that seems to be in my physical make-up, according to the doctors and specialists. It was the left one that was giving me grief now, and as time went on putting up with it grew more and more frustrating. The most annoying thing of all was that after a while I could run perfectly well, but when I tried twisting and turning – simulating match conditions – it would hurt like hell again.

As the weeks wore on and I didn't seem to be getting any

better, I went to the manager and discussed the problem with him. I said I thought I would benefit from getting away for a few days, and he immediately agreed, so I spent a week in Spain. It was good to relax in the sun, but behind the superficial feeling of wellbeing it gave me, I couldn't get my mind off the worry that the longer I went on without getting match fit, the less likely it would be that I would be able to play any sort of part in the first team.

After what seemed an eternity, I did get myself fit again, and having put in two weeks of hard training without any adverse reaction, I was finally available for selection again for the away game with Sheffield Wednesday. It was already the third week in November, and at that point I had appeared in the starting line-up only twice, making four other appearances as a substitute, out of a possible twenty-one games in all competitions.

But when the manager pinned the squad list on the board on the Friday, the name of Teddy Sheringham wasn't on it. I was fuming that I had not been selected. Alex Ferguson called me in and explained that he wanted me to be involved in the Champions League game at Barcelona the following Wednesday, but that he would be happier if I put in an extra couple of days' work on the Saturday and Sunday. The team left on Friday to stay at an hotel overnight. So what did I choose to do instead of training on the Saturday? I went home to London, that's what. Talk about stupid. I don't really know why I did it. I suppose it was frustration at having been sidelined for so long and then, just when I was fit again, I was left out of the squad. I don't know what made me think I had the right to be there, but I suppose it was a bit of a knee-jerk reaction to such a bitter disappointment.

I got back to Manchester for the first-team training on the Sunday in preparation for the Barcelona game, and I thought I had got away with my spur-of-the-moment absence. But the boss knew I had not been in on the Saturday, and on the Monday I was asked to explain myself. I flannelled and tried to beat around the bush by saying I hadn't known I needed to be there on the Saturday, but he saw through that in the blink of an eye. He didn't believe me, he said bluntly, so he was fining me a week's wages and was not going to take me to Barcelona. He wouldn't budge from his decision.

The futility of my actions preyed on my mind all day. In the end I rang the manager and told him, honestly now, that I realised I had been totally out of order, and that it would not happen again. He accepted my apology, but he was not going to change his mind about either the fine or the trip to Barcelona. After that the matter would be closed. I desperately wanted to play at the Nou Camp, which I had seen when I had been in Spain with Nicola the year before. The way I chose to prepare for it was ill advised at the very least. I had taken an unforgivable liberty, and now, quite rightly, I was being made to pay for it. It was a salutary lesson for a thirty-two-year-old who should have known a damned sight better. I was given plenty of time to reflect on it as I sat in front of my television and saw the boys fight their way to a great 3–3 draw with Barcelona.

I hoped the boss would be as good as his word and forget the incident after Barcelona, and he was. I had heard from the odd person here and there that Mr Ferguson was capable of bearing a grudge, but he didn't in my case. The slate was wiped clean. He put me back in the squad the following Saturday for the game against Leeds. I got on to the pitch and played reasonably well as we beat them 3–2 at Old Trafford.

I had a place in the team from the off in the Worthington Cup match against Tottenham. We lost 3–1, and for personal reasons I was not best pleased with the result. There is always a bit of extra ginger in a game against one of your old clubs, and my affection for Spurs made no difference to that – I would have liked us to have beaten them, and I could not pretend otherwise.

As Christmas approached it was time for me to take stock, and I didn't like what I saw. I had been involved in a mere handful of games and had been on the injured list for about three months. There was not much I could have done about the injuries, but I hated what people would be saying about me. There were, I've no doubt, people down south who were writing me off. Coley and Yorkey were going great guns, and I couldn't make any impression on their position of strength. But I had to make myself believe that once I was fit, I would feature again – otherwise I'd have just given up.

Then, disaster of disasters, I got another injury. It was a knee again, but this time the right one. The problem dragged on for weeks and weeks, and finally, after talking to the medical people, the manager suggested I went away for another few days' holiday. This time I went to Barbados with my mum and dad, Nicola and her mum, and we had a great break. I tried to keep fit with some running and the like: it was the end of January, and time was running out.

When I returned the knee was no better, so they gave me an arthroscope, cleaning up the debris around some frayed cartilage in my knee. It was during this time, and the three or four weeks of recovery, that I was at my lowest ebb. The only way I could remain positive was to remind myself that we were still going strongly in all competitions, and there might be some part for me to play when things got really hectic as the season approached its climax. I expressed my unhappiness to the manager, but he told me not to worry: he confirmed that in March and April he was going to need as big a squad as he could get, and he was confident that I would have a role to play for him and for the club.

When I came on as a sub in the FA Cup sixth-round tie against Chelsea at Old Trafford, it was a big day for me. Unfortunately, we could only draw 0–0. I thought I might be useful to the team in the replay three days later, but instead I found myself playing in the final of the Lancashire Reserve Cup against Oldham. What a comedown . . . However, we won 2–1 and I had earned my first medal of the season! I scored one of the goals, too.

Our game ended forty-five minutes before the FA Cup replay, so I showered quickly, made a dash for the television in the players' lounge and got there just in time to see Dwight score our second goal with a lovely chip. It was a brilliantly taken goal, one of the best he scored in a magnificent first season for United. I was glad for him, happy for the club and far from downhearted for myself: now we were in the semi-finals of the FA Cup, and all the time we were still in it, there was a chance that I might still be able to play my part.

In fact I was feeling more and more positive. I still had faith in my own ability, and I knew that on the pitifully few times I had actually got on to the pitch I had played well enough. The manager said he still had faith in me, my fitness was as good as it had been all season and, on the credit side, if I did come more into the action from here on in, I would at least be fresh. It was a question of being patient and biding my time.

I was to feel slightly differently about things a few weeks later. We were still in the European Cup, we were playing brilliantly in the Premiership and our FA Cup campaign could not be going any better. Then came a Premiership game against Wimbledon in early April, four days before our European Cup semi-final first-leg tie against Juventus. I found myself sitting in the stand alongside David May and Wes Brown at Selhurst Park, not even in the first sixteen, let alone the team itself. All my earlier optimism just about drained out of me that night. There was just no way, as far as I could see, that I could come back from this position to be a meaningful member of the first-team squad, whether there was a need for a big squad or not.

By this time Brian Kidd, Alex Ferguson's number two, had left to go off and manage Blackburn and his loss was felt keenly by all of the Old Trafford playing staff. He had formed a powerful link between players and manager and had commanded the respect of us all. The job of an assistant manager can be difficult in that you have to have the confidence of the players at the same time as being the manager's man. Kiddo did it beautifully. In his time he had nurtured the precocious talents of the likes of Beckham, the Neville brothers, Scholes and Butt, to whom he was a sort of surrogate big brother, and yet he identified too with the more seasoned players in the squad, such as Schmeichel, Irwin, Keane and myself. He also knew the game inside out. I didn't know him as well as some of the youngsters did, but in the time we worked together our bond grew steadily stronger. I was sorry to see him go, although I could totally understand his reasons for wanting to move up to the next rung on the ladder and I wished him all the luck in the world.

The consequence of Brian's departure was that for three or four weeks the manager played a more prominent part in the day-to-day activities of the first-team squad and was not able to step back again until he appointed Steve McClaren from Derby to be his new assistant. It was an inspired appointment, because Steve took the job by the scruff of the neck from day one. He had studied the methods of some of the great American coaches in American football and baseball and applied them, very successfully, to football in England in the last year of the millennium. Steve is a pleasure to work with; he represents yet another example of the uncanny knack that Manchester United has of appointing the right people, and a lot of the credit for that has to go to the manager.

Meanwhile, back on centre stage, we were approaching the most vital part of the season and my spirits were as low as they had been all year. We were going into the first leg of the semi-final of the European Cup and I honestly believed at that moment that my own season might well be over. The words of the 'Oh, Teddy, Teddy' chant were beginning to take on an uncomfortable ring of truth. I remembered the night of the away game against Newcastle in March, when I had been on the bench but not got on to the field. That night I was flying down to London to be present at a surprise sixtieth birthday party for Bob Pearson, the man who had given me my first chance in football at Millwall. My debt to Bob was huge, and I wanted to be there, but I was in no mood for it until I met Martin Tyler, the Sky Sports football commentator, who was more of an acquaintance than a friend, but a man I respected. Martin was great. 'Don't give up', he told me. 'There's plenty of time yet.' His words came back to me the night of the match against

Wimbledon, but I was finding them harder and harder to believe. I was constantly arguing with myself. 'Come on, you're still a decent player, you know you've still got something to offer,' I would tell myself.

I was on the substitutes' bench for the first game against Juventus. As I remember it, we were allowed more subs that night – I think it was any three from seven – and I believe, as I look back on it, that the ten minutes I spent on the field as a replacement for Andy Cole represented the turning-point in my season.

I came on when we were 1–0 down and was instrumental in the Ryan Giggs goal that gave us a 1–1 draw. As well as that, I gave the Juve defence something to think about with a couple of cute little flick-ons. I hope I left them with the feeling that if Sheringham, who was not even in the starting line-up, could give them problems in the final ten minutes, then they would have their work cut out to subdue us in the second leg. And ten minutes was all it took.

I left the field that night feeling good about myself and about the contribution I had made in a workmanlike display. I had a personal as well as a professional need to be involved in these games that was all to do with pride in my own performance and being able to hold my head up, but when it came down to it, my private desires were secondary to the greater good of the team. If the team was succeeding, then that made me happy, too.

It was a crazy time. No sooner had one massive game come and gone than there was another one to cope with. This time it was the FA Cup semi-final against Arsenal, our arch-rivals. I was buoyant as we travelled to Villa Park for the game, but then the manager told me that he was playing Cole and Yorke up front and Solskjaer would be on the bench. There was to be no place for me. In a flash, my mood swung from exhilaration to total deflation. I had handled disappointments before, but this was getting beyond a joke. It was starting to become the story of my life.

I sat in the directors' box, slap-bang in the middle of a section of rabid Arsenal fans who were singing that song. When Roy Keane got the ball into the back of the net I gave them hell. I was really dishing it out until David May, who was sitting beside me, tugged my sleeve and broke the news that the goal had been disallowed for offside. Boy, did I feel an idiot.

We held out for a draw and I kept hoping against hope that I might be given the chance to feature in the replay at Villa Park three days later. The fixtures were piling up now and the pressure was unrelenting – if we defeated Juventus and got into the European Cup final, we would have eleven games to play in a mere forty-three days. If we were to pull off the most remarkable feat in the history of European club football and achieve the legendary treble, we would need to use every resource at our disposal, the greatest of which was the depth of strength in our first-team group. The manager had been rotating his squad throughout the season and he had got it unerringly right – the results were testimony to that. Of course, he did have the advantage of being able to pick eleven men from a squad that contained eighteen internationals, and he knew that no matter what he did to change the composition of the team, he would be affecting its strength by probably no more than 5 or 10 per cent. But the fact that the risks he had to take were lesser than those taken by most other managers didn't change the fact that he had taken us through the season without making the merest hint of a mistake. He had said repeatedly that he had faith in every last one of us, and now he proved that in the FA Cup semi-final replay. Having picked Cole and Yorke for the first game, he now put Solskjaer and me into the team in their place. He also rested Ryan Giggs and played Jesper Blomqvist wide on the left. It was right for the team and the situation we were in, and, on a personal level, it was great for me.

I had a hand in the first goal, scored by Beckham, and then things went a bit pear-shaped. Arsenal got back into the game and equalised after sixty-nine minutes, then Roy Keane, our captain and talisman, got sent off. Having been in a position of strength, we were now up against it. I had played pretty well, I thought, but I was nevertheless replaced by Paul Scholes. It was a chastening experience to walk off the field with the jeers of a section of the Arsenal fans ringing in my ears, but I tried to grin and bear it. Most of the time the things football supporters shout at me just go straight over my head, but if there is one club in the world who I can't stand being taken off against, it's Arsenal. As I watched the remainder of the game, some of the insults that were thrown at me were downright vicious, but most were pretty good-humoured, and for all that they were coming from the detested Gooners, I could see the funny side of a lot of them.

In the last minute of regular time Arsenal were awarded a penalty when Phil Neville brought down Ray Parlour. Their supporters informed me once again that, in their opinion, I was probably not going to win anything again, and I must admit I didn't like the look of the situation much, either. I breathed again when Schmeichel pulled off a brilliant save from Bergkamp's spot-kick. We were still in it, but now we had thirty minutes of extra time to contend with and only ten men with which to do so.

The lads played most of the extra-time period defensively,

and the game was heading towards penalties when Ryan Giggs, who had come on for Blomqvist with half an hour to go, scored what was universally – and properly – recognised as the goal of the season. It was a truly phenomenal goal by a footballer who can do things others can only dream about. When the ball was given away by Arsenal's Patrick Vieira, Giggs took possession and embarked on a run that defied belief. He went past one defender, then another and another, two more, and finished it with a searing shot that gave David Seaman no chance and threatened to burst the back of the net. From first touch to final shot it took just seven seconds, but the memory of a truly wonderful goal will endure for a lifetime.

When Ryan scored we had played twenty minutes of the extra time. Ten minutes later we had clinched our place to play Newcastle in the FA Cup final. For the club, reaching the final was a great thrill; for me, reaching it by beating Arsenal was a bonus. We were still on pace for a record; we had run more than three laps without mishap and were now coming off the final bend. The home straight would not be easy and we would have to beat off the threat of a variety of high-profile challengers, but we were still convinced that we could summon up the strength for a final burst for the line.

Three days after the semi-final replay we were at home to Sheffield Wednesday and I produced possibly my best performance of the season to date. I scored one goal in a 3–1 victory and made the other two, and all of a sudden a few people remembered I was still at Manchester United and could still play a bit.

I thought I had a chance of playing in the second leg against Juventus, but Cole and Yorke were the chosen men on that night of pounding passion, a night that looked as if it was going to turn out horribly wrong for us when Filippo Inzaghi scored twice in the first ten minutes. Juve – Deschamps, Davids, Zidane, Inzaghi and all – were a great team, we knew that, but so were we. It was horrible sitting in the Stadio delle Alpi knowing you could do nothing to help. We could identify with our pals out there, though, and we knew without a doubt what they would be thinking: that it would only take one goal to get us back into it and we needed no more than a 2–2 draw to get us through on away goals. Neither the team on the field nor the one in the stand ever lost its sense of optimism that it was going to be OK.

It was somehow appropriate that the man who put us back into contention was Roy Keane, our captain and an heroic figure all season. Those of us in the stand went barmy, and, ten minutes later, our celebrations were even wilder when Yorke scored the equaliser with a great diving header. As of this moment, we were in the European Cup final. After a performance of superb technical merit in the second half, Andy Cole put the icing on the cake by nicking the victory for us with six minutes to go. The mighty Juve had been cracked.

In the next twenty-five days we had to play six games that would either confirm us as Premiership champions or topple us from the head of the table. We had a clear goal-difference advantage over Arsenal, but it was much more important just to keep on picking up points. We drew 1–1 with Leeds, our sworn enemies, then I partnered Yorke in a 2–1 win over Villa. I was on the bench for the 2–2 draw against Liverpool, but played against Middlesbrough, who we beat 1–0. The points were nice, but Arsenal were scoring goals for fun: they put five past Wimbledon and got six against Middlesbrough. From having had a ten-goal advantage, we were now level on points and just one goal in front. There were two games left. It was make-or-break time.

We had Blackburn away and Tottenham at home, and they had Leeds away and Villa at home. The tension leading up to this final phase of the season was unbelievable. I watched the Leeds–Arsenal game on the television with Nicola, and there were times when I could hardly bear to watch. Good as Leeds were, I couldn't see them beating Arsenal, but it was a nice little irony that they, possibly our biggest rivals, should produce a magnificent professional performance to defeat the Gunners with a Jimmy Floyd Hasselbaink goal fifteen minutes from the end. We still had to play those last two matches, but Leeds did us a huge favour that night at Elland Road. I have to come clean: when Hasselbaink put the ball in the net, I was hiding behind the bar in my flat, afraid to look.

On paper, we should have beaten Blackburn convincingly the next night, but Brian Kidd's team were fighting for their lives in the Premiership and they played way above established form. For probably the first time in the whole season, we let the situation get to us a bit, I think, and although we pounded them, they showed outstanding courage in resisting us. In the end it was a goalless draw; less than we had hoped for, but adequate. Now we knew what we had to do – we had to beat Tottenham at home four days later. If we did, it didn't matter what happened when Arsenal met Villa, who had faded so badly after being right up there in the title race for the first two-thirds of the season.

After a season of high achievement and brilliant football, the last three games were the ones that really mattered: the final Premiership match, the FA Cup final against

Ruud Gullit's Newcastle United six days after that and, four days later, the game to end them all against Bayern.

I was lucky enough to be picked to start against my old club, the club of which I had been a lifelong fan, alongside Yorke, while Coley and Ole were on the bench. It was a major boost to me that the manager had demonstrated his faith in my ability to do a job for him in such a vital match. And as luck would have it, Tottenham went and scored the first goal, Les Ferdinand putting an uncanny lob past big Peter. The reaction of the Spurs fans was extraordinary. They knew that with that goal Ferdinand might just be handing the title to Arsenal. I don't think they knew whether to laugh or cry, for there is nothing Tottenham supporters want less than any success for their north London neighbours.

I have to pay credit to George Graham's men for their performance that afternoon. There was nothing left in the season for them, but they played as though they were fighting for survival. It was, I suppose, no less than we should have expected from any side managed by George, a man who had been a formative influence on me in the early stages of my career.

We got back into the game with a superb goal from David Beckham, but my own contribution ended at half-time, when I was replaced by Coley. I could scarcely believe my ears when the manager told me he was sub-stituting me, because I felt I'd done my bit in the first half. Having shown his belief in me, now, I felt, he was bringing me down. He was very consoling, assuring me it was nothing to do with the way I had played and, of course, I accepted that. But the fact remained that my League season was over, and it was a blow for it to end like that.

It should surprise nobody, however, that once again Alex Ferguson had made exactly the right move at precisely the right time. Within two minutes Coley had scored our second goal. After that we played out the rest of the game without trouble or incident. Naturally, I was elated, because after such a stop-start season I had ended up winning the first major honour of my club career, but I have to say that I would have liked to have been on the field at our moment of triumph. It is only a twinge of disappointment, though, and insignificant in the greater scheme of things.

From the Tuesday to the Saturday it was full steam ahead in preparation for the Cup final. At the beginning of the week I was optimistic about getting into the team, but by Friday somehow I knew in my heart I wasn't going to be in his starting line-up. I'd got to know the manager and his methods over the couple of seasons I'd played for him, and I could just sort of tell from his body language that he wasn't going to include me.

My worst fears were confirmed at our hotel on the morning of the match when the boss came into the room I was sharing with David May. He sat down and, coolly and calmly, told me that I was not going to start the game but that he intended to use me at some point, probably after half-time. I took it pretty well, I think, because I was expecting it, really, but I was devastated inside. I thought that at thirty-three, this might be my last chance to win the FA Cup, and now I was going into the game on a promise I had no idea the manager would be able to keep.

In the event my chance came earlier – much earlier – than I had anticipated. There were five of us on the bench – Raymond van der Gouw, Dwight Yorke, Jaap Stam, Jesper Blomqvist and me – and when Roy Keane was injured, only eight minutes into the game, two thoughts passed instantly through my mind. First, that it was a small disaster for us to be losing Keaney, and second, there was no way it would be me who got on to the field. I thought Jesper would be the one, and logically I could have no quarrel with that. But to my surprise, the manager told me to get warmed up and no sooner had I started to do as he asked than he was beckoning me over and telling me to get out there. Yes! I went up front with Coley, with Ole on the right and Becks in the middle. And within a minute, I had scored the first goal in the FA Cup final.

I controlled a pass from Andy, played the ball round one defender and through somebody else's legs to Scholesy. He gave me a beautiful little return pass and I just went on and slipped the ball through the goalkeeper's legs.

On Cloud Nine, I continued to play well as the team's fortunes went up and up. I set up the second goal for Scholes, in the second half, and almost scored another myself when I chipped the goalkeeper and hit the top of the crossbar. This was what this game was all about and I was loving every second of it.

The Man of the Match award I was given after our 2–0 victory was great, but much more important was the fact that I had participated in the game that completed the double for us. We had a lovely meal together that evening, me, my family and my friends, and got to bed ahead of the 2 a.m. curfew. Nobody was going to take advantage of that, there was too much at stake in four days' time.

Two down, one to go. But would I be given an opportunity to help my club in their bid for the longed-for treble? In the previous few weeks I had played better than at any time in my two seasons with United – including the early months of 1997–8, when I was scoring a few goals. I felt I had proved that I was a big-match player who could rise to the occasion, but at the same time I prepared myself for the possibility that I might not get a place.

And that, of course, was how it turned out. The manager told David May and I on the Monday that we would not be playing from the start, but that we should prepare ourselves for anything. We both put a brave face on it, but I know I can speak for David as well as myself when I say that we were terribly disappointed.

The Nou Camp stadium is everything you could imagine, and more. We each had a locker – mine belonged to Sergi, the little left back – and we trained on the pitch on the Tuesday night. It was a wonderful playing surface, like a bowling green. If I didn't get to play on this field of dreams the next evening, I knew I would regret it for the rest of my days. In these circumstances, knowing you would get a medal if you were an unused substitute was just beside the point. Playing in a match of this calibre at such a terrific arena is the pinnacle of a footballer's life at club level. It doesn't get much better than that.

On the big night a dew on the ground made it a perfect surface on which to play a European Cup final. As I watched from my place on the sidelines, we suffered an early setback when Basler blasted a free kick past the defensive wall and into the net before Peter Schmeichel, the old warhorse who was keeping goal in his last game for the club, could move. But we were not downhearted. We took the game to Bayern who, strangely for a German side, seemed hell-bent on feeding long balls to their central striker, the powerful Carsten Jancker. It was a bit at odds with what we had come to expect of German football, with its considered, practical approach to the game and its nuances. Organisation was their watchword, and they usually played solid keep-ball, moving the ball through the midfield and getting the opposition running about. And here they were playing like Wimbledon. As for us, we were not at our most convincing in the first half. Sure, we were taking the game to them, but we could not quite seem to make it gel.

At half-time the manager came over to me and told me that if things had not changed, I should get ready to go on after about twenty minutes. Well, we still hadn't broken them down by the time those twenty minutes of the second half had elapsed, and I was straining at the leash. Already the Germans were showboating. That infuriated me, because I felt it showed that they didn't respect us as opponents. So when my chance came to run out on to the pitch, I wanted us to win so much it almost hurt. We chucked everything at them, but still could not seem to make the final, telling thrust and the game moved into the last few minutes with us still trailing 1–0.

We would have to produce something special quickly, because we had played eighty-eight minutes without scoring, despite coming close to it on several occasions as the tempo hotted up and the final whistle got nearer.

We never lost our belief. We knew that we were a good side, and that we should win the match. But with two minutes to go, it didn't look likely. And then we won that corner on the left, and David Beckham trotted out to take the kick. As we took the corner on the left, I didn't even realise that Peter Schmeichel had gambled all and had joined us in the Bayern penalty area . . .

And the rest, as they say, is history.

Chapter Two

Leaving Tottenham

Fate has some surprising twists in store for us all, and you never know what is around the next corner. It is strange, when you think about it, that it took one of the saddest events of my life to present me with the opportunity of realising that great dream of winning the treble with Manchester United.

It was the end of a love affair. Like all such grand passions, it did not end without pain, hard words, recriminations. The wounds went deep, and will remain with me for ever. The break-up left me confused and hurt but most of all angry. There is no hope of reconciliation: words were spoken which can never be erased.

Ever since I was a kid growing up in Highams Park, on the north-eastern outskirts of London, I had loved Tottenham Hotspur. When I was kicking a ball about with my mates I wasn't on the Rec., I was at White Hart Lane; I wasn't hoofing it between a couple of piles of coats, I was scoring the goal that gave my favourite team the League title or the FA Cup.

Years later, the dream became reality. Me, the lad who

had been good enough to play for my county only once. Me, who had once suffered the indignity of being lent to Fourth Division Aldershot, long-since defunct as a Football League club. Me, Teddy Sheringham, professional footballer. And yes, I did score goals for Tottenham. I got to play for England, and to make a success of it. Life should have been good, and it was, for a while – under the man who brought me back to London from Nottingham Forest to play in the famous white shirt with the cockerel on its breast and who ultimately made me what I was. Terry Venables was that man's name, and I shall never be able to thank him enough for what he did for me.

Yet even in those early days there was trouble in the air. Venables, hailed as the saviour of Tottenham when he joined them in 1991 as chief executive, was having a spot of difficulty with the chairman, and it was eventually to lead to his departure from the club he had once played for himself. The chairman, Alan Sugar, had made his mark in the world with his company Amstrad, the firm which brought the personal computer to the masses. Like all successful men, he was used to getting his own way, and it did not seem to matter to him whose feelings he hurt in the process.

Unfortunately, you can't treat human beings in the same way as you treat bundles of computer chips. I have always found that good man-management calls for an ability to listen to what the other bloke is saying. You don't have to agree with him, but at least you listen. Alan Sugar didn't listen. Alan Sugar did handle people as if they were no more than bits of hardware. It might have been the way to run a giant electrical firm, but it sure wasn't the way to run a football club.

In Terry Venables, Sugar met his match. Venables, thank heavens, has never been the sort of individual who will do as he's told if he thinks that what he's being told to do is wrong. He had all sorts of run-ins with Sugar, and, as everybody in football knows, it all ended in tears when Terry was ousted from the club.

When he brought me to White Hart Lane in 1992 I believed that we were on the brink of achieving great things. In my one full season with Terry at the helm there was a sense that we were working towards making the club one of the best in the country. I always got on really well with him. I appreciated him and I felt he appreciated me, both as a footballer and as a person. Unlike the chairman, he did listen, regardless of whether he agreed with my view of things. I think he liked me, in the same sort of way as he liked Neil Ruddock, a guy I'd played with or against ever since we were kids.

When Terry eventually left the club, 'Razor' Ruddock kicked up a big fuss and his wife was pictured outside Sugar's house protesting about Terry's departure. I didn't want to get involved with that kind of thing. When you sign for a club, sure, you sign for a particular manager, but you also sign for a tradition, for what the club means to you, so although I was upset, I knew that life would have to go on. I didn't want to throw away my future with the team I'd always wanted to play for and do well with for the sake of an outburst that wouldn't do anyone any good. I'd seen other managers I liked and respected get the sack. It's a sad fact of life in football. I took the view that I didn't know all the ins and outs of everything, so although I was upset I made up my mind that I would do my best for the new manager and give him my best shot.

Ossie Ardiles, another of White Hart Lane's favourite sons in his playing days, was chosen to replace Terry after he resigned from West Bromwich Albion at the end of the 1992–3 season, and for a while I thought things were looking up. It seemed as though my dearest wish – that Tottenham would sign top-flight players and make themselves a power in English football – was going to come true. But from such promising beginnings our development was allowed to stagnate. Ossie brought the German sensation Jürgen Klinsmann to the club at the start of 1994–5, and although he had one great season with us, other signings, notably the Romanians Gica Popescu and Ilie Dumitrescu, were not nearly as successful. In spite of Klinsmann's brilliant if short-lived presence, it became pretty obvious that my hopes that there might be a new spirit abroad at Tottenham had little if any chance of coming to fruition.

After a long honeymoon period, Ossie's folk-hero image took a battering and the fans, like me, sensed that the wheels were coming off Tottenham's attacking machine. Ossie's position grew more and more difficult and in the end he had to go, for the sake of the club, and not least for his own. He was eventually fired in November 1994. By the end of the season his three foreign stars had left as well.

It was said that the next manager, Gerry Francis, would be given the buying power to transform the club's fortunes, but I got the feeling that the club – and particularly the chairman – had been stung by the Klinsmann, Popescu and Dumitrescu transfers. Indeed, the chairman let it be known that he felt he had got his fingers burned the year before and wasn't going to allow it to happen again. 'Carlos Kick-a-Balls', he called the big-money foreign players, and 'Johnny Foreigners'. He said he wasn't going to spend major amounts of money for players to come in for a year then leave. He said he wanted commitment and team spirit. I, too, firmly believe in those virtues, but you must have the quality there in the first place before you can even think of getting the team ethic going.

Sugar's attitude may have been partly understandable, but it wasn't the way to move the club forward. It was a desperate period for me. There I was, playing my heart out for a club whose ambition, as far as I could make out, was zero. We weren't even competing at the top level, let alone getting close to winning major honours. And yet still I was so passionate about helping the club on to bigger and better things that I wasted more than a year of my career and my life keeping my doubts and frustrations to myself.

During that time, a lot of people – Spurs fans included – told me I should get out. 'It's not doing you any good,' they said. 'Move to another club before it's too late.' They were right – I know that now, but in the back of my mind I still clung to the hope that things would change; that we would become a really strong outfit and end up winning things. I wanted Tottenham to be like the Tottenham it had been in the eras of Glenn Hoddle the player and, later, for a while, Ossie Ardiles the manager. In my eyes, it was the best and most stylish club in London – it still is, in spite of everything. But it just wasn't happening.

As if that wasn't enough to get depressed about, there was also my relationship with the chairman, which started off OK, became indifferent and finished in a complete breakdown of communication. I've no doubt that I played my part in that, but only because I've always been a straight talker who states his opinions honestly in the belief that people respect you for that. I found out pretty swiftly that Alan Sugar did not like plain speaking when he was at the receiving end of it and did not respect me for it.

My first impression of the chairman was created at a meeting he had with the playing staff to give us a new-season pep talk, when he walked in wielding an unusual visual aid – a baseball bat. He had got on in business, he told us, by knocking anyone who was in his path out of his way, and he expected us to do the same. We were a bit nonplussed. Clearly he viewed football as a business, and I wondered then how much he knew about the game itself.

The first conversation I remember having with him took place when he came to our training ground at Mill Hill one day. The facilities there were terrible. We used to have four showers that operated for about three seconds at a time, and you had to keep pressing a button to get the next three seconds' worth. A nice hot bath after training, a bit of massage maybe, some nice towels, soap and shower gel shouldn't have been too much to ask for, but there was none of that. Anyway, the chairman was taking a look round the changing rooms and in passing he asked us all in a general sort of way if everything was all right. It wasn't, so, being the kind of person who speaks his mind, I said that the facilities were a disgrace. I wasn't being mouthy or anything: the question had been asked and I was just pointing out that I didn't think things were very good.

To be fair to the chairman, within a couple of weeks we had a bath installed and the changing rooms were sorted out. I thought that reflected well on him; that he was the type of man who got things done. However, later events seem to indicate that he did not take kindly to my response and never forgot it.

About three months after Ossie's arrival, we were playing Manchester United at Old Trafford when I felt something go in my right knee and had to go off. I was told that I would be out of action for only a couple of weeks, but that fortnight became a month, then six weeks and then two months. It was a worrying time for me, because it got to the point where I didn't know if I was ever going to play football again. I was pretty desperate, to tell the truth. Anybody who's ever played professional football will tell you that at times like that, when you're sidelined with what you fear might be a career-threatening injury, you need a bit of reassurance, a quiet word of encouragement. So what did I get from the chairman? A rollocking of the first order.

I was in the treatment room one day when Sugar walked in, and without even asking me how the knee was doing, launched into a tirade the like of which I had never heard before. I was a Terry Venables man, he said; I had no commitment to the club; I was feigning injury. It was an astonishing attack and, coming as it did three months or so after the damage to the knee, when my worries were at their height, about the last thing I wanted to hear. I was shocked at first, then angry, and I told the chairman I was amazed by what he was suggesting. 'How dare you question my professionalism in that way?' I snapped. 'Don't ever accuse me of anything like that again.'

I was at a really low point just then, but in spite of Sugar's insults I did get mended – though it was not to be the last time it gave me problems. The medics eventually went into the knee, found a tear in my cartilage, which was finally removed, and gave me a couple of arthroscopes and some injections which cleared up the trouble. I was pleased, naturally, that I still had a Premiership career, but Alan Sugar's words that day have stayed with me ever since. Nobody had ever questioned my professionalism. It was something I prided myself on. In retrospect I felt it said more about Sugar than it did about me, and tried to forgive him. It'll be a long time before I forget, though.

That was the first confrontation I had with Sugar, but it was far from being the last. The next came when I agreed to sign a new contract. I had spoken to Ossie about it, and everything was progressing nicely until the chairman got involved, from which point things went rapidly downhill. He brought the same style to dealing with the issue as he had shown in the treatment room that day. He didn't speak *to* me, just through me or down to me. His approach did not feature any consideration of what points we needed to talk about to sort out a deal. He just waded in with all guns blazing. 'Are you going to sign or not?' he demanded. 'Do you want to be at this club or not? If you do, sign. If not, do the other thing.' I thought it was a very strange way for somebody to be talking to a person he presumably wanted to stay at the club. And I wasn't picked out for special attention: I found out afterwards that he apparently treated everybody the same way. It was an illustration of his view of what football and footballers were all about. With him everything was black or white, with no room for discussions or negotiations about anything.

I came pretty close then to telling him what he could do with his new contract, but thinking about the situation calmly, I reasoned that whether or not I got on with the chairman didn't really matter when it came to me doing my job. OK, I didn't like the way he did business, but running the club was his responsibility. I'd let him do that the way he wanted if he let me get on with being a professional footballer. Reaching this conclusion had one big bonus: it taught me how how to play the game. I knew exactly how I would behave towards him the next time anything like this happened. From that moment on, my relations with Sugar were hardly cordial.

I began to feel increasingly alienated from the chairman. In the summer of 1995, Klinsmann and Popescu were sold. Under Gerry Francis, we had achieved mid-table respect-ability, but no more. In the close season I was at a press function at the Sports Café in the Haymarket launching a new boot with the people I had a deal with at the time. It was a day or two after Gerry had lashed out £4.5 million for the Crystal Palace forward Chris Armstrong, who had been in a spot of bother with allegations of drug-taking, and the press men there asked me what I thought of the signing.

I must confess that Chris's arrival had surprised me a bit. Nicky Barmby was still at the club at the time, and he had been told that he would be playing up front with me, the following season, which was only a couple of weeks away. I said I was pleased that Chris was coming, but added that I didn't really know that much about him. I admitted to my slight surprise at his signing, and I said that, having played up front with Barmby under Terry Venables, I was looking forward to doing so again. That was the extent of my comments. There was no way I was going to slag off Chris just when he'd joined the club, but of course I was wondering whether what I'd been told about Nicky and me playing together was now perhaps not going to happen, and where Chris's presence in the side would leave Nicky and myself. However, the tabloid press, ever-alert to what they perceived might be a story, knew that a press conference had been called at Tottenham at four o'clock the same afternoon, which turned out to be the announcement that Darren Anderton had signed a new contract. The chairman, who was in attendance, was confronted by the press, and, as later events were to prove, immediately went on a slow burn.

The next morning all hell broke loose when certain sections of the press reported that I couldn't believe Tottenham had paid £4.5 million for Chris Armstrong. I was totally astounded, but I shouldn't have been: I knew how the press worked, changing quotes and putting their own spin on them to build up the particular story they were after. It had happened before and it would happen again. To add insult to injury, there were one or two other things which the tabloid boys turned round for their own ends. For example, I had been asked how I thought Arsenal were going to do the next season, and had said that they had a good manager – Bruce Rioch, once my manager at Millwall – coming in, and some good players, and I thought they might have a much better season. In the papers that became: 'Sheringham says that Arsenal are going to have a much better season than Tottenham.' I did not utter those words, or even suggest such an opinion.

The following day we were due to report for our first day of pre-season training. Feeling that I had to nip this thing in the bud before any more damage was done, I got Chris's telephone number from the club and rang him. He wasn't in, so I left a message on his answering-machine assuring him that I had not said what I had been quoted as saying in the papers, that I was terribly sorry that it had come out the way it had and saying that I would see him at training the next day. When Chris came home and listened to my message, he immediately called me back to tell me not to worry; he knew, he said, the way some of the press angled stories to suit themselves.

And that, I thought, resolved the matter. Knowing Alan Sugar, and given my increasingly frosty relations with him, I suppose I should have known better. When I got to the training ground Gerry Francis came over to me and told me that the chairman had got the hump with me. I explained to Gerry what had happened, but I could tell from his reaction that he wasn't fully convinced that I was telling him the truth. Either that, or he was under pressure from Sugar and didn't quite know how he was going to smooth things over with him.

The next morning I received a letter from the chairman

in which he told me I was a disgrace to have criticised the club in the way I had. To this day I don't know whether Gerry Francis relayed my feelings to the chairman, but whatever the case, Sugar fired off the letter anyway. He concluded by saying that if I did anything like that again, I would be fined two weeks' wages. It was simply Sugar believing what he wanted to believe. Not for the first time, I wondered how anybody could just flip like that without speaking to me first to get my side of the story. After all, he had had plenty of dealings with the press himself and must have been aware of the gift some of them have for twisting your words out of all recognition. But no, he chose to judge the issue apparently without making any attempt to find out the truth, and that is just a basic lack of courtesy. Apart from anything else, if I had been unhappy about the Armstrong signing I would have lost no time in making my feelings known to Sugar – he'd heard me speak my mind often enough to realise that. As it turned out, although Nicky was less than chuffed, I had no problem about it.

In my second season under Gerry, we played West Ham at home and lost 1–0 to a side who should never have beaten us. Our pitch was terrible that season, and that day it was atrocious; it was worse than playing out on Hackney Marshes. There was four inches of mud on the top, and you couldn't keep your footing, never mind hope to play any football. In a game you have your eye on the ball only about half the time. The rest you spend monitoring what's going on around you, looking for openings and opportunities. You couldn't do that on this pitch; you had to watch where the ball was going, which bobble it was going to hit next, the whole time.

After the game, Sugar came in with Claude Littner, his right-hand man, who asked me if everything was all right.

I told him how appalling the pitch was and I must admit I used some pretty choice language. I felt very strongly about it: our pitch should have been helping us, not hindering us, and I was fed up with it. It just wasn't good enough, I told Littner. We were playing Second Division clubs in Cups and we were being brought down to their level. We kept hearing that things were going to change, but time was passing and nothing was being done. I think I was right to speak out about it – the situation was ridiculous for a Premiership club. But I'm pretty sure Sugar overheard my complaint, and that was probably another nail in the old coffin.

It was against this turbulent background that the saga developed which finally resulted in my departure from the club I loved more than any other in the world. By the time the 1995–6 season drew to a close I was seriously unhappy about the direction Tottenham were going in – or, to be more accurate, about the fact that they didn't seem to be going in any direction at all. But at the bottom of my heart I still wanted to play for them, and to aim for success with them, even under a chairman who seemed hell-bent on imposing his will on other people's lives and careers without giving a second thought to their true views or feelings – for there were only two sides to any argument with Alan Sugar: his and the wrong one.

I'd spent hundreds of hours in that year and a half pondering my future and the options I had. I couldn't leave Tottenham if I wasn't going to move onwards and upwards. The 1996–7 season was upon us, and it became clear to me that if I was going to join a new club I couldn't stay in London. There was no way in the world I could have gone to Arsenal, and although the thought of joining Chelsea crossed my mind, at that time they were perhaps one level down from what I needed. It seemed to me that the only clubs where I could advance my career were Liverpool, Newcastle or Manchester United.

The crunch came when we were beaten 3–1 by Arsenal at Highbury in the Premiership on Sunday 24 November and followed up that disaster by going down 6–1 to Bolton in the fourth round of the Coca-Cola Cup three days later. Those two defeats brought it home to me that the club was going nowhere, and I felt I had simply got to the end of my tether. I spoke to Gerry a couple of days after the Bolton game and said that I was going to have to ask for a transfer. His immediate reaction was that there was no way he could let me go, but he promised he would speak to the chairman about how I was feeling. He was very upset that I had asked to leave but he was as good as his word. He soon came back to me with the chairman's response: I couldn't be allowed to go right then, but if I still felt the same way at the end of the season, my transfer request would be granted. However, Gerry added, he was confident that, come summer, I wouldn't want to leave because of the plans he had for the club.

That was music to my ears, exactly what I needed to be told. I didn't want to go in the first place, but Tottenham was not going to become a great side unless some big-name signings were made. Over the following couple of months there was a lot of talk, but nothing much in the way of action. Then Gerry signed John Scales, Ramon Vega and Steffen Iversen, all very good players, but I didn't feel they were quite of the quality we needed to move the club onwards: I still firmly believed that it would take the arrival of some £6 million or £7 million players to take us to the level where we could genuinely challenge for honours. And I made my feelings known.

The chairman told me that he wasn't going to fork out for players like that and then pay them £25,000 to £30,000 a week, but in the same breath he asked me who I thought we should be signing. I suggested Paul Ince, but Sugar retorted that Ince was one of those £7 million players, and he wasn't going to pay that for a twenty-nine-year old, plus the £30,000 a week Incey had been asking for to leave Inter Milan. Then I mentioned Rob Lee. I was confident that he wouldn't cost that much, and Sugar wouldn't have to pay him as much as Ince was asking. True, Rob would be on the next scale down from Ince, but I knew from my England experience that he was a great player. The chairman didn't react one way or the other, but his lack of subsequent action showed that he had not really listened, or that if he had, he thought he knew better than me.

The result of all this hot air and speculation was that precisely nothing was done, and we ended the 1996–7 season no nearer to making Tottenham the club I knew it had the potential to be. A few signings were made but there was never the sense of excitement to the place there had been when Jürgen Klinsmann had joined us. Our last game of the season was on 11 May at White Hart Lane, against Coventry City, who had to beat us to stay up. Gordon Strachan's team did precisely that – another frustrating night for anybody who loved Tottenham, if a great one for the men from Highfield Road.

After the game I had a meeting with Francis and Sugar. On the face of it, it was about a new contract, and as they were probably under the impression that I wanted to sign again, perhaps they were a bit unprepared for what I had to say. And they were not wrong about that, I did want to sign – but this time it wasn't just about me getting the best deal, about being a top earner. I wanted to know that they were committed to going out and spending some significant money on some really good players. I wanted the club to have the buzz it had had when Jürgen Klinsmann had been there. I wanted assurances from the chairman.

He wasn't about to give me any. 'I'm not going to say that,' he said. 'I'm telling you I'm going to get it right, and that should be good enough for you.' Do as you're told, Sheringham, you're just a footballer, I know best, he seemed to be saying. I felt like an impertinent schoolboy who had been caught cheeking the headmaster.

I wasn't having that. I had been patient, I had done right by them. I'd had a pretty good season personally, and I reckoned that gave me a stake in the future of the club. 'I'm one of your top players, and I'm telling you that it is just not good enough, so I'm asking for a transfer,' I replied.

He didn't hesitate for a moment. If that was what I wanted, he said, then I should put it in writing and they would make me available. It was a hugely different outcome from the one I had expected when I walked into that room. I had gone in to talk about signing a new deal with Tottenham Hotspur, and now I was about to walk out with my name on the transfer list. I was a bit stunned, but I suppose deep down I was not all that surprised.

Gerry asked the chairman if he could speak to me alone. Sugar didn't like that at all, but eventually he did leave the room. Gerry asked me what I was doing. 'I thought you wanted to stay at the club,' he said. I told him that I did, but only if certain conditions were met. Gerry suggested that I let him have a chat with the chairman – he was confident he could talk Sugar round. I agreed, and asked him to bear in mind that when all was said and done I *did* want to stay. Sure, I wanted to sign a good, improved contract, but most importantly I wanted to stay and play with great players.

Gerry rang me a day or two later to say that the chairman wanted to speak to me again. When Sugar phoned, he told me he was prepared to offer me a four-year contract, but I said I wanted five, because at the time I had been at the club for five years and another five would take me up to a testimonial. Sugar said I couldn't guarantee that I would still be playing first-team football at thirty-six, and he didn't want me on the high wages I would be earning on a five-year contract when I reached that age. What he would do, he said, was to ask Gerry Francis whether he thought I would still be playing in the first team at thirty-six.

Sugar said he would call me back that night, but I waited for a week or more before he rang again, on Tuesday 20 May. He expressed surprise to find that I was not best pleased by the length of time it had taken him to respond. Moving on to the point of his call, when it came down to it, he said, the manager had not been able to give him a categorical assurance that I would still be a first-team footballer when I was thirty-six, so the offer stayed as it was, a contract for four years.

Since he had kept me waiting for a firm offer I felt I was entitled to some time to think it over. I said I would consider what he had had to say and would get back to him. I was about to leave with the England squad to play South Africa at Old Trafford. Three days later, the day before the international, I received a recorded-delivery letter from him at Mottram Hall Hotel in Cheshire, where England were staying, in which he said that as I had not got back to him, his four-year offer had now been withdrawn. He was now making me a new offer –

for three years. 'Further to our last telephone conversation on Tuesday, May 20, I did actually try to get back to you straight away to inform you that the offer made to you, as is always my custom, was open for your consideration for 48 hours,' he wrote. 'Furthermore, I am told that the club have repeatedly tried to contact you at Mottram Hall Hotel, where you are staying, and in fact left up to ten messages on Wednesday and Thursday for you to return the call. The obvious reason for them trying to contact you was to inform you that the offer made to [you] would be open until Thursday, May 22 at 5 p.m.'

Now, I am not saying that those messages were not left, but it seemed pretty strange that I had not got so much as one of them. This wasn't a £15-a-night B&B we were staying in, it was a five-star hotel accustomed to dealing with high-flying businessmen and whose staff are well used to taking and passing on messages. That was my first reaction. The second was one of indignation. Sugar had kept me hanging on for a week for a phone call he had assured me would be made the same night, then had the barefaced cheek to write to me when it was too late to tell me that actually I'd had only forty-eight hours to think about it. It might well have been his custom to give people two days to reply to him, but he didn't seem to think that out of courtesy he should abide by his own rule himself.

I played in the England game and on the morning of Monday 26 May I rang the Tottenham chairman from my home. There was now only a three-year deal on the table, he informed me again. I told him that was not acceptable and that he could expect to receive my transfer request the next morning. I put the phone down, thinking that that was the end of it. I had made my decision, and that was that. The phone rang again a couple of minutes later. To my surprise it was Sugar, asking me whether, if a four-year deal was back on offer, I would consider it. I asked him what he meant by 'if'. 'What are you doing now?' I said, puzzled. 'Are you offering me a four-year deal?'

'No,' he said. 'I'm just saying if it was a four-year deal, would you accept it?'

I replied that it didn't really matter whether I would or not, since I had not been offered it. He was asking a hypothetical question, and therefore my answer was none of his business. 'All I can talk about is this three-year offer, so why are you coming back to me with such a ridiculous question?'

He said something pretty lame – he was just wondering what I would have said if he had put a four-year contract in front of me, or something like that. I told him not to worry about it, and put the phone down.

Barry Nevill, my agent, and I decided not to announce anything until after England's all-important World Cup qualifier against Poland the following Saturday. As soon as the news that I was on the transfer list was broken, I went off to France with England to play in Le Tournoi, the four-nation tournament involving ourselves, the hosts, Brazil and Italy. I did a lot more thinking about my future while I was in France but it always came back to the big three: Manchester United, Liverpool or Newcastle. Premiership champions Manchester United would have to be my first choice, because of the players they had and also because of one they no longer had: Eric Cantona had just announced his retirement, and I thought his departure might leave a role for me at Old Trafford. I hoped against hope that manager Alex Ferguson might feel the same way. But at the same time the thought of playing with Robbie Fowler at Liverpool or Alan Shearer at Newcastle was exciting, too.

I knew that Alex had tried to buy me a couple of years before, but the first comment I read from him on the question of my availability was that his club would not be prepared to pay £6 million for a thirty-one-year-old. When Alex says something like that he usually means it, so I put a move to Old Trafford out of my mind and reconciled myself to the fact that a potential move to Manchester United had probably come a little too late in my career. His remarks were fair comment, but having said that I don't think my age has any effect on how I perform. I think I've got a bit better with age, actually – it's not as though I'm a winger who's lost his pace and is on the way down. But that really didn't come into it any more: Alex had spoken, and I thought that was the end of it.

I'd read that my next two options, Liverpool and Newcastle, were both interested and I was equally excited about both of them. Remember, I was looking at them from the perspective of a Tottenham player – the Tottenham which didn't win anything; the Tottenham which had a distinguished past but not much of a future. Both clubs were bigger than the one I was leaving, and both had better prospects of the kind of success I wanted to play my part in achieving. Meanwhile, in France, England won Le Tournoi with a results list that included a victory over Italy, who were going to be the biggest potential stumbling blocks to our winning a place in the World Cup finals. I was delighted to have contributed to a good England performance, and as soon as I got back from France I went on a two-week holiday to Miami with three of my friends. I made sure I kept in touch with the folks back home, and while I was away all the talk revolved around a move for me to Liverpool or Newcastle.

I got home on the morning of Thursday 26 June, and

replayed the thirty-odd messages which had accumulated on my answering-machine. Two of the last five were from my dad and one was from my mum, all telling me to get in touch as soon as possible. They obviously weren't panic calls, so I knew there was not a family crisis or anything like that, but both my parents sounded excited. Neither of them let on that anything was up, however. I phoned my dad straight away and asked him what the problem was. He said that Tottenham had been on the phone and that they'd agreed a fee with a Premiership club who wanted me to go and talk to them. When I asked him which one it was, he said, 'Guess.'

'Liverpool?'

'No.'

'Newcastle?'

'No.'

'. . . not *Manchester United*?'

There was a smile in his voice when he told me, yes, it was. I couldn't take it in. It was like a dream come true.

Dad gave me a number for Martin Edwards, the Manchester United chairman, and I rang him immediately. He asked me if I would be interested in talking to him. 'Interested' was the understatement of the decade, the way I felt at that moment. I said that of course I would like to talk to him. I shouldn't embark on a long drive while jet-lagged, he said: I was to get on a plane to Manchester. If he'd asked me to, I'd have flown up there without the aid of an aeroplane.

I'd arrived in Manchester by 8.30 that evening, having told nobody but my close family and advisers that I was meeting the chairman of Manchester United for dinner at nine o'clock.

I must admit that initially I was a bit worried to find

that Alex Ferguson was not at the hotel where I'd arranged to meet Martin Edwards. You hear so many stories about chairmen buying players who turn out not to fit in with the manager's plans. But I was assured that Alex was looking forward to working with me and wanted me to sign for United, and that was good enough for me.

Excited though I was, as I talked to the chairman the effects of the long flight back from the States began to take their toll, so we agreed to meet again the following morning at 9.30. At our second meeting I told Martin Edwards that if he could do a couple of things for me I would be delighted to sign straight away, he agreed, and the deal was completed. I had become a Manchester United player within twenty-four hours of returning from my holiday.

I was going to be playing for the most famous football club in the world, and I was ecstatic that such an unhappy period of my professional life should have come to such a happy conclusion. I was joining a great, great club, and at last I was free from the influence of Alan Sugar, a man for whom I had long since lost any respect. Everything was perfect.

Or was it? Not quite, because my nemesis, the dictatorial Mr Sugar, still wanted to have the last word. I had signed my contract and was waiting to complete the formalities in the chairman's office at Old Trafford when I was told that Sugar was on the phone for me. He didn't mince his words. 'Now that we've let you go to the club you wanted to join and you're happy, I don't want to see any shit in the papers about me or Tottenham, or I'll be after you,' he said. 'I'll hound you down and get my own back.'

He wasn't getting away with that. I told him not even to think about threatening me. I would do exactly what I wanted to do. If I wanted to write something about him one day, I would, and if I didn't, I wouldn't, but I wasn't about to make any promises. It isn't my style to make promises I can't keep. So I left him to wonder whether one day I would tell the truth about my life and unhappy times with Alan Sugar. Well, I would; and now I have.

It's ironic, really. Not that long before my move he had declared to me that he would never give £6 million or £7 million for a player and then pay him megabucks in wages. So what did he do after I left? He spent £6 million on somebody who was the same age as me – Les Ferdinand – and ended up paying him a lot more than I was negotiating for. Alan Sugar a man of his word? Draw your own conclusions.

Chapter Three

Early Days

Anybody walking down a quiet suburban street on the north-eastern outskirts of London on a summer evening in the late seventies would have heard a couple of young voices raised in hot dispute about something that was quite obviously more important than life itself. The owner of one of those voices, the elder child by three years, would be the peacemaker; the younger one would, more often than not, be complaining vigorously about what he saw as a gross injustice. That was my big brother, Jimmy, and me, and we would be playing 'Goals' in the alleyway between our house and the house next door. The kerfuffle would in all likelihood have been caused by my claim for a penalty, or a goal, or something equally crucial. More important than life itself? To us it was.

My brother and I grew up in a football family in Malvern Avenue, Highams Park. Our father, Paul, a policeman, was a very good player himself and he brought up his two offspring to share the love of the game he'd had all his life. There was hardly a moment in our house when at least two of us were not talking about the beautiful game. Dad played in police leagues and also appeared for the Watney Mann Saturday team. Jimmy and I used to go and watch him, although as I remember it we spent a lot more time playing ourselves on the side of the pitch.

Although football was always number one with me, I was a pretty good all-round sportsman. I liked table tennis and was particularly good at tennis. My mum, Shirley, and my dad had always played, so as soon as I could hit a ball I used to go down to the local club with them and Jimmy and join in. Every year when Wimbledon was on we used to get the bug and end up playing doubles, Dad pairing off with me because I was the youngest and weakest. We had some good games: I can't vouch for the standard of tennis, but they were always very intense!

I'm often perceived as a laid-back character, and I suppose to a certain extent I am. It must be in the genes, because my dad is one of the most relaxed people I have ever met in my life. He played his football much the same way. By the time we were watching him he was playing centre half, but in his younger days he had been a centre forward, and that made up my mind for me – there was never any doubt where I was going to play.

I loved football almost from the time I could walk. At my first school, Selwyn Primary, I spent every second of every break playing the game in the playground. Even then I was the striker, the one who hogged the ball in front of goal. Even then I relished a challenge. Even then I was the one who was going to be a big star one of these fine days. And I must have been pretty useful, because when I was in the first year I played pick-up games with the fourth-year boys, even though strictly speaking it wasn't allowed. My brother was in the school team, which was the height of glamour as far as I was concerned. There would be him and the others from his year, and little Teddy, three years younger. I did OK, I think – I was the smallest by a long way, but I can't remember being outclassed by the big boys.

My first organised team was the Cubs side, and I shall never forget the moment I was first picked to play for them. The manager was going through the team, and when he got to number 7, and I wasn't in, and then 8, and still no mention for me, I was sure I'd been left out. As 9 passed me by and so did 10, I was beside myself. I wasn't going to get in, even though I thought I had done enough to impress him. I was on the verge of tears. Finally he got to 11 – it was me. I was in. I was going to be the little left winger. I was ecstatic. I was going to play in the same side as my brother, who was a hero of mine. I think I was seven years old at the time, and the rest were all about ten.

Word must have filtered back to Selwyn, because it was not long before I was playing in the third-year team, even though I was still in my first year. To me the biggest thrill in life was scoring goals, and I got more than my share as a kid. The schools round our way used to play in a league and two cup competitions, the McEntee Cup and the Birmingham Cup, which was the bigger event of the two. The Selwyn team, starring E. Sheringham at centre forward, won all three competitions in various years. I think the best moment of my early life was when the Selwyn team played in the final of the Birmingham Cup at the George White ground in Walthamstow. It was a great little pitch to play on, the best in the area, because it was enclosed, which made you feel as if you were playing in a stadium. We won 8–1 and I scored five. I was ten, and already I'd had a career highlight.

I don't think there was one particular instant when

it struck me in a blinding flash that I wanted to be a professional footballer one day. I came at it from another direction – I never thought I would be anything else. One thing I do remember is having an interview with the careers master at school when I was about fifteen and telling him that I was going to be a pro footballer. He slapped me straight down. 'You can forget that, son. If you were going to be a pro, somebody would have picked you up long before now.' I could have gone one of two ways at that point in my life. I could have believed him and started looking round for something else to do when I left school. The option I took was to roll up my sleeves and try to prove him wrong. If I hadn't been so determined, it might all have ended there and then.

I suppose I must have been about eleven or twelve when I first went to watch the professionals with my brother. At first we went to West Ham, and I enjoyed that, but I didn't discover what being a true fan was all about until I went to Tottenham for the first time when I was a little bit older. I was hooked. I always got to White Hart Lane early to watch Glenn Hoddle go through his warm-up routine, doing his tricks, keeping the ball up, spraying it all around the pitch. I was mesmerised by what he could do with a football.

Even though I was a pretty decent player in local schools football, I was no great shakes at a higher level. I did play for Waltham Forest district team, but although I had good skills I was a little bit diffident in the way I played. It seemed to me that all the better players were big boys, and I was never that sturdy. I got just one chance to play for the county side. There was a young player round our way called Dave Matthews, who was on West Ham's books and a regular county player. I was given my single opportunity when Dave was injured, played in precisely half a game and was never asked again. If anybody had told the county officials that the skinny kid to whom they had given half a game would go on to play for England, they would have laughed, and nobody could have blamed them.

Out of school I used to play for a team called Discus, until a man by the name of Maurice Newman, who was the manager of another kids' team, Beaumont, in Leyton, turned up unexpectedly at my house one day and asked me if I would like to go and play for them. They had great players, he said, and he thought I would fit in. Maurice was the first person ever to have any real confidence in my ability. I played for Beaumont from the age of thirteen to fifteen, and all the while he would constantly be telling people how good he thought I was. It always surprised me a bit, to be honest, because although I knew I was a pretty reasonable player for my age, I felt that there were quite a few better players than me in the team.

Having said that, I think I was always pretty confident as a young player. Confident, and a bit flash, if I'm truthful. Even then I wanted to score the great goals, the clever goals, the goals that people would remember. I know better now – as long as it goes over the line, that's good enough for me these days. I can't remember goal tallies or anything like that, but I do remember the goal that earned me my first mention in the local paper. It was scored for Beaumont after four seconds – and we hadn't even taken the kick-off. The opposition had kicked off and passed the ball back. I ran straight through, and as they tried to pass it across, I intercepted it, pushed it forwards and slotted it past the goalkeeper. It was my first taste of stardom, and I just loved it.

Our goalie in that match was Perry Suckling, who later also made a career out of the game with Crystal Palace and England Youth. He often got his name in the papers for saving penalties.

Football was such a major part of my life that I never had much time for the academic stuff. I was pretty good at maths and English early on, and I think I was considered fairly bright for my age, but as soon as it started getting complicated – you know, Pythagoras and all that stuff – I started to question the necessity for knowing all this. I was going to be a professional footballer, you see, and they didn't need to know Archimedes' Principle.

Heaven only knows what I would have done if I hadn't gone on to become a footballer, because in my latter days at Monoux, an all-boys school I attended to complete my education, I never thought about anything else. I went for a trial with Tottenham and Robbie Stepney, who was coaching the youngsters there, collared my dad one Tuesday evening and asked him if there was any chance of giving me a kick up the rear to liven me up a bit. 'He's got all the talent in the world,' Robbie said. 'He just doesn't do the business when he has to.' Dad told him I was like that at home as well, and he didn't honestly think there was much chance that I'd change.

I didn't know any of this until I joined Spurs from Nottingham Forest years later, and Robbie, who is still at White Hart Lane today, told me the story. I think he was right, now I look back on it, but if I was too laid back then it was because I was my father's son. He's been like that all his life and will never change now, thank goodness. He still plays squash and he's the same on the court as he was on the football field: always in the right place at the right time, and never seeming to have to hurry to get there. And he never takes three little steps if one big one will do. When he played football he was always going nineteen to the dozen between his ears, though, and I think I'm a bit like that too.

So if I seemed a little too casual, underneath I was always hungry to learn. You can look at other players in the same team as yourself when you're sixteen or seventeen and think you can do what they can do, but if you want to keep your place in the team you have to progress to the next step. You never stop learning in this game, and the moment you allow yourself to think you know everything is the moment it will all start to go wrong for you.

I probably started to become the player I am today at quite a young age. For instance, when I went on to play at Millwall, in our successful days, the guys used to play the long ball to me or Tony Cascarino – we both had the ability to win it in the air. The bigger of the centre halves used to pick up Cas and the smaller one used to pick me up. It was a pretty direct route, but even then, ten years ago or more, I used to like to come off my marker by 10 or 15 yards, link things up and go on from there. It was natural for me to do that; certainly no manager ever told me to play that way. They didn't tell me not to, either, which is just as well, seeing how my career and my role in various teams has developed.

I went for another trial, at Leyton Orient, when I was about twelve, because my brother had also had a trial there. But that sort of fizzled out, and so did a spell I had training at Crystal Palace. Palace actually wrote to me thanking me for going over to them and wishing me the best of luck for the future, but telling me they wouldn't be needing me again. I didn't get to play many games for either of these clubs, and with the Tottenham thing fading away as well, it seemed as if I just wasn't going to make it.

It was Millwall who gave me my chance to fulfil my

lifetime's ambition to become a pro player, and at Millwall that I spent one of the happiest spells of my career. I was coming up to sixteen and school-leaving time, and still nobody had beaten a path to my door begging me to join them. One afternoon I was playing for the youth team at Leytonstone and Ilford, an Isthmian League club in east London, against Millwall's youth side, and scored both goals in a 2–1 win. After the game Millwall's chief scout and their youth-team manager came up and asked me if I'd like to go there for a six-game trial. I said I'd love to, though I didn't even know where Millwall was, much less anything about the club itself. Anyway, they explained how to get there, and I promised to be there whenever they wanted me.

I shall never be able to thank those two men, Bob Pearson and Roger Cross, enough for the chance they gave me. They put me into a game – against Charlton Athletic – for the younger of two teams they ran in the South-East Counties League and I thought I put in a pretty mediocre performance. I played in another match, and I wasn't too impressed with myself in that one, either. But it's no wonder I felt I had put up a lousy showing in my third game: they had shoved me into a game for the older South-East Counties sides. I was fifteen and I was playing with eighteen-year-olds.

I certainly wondered why they had chosen to play me in the better, older team when I had not exactly shone in the younger side. Bob Pearson had obviously seen something in me that made him think I was worth encouraging.

Bob is a special person to me and dozens of others; one of those rare people you feel privileged to know. Players all over the country who he discovered keep in touch with him, as I do. He is still in football, and he never tires of telling me how he went round saying to people, 'You think what you like, but I'll show you this kid's a good player, and he will be even better.'

I played a fourth game, on the astroturf at Queen's Park Rangers, and once again I didn't exactly set the world alight, at least in my own eyes, so it was a huge surprise when we got a letter inviting my Dad and me to be Millwall's guests at a first-team game at the old Den. That was thrill enough, but it was nothing compared with how I felt when Bob announced after the game and that he'd like to sign me to a two-year apprenticeship. I was just so excited. It was what I'd always wanted to do, and although I had never considered anything else, I think even I was beginning to doubt that I was ever going to interest anybody enough for them to want to take me on.

My only concern was how I was going to get myself backwards and forwards from south London. I asked if there was a chance they'd let me buy a little moped, but they stamped on that idea in no time. 'It's buses and trains for you,' they said, 'and just make sure you get here on time, too.' The journey involved a bus and three trains, but I would have walked if I'd had to. There I'd been, starting to tell myself that I wasn't going to make it, and now I was going to be playing football for the next two years of my life. My wages would be only £25 a week, about a quarter of what some of my mates were earning, but I didn't care. Money didn't come into it. I still had to pinch myself occasionally to convince myself that I'd taken this first, all-important step. I had been so lucky. OK, so I'd scored dozens of goals as a kid and I'd been very good at school level, but I hadn't made much of an impact in district and county football, let alone got anywhere near an England Schoolboys cap. But through it all, first Maurice

Newman and now Bob Pearson had believed in me. It was a very good feeling to be held in high esteem by people I respected.

I enjoyed my early days at Millwall. It was hard work – very hard at times – but it was worth it. I was with a bunch of other young hopefuls with whom I shared a common aim: making a success of our careers. Some of us did; others fell by the wayside, and I have a lot of sympathy for those who did not progress. I know what it would have meant to me if I'd been thrown out after my two years. It can be the worst moment of a young life.

You developed a knack of being able to identify those who had a chance of making it. One who certainly did was a lad from Kent with whom I struck up an immediate rapport when he arrived at the club. His name was Neil Ruddock, and our paths were to cross again and again as our careers developed. Even though 'Razor' is a couple of years younger than me, he and I played in the Millwall Under-18 side together when I was a first-year professional and he was an apprentice. It will make a few people smile when I say that Neil was a nippy left winger who was a great crosser of a ball and made a stack of goals for me. Neil always had that little bit extra. He was not going to stay in the lower Millwall teams for long, and so it didn't come as any great surprise when George Graham, the manager at the Den at the time, came down the stairs and told us that Tottenham had made a £50,000 bid for him, which Millwall had accepted. I was glad for Neil, but at the same time I was wildly jealous. I couldn't believe they'd singled him out among all of us and all the other youth teams around. I was sick: not only was my mate leaving, but he was going to the club I loved above all others.

George Graham had come into my life not long after I

started my apprenticeship. Peter Anderson had been the manager when I first arrived but had left soon afterwards, to be replaced temporarily by Barry Kitchener. Everybody on the playing staff wanted Barry to get the job full-time, but it was not to be. He had been in charge for only a few games when Graham was brought in.

I'm not sure what attracted George to Cold Blow Lane. We had a tiny squad, so small that I had to play for the youth team on a Saturday and the reserves in midweek and was on the verge of being in contention for a first-team place as well. But George soon put an end to any first-team-football pipe dreams I might have entertained. I was a flash kid in those days, a real showboater with a repertoire of all the flicks and touches. I still wasn't interested in scoring boring goals – they had to come from benders into the top corner, or chipping the goalkeeper, or something. When they came off, they looked great, but the trouble was they didn't come off very often.

George, then in the early days of his managerial career, wasn't having any of that. Even then he was a realist. The glamour could come later, he reasoned, let's just score a few goals first, never mind how we score them. He's still the same today: gritty pragmatism rather than romantic flair is his watchword, and it's made him one of the most effective managers in the modern game.

He soon got hold of me and told me in no uncertain terms to cut out the fancy frills. He used to drum it into me until I was sick of it. 'Just get on to it,' he'd say, 'and don't worry about the flashy stuff, just hammer it through the goalkeeper's legs, either side of him, whatever, just make sure it goes into the net.' I'm ashamed to say that I thought I knew best. So what if the manager had been one of Scotland's most distinguished players of the modern era? I had the skill, and I was going to use it. I should have known better than to try to get the better of George. The next time I had a chance I tried to score the definitively spectacular goal. George was watching. 'I've told you once, I've told you twice, and I'm not going to tell you again,' he said. 'Just get the ball in the back of the net.' Even then I wouldn't admit defeat. I'd scored goals like that before and I would score them again. I would show him. Then I'd be crowing, 'There you are, boss, see that? I told you I could do it.' He would smile grimly and tell me to have it my own way.

But finally George reached the limits of his patience and he gave me a right roasting if I tried the classy shots at goal, even in training. The other players told me the manager couldn't stand the sight of me. So conceited was I, I didn't appreciate that he was actually trying to teach me a very valuable lesson. I just thought he hated me, because the other players told me he did. He didn't pick me for the first team very often, either. It was not until the next manager, John Docherty, came in and told me exactly the same thing that I began to come to the conclusion that he and George might have a point and that I'd better start paying attention to all this. George might have hated me, but John couldn't have done because he didn't know me from Adam – or so I thought. As it turned out, he did, but that's another story.

By this time I'd had another salutary lesson of just how fragile your grip on your career can be in those formative days. I had made my Third Division debut for George on 15 January 1984 in the London derby against Brentford and missed a sitter in the last ten minutes in a 2–1 defeat. It was a header I saw late and put straight into the arms of the goalkeeper. I remember that Paul Roberts had left

Millwall for Brentford, and the Millwall fans gave him a terrible time. He did himself no favours by shouting back at them, and the situation came to a head when a Millwall supporter ran on to the pitch and took a swing at him. I thought my missed goal would mean that this had been my last chance for a while, but I kept my place in the next game, away to Bournemouth.

It was in that match that I scored my first goal in the senior game. That gave me a terrific feeling after working and hoping for it for so long. Every time I celebrated a team-mate's goal I wished it had been mine, and now, at last it was. I can still remember the sheer thrill of it. I was in the corner of the 6-yard box, controlled the ball, cut inside with my right foot and scored low and hard from about 8 yards. I notched up another as a substitute in a 4–3 win after extra time in the Associate Members' Cup against Gillingham. Yet in spite of my exhilaration at these milestones I was still nowhere close to being the finished article – far from it – even if I thought I was doing OK.

George obviously realised this, because he gave me only one substitute appearance in the 1984–5 season and then sent me off to play for Aldershot on loan for a month. I hated it. Aldershot, who played at the Recreation Ground, a quaint, run-down little stadium in the middle of a public park, were in the Fourth Division. As I was still living at home, that month involved a lot of travelling, too. I used to meet Phil Coleman, a non-contract player with Aldershot – the brother Nicky, my team-mate at Millwall – at a café just off the Chiswick roundabout in west London and he gave me a lift from there.

In my cocky naïveté I thought that because I'd been playing in the reserves at Millwall I would go off to

Aldershot, score a pile of goals and be an instant hit. What an idiot – I couldn't have been more wrong.

The football was a huge culture shock. I got kicked up in the air every week, I felt slower than ever and because people in the bottom division were not as sharp, they couldn't read what I was trying to do. My first game for Aldershot was in the Freight Rover Trophy against Orient on 5 February 1985. We lost 1–0, but I remember thinking I'd played quite well. 'I'll show them here what I can really do. I'm going to enjoy this,' I said to myself. I didn't. For the next five games I didn't get a kick.

My last game for Aldershot was typical of my whole experience there. We played against Northampton, who had a 6-foot-4 centre half by the name of Wakeley Gage. It was awful. I can remember with crystal clarity our centre halves whacking the ball up to me and good old Wakeley heading it back 40 yards at them and clattering me about the head, legs and ankles at the same time. I thought then that this was no place for me to be playing, but the truth was I was my own worst enemy. I was a slightly built youth, not as big or filled out as I later became, and I held my body in all the wrong positions.

I had been told by George Graham that I was going to Aldershot for experience, but it was not until much later that I discovered that there had been a bit more to it than that. When John Docherty arrived to succeed George, who left at the end of the 1985–6 season, he told me that at around the time I had been farmed out to Aldershot, George had offered me to him, Docherty, then the manager of Brentford, for £5,000. John had said he didn't want me. When I heard this I thought I could be on my way at any time, but thankfully John put me in the first team and I did OK for him.

It was good for me, I suppose, to have gone to Aldershot for a couple of months. But it was a trying interlude, in which I played six games, scored not a solitary goal and got clattered from pillar to post in every one, and I seriously began to doubt if I was going to make it in football. My saviour was Roger Cross, the Millwall youth-team manager, who, along with Bob Pearson, had brought me to the club in the first place. Roger was brilliant for me. He had only just finished playing himself, and he was a lot like me – not the quickest, quite clever, could score a goal – and I think he saw a bit of himself in me. I liked his practice sessions, which were all geared to finishing. I went to see him one day in despair and told him that I didn't know where I was going, people were playing me offside and I wasn't getting involved in games. He said not to worry, I was doing all right. There would be games I wouldn't get involved in; that was the way of the world for strikers. If I kept on plugging away I would be OK.

I listened to what Roger said and realised that it made a lot of sense. There was no point in whingeing, because that would only make things worse. I began to think that perhaps there was a future for me after all, even if I was playing for a manager who disliked me intensely. And everything did work out eventually. But Gorgeous George had one more trick up his sleeve to play before he would allow me to graduate from struggling youngster to fully fledged professional footballer.

Chapter Four

Life at the Bottom – And at the Top

'Do I want to go *where* to play?' I spluttered.

'Sweden,' said the manager.

He had been contacted by somebody at Wimbledon asking if he had any bright young players who might like to gain more experience by going to Sweden for the whole of their season, which ran from April to October. I didn't want to go to Sweden. I didn't want to go anywhere but the Millwall first team, but there didn't seem much prospect of that. It was a month before the end of the 1984–5 season, and having played ten games for the team in 1983–4, I thought I might have a chance of establishing a more regular place. I felt I had done all right in that first year, scoring a couple of goals, but I was coming to believe more and more that not only did George Graham not like me as a person, but he didn't fancy me much as a footballer, either.

As a consequence I had made just one appearance in the first team, in 1984–5, coming off the bench to play in a 1–1 League Cup game against Chelsea in October. After that nothing, except the miserable spell at Aldershot. No sooner, it seemed, had I returned to the Den from that gloomy garrison town than Graham was packing me off to Sweden, of all places.

'Why would I want to go to Sweden?' I asked. 'There's a month left in our season, and I want to try to get into the first team again.' The manager almost chuckled. I could forget that, he said, because he wasn't going to pick me.

It would be an exaggeration to say that I was devastated, because I'd got used to being knocked back under Graham's managership. With the benefit of hindsight I can see that he was only trying to make me understand what was required of a professional footballer. In those days I was merely a young man who was playing football for money, and that's not the same as being a good professional. I was disappointed, though. I couldn't imagine how a few months in Sweden was possibly going to do anything to advance my career. It wasn't as though I was being sent to a particularly prominent club – Djurgarden, it was called, a Swedish League Second Division outfit in the suburbs of Stockholm. But I did agree to think it over, and I did a lot of soul-searching. Apart from the fact that the visit didn't seem to offer much obvious value to my football, it would mean moving away from home for the first time. Our family has always been very close, and in spite of my slightly flashy demeanour, I wasn't nearly as confident as I might have seemed.

Yet in the end, I decided that I might as well go. George Graham had ruled out any likelihood of me getting a first-team game before the end of the season. It was a chance to travel and to see another part of the world, to test my wings away from the family unit and to sample playing football for real money instead of the £6 win bonuses I earned in youth teams. The more I thought about it, the more it appealed to me. It turned out to be one of the best decisions I've ever made. I was at Djurgarden for seven months, and not only did I thoroughly enjoy the experience, but it gave me my first taste of success.

I took me a bit of time to settle in, but once I had I managed well. Initially I stayed with a Swedish lad called Leif Neilsen, who worked in a bank by day and went to training with me in the evenings. Another player, Kenneth Johansson, lived in the flat downstairs and the three of us used to get to training early so that we could get in some extra practice. After a month or so I rented a room in a luxury apartment in the city centre, which was owned by an elderly couple who divided their time between the city flat and their house in the country. I would never know when they were coming back, so I couldn't have parties or anything like that, but it didn't stop me from getting up to one or two high jinks.

My brother had always played for clubs like Redbridge, Dagenham and Grays Athletic, and I would characterise the game in Sweden as something like the football played at those clubs in style and standard. I wasn't at all prepared for the way they went about things in Sweden. I had become used to something completely different back home: at Millwall the football was tough but fast and quite skilful, and Aldershot was the same, except for the speed and the skill. In Sweden, ruthless it wasn't. It was decent football, but at the start I thought it was a bit nicey-nicey, until I realised that what these guys lacked in hardness they more than made up for with technique. One of their stars was Stefan Rehn, who went on to play for Everton and eventually became a Swedish international. His skill was matched by his ambition, and it was good to play in the same team as him.

We trained every night for three hours in the main stadium, which was like a mini-Wembley. It was beautiful – quite a change from the Den, which wouldn't win any prizes for its looks. Our ground was the old Olympic stadium in Stockholm, which had facilities beyond the experience of a boy from Millwall. We used to get pretty decent crowds for home games – 9,000 wasn't out of the ordinary. The pitch was fantastic; even the balls we used in training were miles better than anything we could afford at Millwall.

All in all, it was time well spent. I had the use of a nice apartment, an old BMW car, my basic meals paid for and a decent wage. I wasn't at all homesick in Sweden: funnily enough, the only time I felt a brief flash of homesickness was the one occasion when I returned to England to attend my brother's wedding. While I was home I went to watch Millwall play, of course, and saw my mates, and I suppose that reminded me of what I was missing. I wasn't the most gregarious or forthcoming of people in those days, so I had to get used to coping on my own in Sweden, and I did a lot of growing up in that summer, both on and off the pitch. I was forced to stand on my own two feet for the first time, to survive in a big city, where there are always unscrupulous people who will try to separate a young fellow from his money. I think I lost a bit of my innocence, but that was no bad thing. I was bit lonely at times, but I learned to deal with it, and that was a valuable lesson as well.

On the field, I very quickly came to understand that in being paid to win games for my team, I was playing not only for my livelihood but those of my team-mates as well. You must never, ever forget that when you're a professional footballer. You have a responsibility to yourself, of course, but you also owe something to the lads you play alongside. When you're playing for money that can make a difference to people's lives – we got £40 for a draw, £80 for a win – you really try to win every time you set foot on the pitch. For the first time, the importance of what George Graham had been telling me back at Millwall began to dawn on me. It truly *didn't* matter how you got the ball in the back of the net.

Djurgarden had already played five of their twenty-six games before I arrived, but I featured in all of the remaining twenty-one and became the club's leading goalscorer with thirteen goals. Sure, there were a few of my favourite flashy efforts among those thirteen, but many were scored by less complicated methods. Those goals helped us to win the Second Division North title. We then got through a two-leg play-off to earn a place in the Premier League. It was a bit tight near the end, though. Our opponents were the Second Division South champions, a team called GAIS from Gothenburg. We'd played out a defensively dominated goalless draw in the first match, and the second leg finished – after extra time. I scored the goal that kept us in contention and took us on to a penalty shoot-out. As I stepped up to take my spot-kick I thought of what George Graham would have said had he been there: 'Now, don't be flash, just keep it simple, OK? Just hammer it.' So I did, and it went in. For the first time in my professional career, I had won something. It was a fantastic feeling. It was to be three years before I experienced it again.

I got on well with the other players at Djurgarden, and I still consider them my friends, although I haven't seen any of them for years. Left back Gary Williams, from Tranmere Rovers, was also at Djurgarden for the season.

He had been there before, and spoke some Swedish. He was a typical Football League professional whose style I could identify with, and he took me under his wing. English footballers sometimes have language difficulties playing in foreign countries, but in Sweden I had no problems. The first-team squad, with very few exceptions, spoke good English, and the manager was fluent. The training was conducted in Swedish with my tactical instructions being translated into English for me. And I went to Swedish classes once a week after training and managed to learn a bit of their language as well.

When my spell in Sweden was coming to an end, there was a lot of talk about Djurgarden signing me on a permanent transfer, but I wasn't really interested. I'd enjoyed playing there, but I didn't want to stay on: it was just a stepping-stone in my career. And it must have taught me something, because when I got back to England George, at last, began to give me a few games in the first team. More often than not I was a substitute, but at the end of the 1985–6 season – our first back in the Second Division after winning promotion from the Third the year before – I had made eighteen appearances, and had been in the starting line-up for the final seven games.

At the end of that season George left to go to Arsenal. We had done pretty well in our first year back in the Second Division, and although I think George had the same sort of soft spot for Millwall as I did, when the call came from Highbury, of course he couldn't turn it down. A couple of years earlier I would have been delighted for George to have gone. Not only did I think he hated me, but if I'm honest, I'd have to say that I didn't like him much, either. It was only after he had left, and after I matured a bit, that I realised how good he had been for me. He was a very ruthless character; he had decided what he wanted from me and wouldn't be content until he got it, by hook or by crook. To the last I didn't enjoy playing for him, but when I look back now I have to admit that he must have seen something in me that could be developed to turn me into a decent player. He might have wanted to bring out what talent I had for his own ends, or at least the club's, but the way he handled me – including the chastening two months at Aldershot – was exactly right for the kind of player, and person, I was in my late teens.

George was the first of a series of great managers I've played for. I've been blessed in that respect. Just look at some of the names: as well as George Graham, I've been managed by Brian Clough, Terry Venables and Alex Ferguson – a real *Who's Who* of excellence in the art of managing a football club. They have all helped to make me into a better and more rounded player, and there is no question that I would not have gone as far in the game as I have without them.

In many ways the next manager at Millwall thoroughly deserves to be included in that list. John Docherty joined Millwall from Brentford, where he had shown that he was a manager and coach who dealt in both practicalities and dreams. He was a very clever manager who seemed to have an instinctive knack for getting the best out of people. It was John who made me, for the first time in my career, a regular first-team player. You should never forget the man who gives you that first real chance to stamp your mark on a team and a club. Along with a few others, I used to spend a lot of time with John. He was a bit of a lonely man, I think. He liked nothing better than to sit in his office, light up a cigar and reminisce about his life in football. He used to tell the same stories over and over again. Bob Pearson, who knew him pretty well and had heard the yarns fifty times before, would give him a sideways look, smile wryly, make an excuse and leave. But we stayed on, because he was never boring. His stories were always the same in every detail, so either he was very good at remembering his script, or the incidents he told us about really happened.

I established myself as a first-choice player in my first season under Docherty, 1986–7, and it was a pretty steep learning curve. The club was a bit strapped for cash, I think. It must have been, because otherwise we wouldn't have persisted with our main strike pairing. I spent that season playing up front with a young lad called Michael Marks, who was only eighteen. I had played fewer than a dozen first-team games myself, and I was the experienced one, for goodness' sake, trying to bring this boy along. It was a peculiar feeling.

It was a real dogfight against relegation all season. We had to battle like fury to save ourselves from going back down into Division 3 after only two years in Division 2. I scored thirteen goals in the League and Marks got about ten, I think. Talk about boys doing men's jobs. It worked, though – just. We stayed up, if only by the skin of our teeth. Happily it was the last season of bad times for quite a while.

In the summer of 1987 the club must have come into some money, because Docherty was able to embark on a programme that, by Millwall's standards, constituted a spending spree. His major signing was Tony Cascarino from Gillingham for £200,000, but others came to the club who were nearly as important. Wingers Kevin O'Callaghan, Jimmy Carter and George Lawrence, and centre half Steve Wood, were all perceived, by Millwall fans at least, as big signings. For me the strengthening of the side was great for two reasons: first, it meant that I would be playing alongside better players, and secondly, their arrival would take a bit of the burden off my shoulders by adding their experience to the team.

It was a terrific team for the level we were playing at. Tony played alongside me, we had some quality on the left wing in O'Callaghan, and Lawrence was an experienced hand coming in on the right flank. We also had Terry Hurlock and Les Briley in the middle – perfect performers for our style of football. Wood and Alan McLeary were an effective pairing at centre back, two clever, thinking players who were great readers of situations. They were never eye-catching, but they did a fine job for us. Right back Keith Stevens was very solid – nobody used to get past him – while Nicky Coleman at left back, who had come through the youth ranks with me, was a highly competent player. Brian Horne in goal completed a team that was perfectly balanced for the job it was employed to do.

It was also a side that wrote several pages in the Millwall record books, because it took the club to the First Division for the first time in their history. So it was an amazing time – for fun, for team spirit, for being on the same wavelength as an excellent manager, for the sheer enjoyment of playing the game, it was as good a team as I've ever played in. Sure, I've played with better players, in bigger teams; I've had the thrill and the honour of playing for my country, but with all due respect to all of them, none has given me more pleasure than I got from my time down in south London.

That year – 1988 – was a red-letter one for me. As well as becoming a Division 1 player for the first time, I also became a father. Denise, my girlfriend of a year or so, gave birth to Charlie that April. Although my relationship with Denise eventually ended, Charlie remains the apple of my eye.

So everything went well for me and for Millwall all season, but there were highlights as the end of the season approached and the drama increased, each game becoming more important than the last. I think the moment we finally convinced ourselves that promotion was just round the corner was on a cold Tuesday night at Elland Road at the beginning of April 1988. We knew we had to win, and it was a daunting prospect. Leeds were a First Division side which had come down and we were a little team which had dragged ourselves up from the lower reaches of the Second Division. We beat them 2–1 and there was an amazing feeling in the dressing room after the game. We'd had to defend like fury, but we had all stuck together with a feeling of common purpose, the sort of feeling that comes only from playing a lot with the same group of people and wanting to do it for each other.

The game which won us the Second Division title was against Hull City on 2 May 1988, a day that will for ever be stamped on my memory. We had to get some sort of favourable result at Boothferry Park to guarantee promotion, or at least a place in the play-offs. It was a night of almost unbearable tension which ended with us winning 1–0 in front of a crowd that contained an estimated 4,000 Millwall supporters. The fans came on to the pitch: they thought it was all over, and it was now. Grown men, Millwall supporters all their lives, were crying their eyes out. There were a few players reaching for the tissues in the dressing room afterwards as well. I'd been part of a team that gained promotion in Sweden, but that experience didn't begin to compare with this. I was on home territory now, playing with and for people with whom I had an emotional bond. We partied all night at the hotel where we were staying. We were the team who had achieved the biggest moment in Millwall's history, we knew how good we were and we couldn't wait for the following season.

We still had one game to go, against Blackburn at home the next week, and it was a great shame that we lost it 4–1. But we had only ourselves to blame – we had been celebrating all week. We desperately wanted to put on a good show for the fans, but we had exhausted ourselves on the pitch all season and off it for a week. The bad performance didn't kill the atmosphere, though – it was like a big night in a European competition, with banners flying and the fans in good voice. We didn't want to lose, of course, but utimately it didn't really matter. We were the champions, and nobody could take that away from us.

It was a fantastic night, a night when a little thing like a 4–1 defeat was soon forgotten. There was a carnival atmosphere down the Old Kent Road as we caroused in the Frog and Nightgown. Our wives and girlfriends joined the party, including Denise and our son Charlie, who was only two months old. It was his first taste of night life.

John Docherty drove down the famous old street waving the Second Division trophy in the air. Because he was a chap who kept quite a low profile, few people recognised him at first. When they did, they started chasing him and the boss got scared and drove off like the wind before somebody did something silly. There was talk of taking an open-topped bus down the Old Kent Road, but the police wouldn't allow it for some reason. It was a pity, because we wanted to put on a show and thank the fans who had supported us through thick and thin in the Third and Fourth Divisions.

I loved playing in that team. Everybody was so willing to work for each other, and together we made things happen. It was the culmination of all I had worked for, and it made all the hardships of my early career truly worthwhile. I maintain to this day that Millwall was the toughest-ever place for a young lad to break into a team, and it probably still is. I had a hard time with the fans for a while. At the start they were prepared to give you a chance because you were new and fresh, so for ten games they would treat you as though you were a world-beater, but after that they absolutely hammered you if you made the slightest mistake. I remember one chilly, wet Tuesday night at the Den, with about 2,500 people rattling around in the stands, when I was going through a bit of lean spell. A fan who thought I was bit slow in getting to one ball yelled out, 'Oi, Sheringham, get that ****ing piano off your back.' The insult echoed round the stadium to general laughter. I remember wishing I could tell that supporter and his jeering friends that I was doing my level best, but of course you couldn't do anything like that. If you did, they would have won. When that sort of thing happened, you had two options. Either you could say, 'OK, pal, get a laugh out of me for your mates if you like, but if you think I'll go under, think again, because I'm going to show you in the end.' Or you could just fold up on the spot.

And it would have been easy to buckle. In my time at the club I saw a few pretty good youngsters who faded away because they couldn't take the stick from the crowd. If you could survive it, you could survive anything. I survived, and came out of it a stronger, more resilient player. The other bonus was that if you stuck with it and won over the fans, they would support you through thick and thin. There was a great community feel to the whole club, from Lil, the tea lady, to the chairman of the board. I soaked it up that first night I went to the Den to watch the first team with Bob Pearson. They got beaten about 6–1 by Grimsby in front of about 2,000 bedraggled fans. There was no glamour in that at all, but I so much wanted to become part of it that I was overjoyed when Bob offered me apprenticeship forms. It was only in our first year in the First Division, when we were playing at Old Trafford – Millwall, for goodness' sake! – that you realised how far you and the club had come together. And that same family feeling was still there the day I left.

Chapter Five

Life at the Top – And at the Bottom

I am pleased I took the path I did to find my way to the top of the game. I'm sure that people who signed for Tottenham as kids and are still playing for them are also happy with their own routes to success, but I wouldn't change anything about my career. I really appreciate the lessons I've learned, even in the bad times. I did it my way, as the song goes, and I'm glad I did.

It was for everybody connected with Millwall that I was playing, as well as for myself, in that memorable 1987–8 campaign, during which I first began to get myself noticed a little in the world outside the Den. I think it had something to do with the fact that I was playing alongside Tony Cascarino. He was a Republic of Ireland international and was commanding a regular place for his country, he had cost a lot by Millwall's standards and he was delivering the goods. I'd like to think I helped him a bit, too, but in a season in which we were neck and neck in the goalscoring stakes – I got twenty-four in the League and Cup and I think Cas got something like twenty-three – I certainly benefited from his presence. All of a sudden people were beginning to pay attention to Millwall.

At the time I'd had no thoughts whatsoever about playing for anybody else. I loved my club with a passion. Like all kids, I'd dreamed about one day playing for a big side, but I don't think I would have been any good at all at a higher level in my early years. In any case, I was enjoying my football. The camaraderie and the team spirit were brilliant, and the only other time I've ever felt anything like the same atmosphere at a club was, funnily enough, the day I walked into Manchester United for the first time. The sensation when you walk through the doors at Old Trafford is exactly like the one at Millwall, only a hundred times stronger. Just as there was at the Den, there is an overwhelming feeling that everyone, from the chairman down, is part of it all and is valued by the club. It is such a friendly place: everybody talks to and respects everybody else. You can't buy that feeling. It has to be worked for. And once you've experienced it, you never forget it.

Although Millwall must have slotted in some of the bits of the jigsaw to produce the player I am now, my style didn't really play a huge part in John Docherty's thinking. His was very much a direct, long-ball strategy. It was intended that Cascarino would win the ball, then we'd get the next ball and make sure the opposition didn't clear it, work them hard and break them down that way.

I must have been reasonably successful at the Millwall style, because I remember Terry Hurlock coming back from an England B game and, over a couple of beers one night, telling me, 'Ted, none of them have got what you've got. You can do it if you want to, you know.' I really admired Terry – he was a superb, clever player and had a great character – and it meant a lot to me that he'd taken the trouble to tell me that. He didn't have to say it, and he wasn't the sort to butter you up for the sake of it, so I felt I should take his words seriously and really go for it. After all, if I continued to improve, who could tell where it might lead? This was the first small sign I saw that, provided everything went well, there might be something really good in store for me.

That wonderful promotion year left everybody at the club buzzing. We were dying to get into the First Division and test ourselves against the likes of Tottenham and Manchester United. We were so confident; we really thought we could be a team to watch. We could not do other than respect the teams we were going to be playing, but we honestly felt that we had what it took to become a force in the upper echelon. This always happens with promoted teams, but more often than not that confidence is undermined by the harsh reality of life at the top. Ours, incredibly, was not.

I can honestly say that in the beginning none of us gave a second thought to the money we were earning. Our average wage was about £450 a week, which the club couldn't increase in case we went straight back down – a big wage bill in the Second Division would have sent the club to the wall. So the management compensated us by putting us on a fantastic bonus scheme. Our appearance money amounted to about £200 and we had a crowd bonus, banded according to the attendance, as well. The ground at that time held 23,000, and if we filled it we got another £450. After our good start at home to Derby, the ground was full for the next home game and with the appearance money, win bonus and crowd bonus on top of my basic wage, I took home nearly £1,650 that week. I had never known such riches before. Two years earlier I had been on £110 a week. We needed to go on playing well if we were going to earn good money. We did, too – and we kept the crowds coming for most of that season. If we played the likes of Manchester United, Tottenham or Arsenal we always got a full house.

We used to go out for our warm-up and estimate what sort of gate we'd got that day, and if it was a good one, we'd be in high spirits, rubbing our hands together at the prospect of bonuses and cracking jokes about them with one another. At one time I used to add a bit of extra excitement by joining my friends in a bet on me scoring the first goal. After a while, though, that additional interest started to prey on my mind. I was afraid that one day I might go for a shot at goal when I should have passed to someone in a better position. So I stopped making bets before anything like that looked like happening. But my mates carried on the tradition – and did pretty well out of it, too.

Mind you, it could just as easily have gone horribly wrong. If we'd gone to Manchester United in the first week and got battered 6–0, then lost 4–0 to Tottenham and gone on to another thrashing at Liverpool, the bubble would have burst with a resounding bang there and then. But it didn't happen: we were on a roll, still high on adrenaline from the previous season, and it didn't peter out for ages. It was a crazy, exhilarating time. There we were, little Millwall, in our first season in the First Division and topping the table until about March. Everybody said it couldn't last, and of course it couldn't and it didn't, but we gave them all a run for their money. We were beating the best teams when we shouldn't have been and getting away draws to which we had no right.

Our first game in Division 1 was a 2–2 draw at Aston Villa, in which Tony Cascarino scored both our goals. In our first game at the Den the following week, I scored the only goal, a scruffy sort of an effort that eluded Derby goalkeeper Peter Shilton, hit a post and allowed me to nip in and score from about a yard. I'd only had to tap it in, but to me it felt like the greatest goal of all time. It meant that both Cas and I had a record – he had scored the first Division 1 goal in Millwall's history and I had scored the first at home.

It was all a big adventure for the club. It was the first time John Docherty had managed at anything like this level and he and we players were in unknown territory. Probably the first real highlight of 1988–9 was going to Liverpool in November. When we took the lead through Paul Stevenson after eleven minutes we all sort of looked at each other, and without saying anything we knew what we were all thinking: 'Blimey, we're one up away at Liverpool. We can actually win this.' We had only two players who had ever played in the First Division and yet we were actually ahead at Anfield. Like most dreams, this one didn't come true. They equalised soon afterwards and then they really pounded us, but they just couldn't get the winning goal.

Marking me was Alan Hansen, who was the best central defender I have ever played against. He would just drift past me – I wouldn't even see him. At least, he was supposed to be marking me, but it ended up the other way round: I was trying to stay with him, but I could never get near him. There was no comparison between him and the rest of his team and us, and yet we got a 1–1 draw. It was the result of the season to date. There were not many better in the whole campaign.

Our first major home game was in mid-September, against Everton, whom we beat 2–1, both goals coming from Cascarino. We weren't beaten until Middlesbrough did us 4–2 at Ayresome Park on 29 October. I was playing against Gary Pallister, with whom I often swapped stories about the games we had together in the lower divisions when we met up at England training sessions.

In the Second Division we had dictated games, imposing our style on amost every side we came up against, getting the ball in the channel in our simple, direct way. But now we needed to find a style which suited the division we were playing in. It was not until Frank McLintock, who was later to become my agent for a while, joined John Docherty on the management team that we began to develop one. John had never played much at the highest level, and furthermore he had achieved success with a team that was moulded in his own image: direct and down to earth. Frank, however, had been a cut above John as a footballer and had played in better teams. There was a fundamental difference in their respective philosophies: John didn't think we were sophisticated enough to play the way Frank wanted, and Frank felt that we would never make ourselves an enduring force in the First Division if we kept playing the way we were. So the compromise was never completely comfortable, but in our first year it worked all right because of our high morale. It was not found seriously wanting until our second season in Division 1, a season that ended in tears. The truth is that eventually we got fatally trapped between two styles.

My maiden game against my boyhood heroes, Tottenham, came along on 10 December. We were in the top three at the time and our expectancy levels were high. We thought we would win, but they beat us 2–0 and gave us a footballing teach-in in the process. I also learned a valuable personal lesson. Paul Gascoigne was in the Spurs team that day and he hit me with the hardest fair tackle I had experienced since Wakeley Gage had booted me up in the air at Aldershot. That one tackle taught me a lot: I just had not expected it from such a fancy sort of footballer. It was 100 per cent fair, but it knocked the stuffing out of me all the same. It made me realise that there was more to football at the top level than just being a fancy dan.

My first match against the great Manchester United was in January 1989. We feared we might get beaten by six or seven goals, so I suppose a 3–0 defeat was not too bad. They were simply unbelievable that day, and Mark Hughes in particular was magnificent. He battered Steve Wood, no mean performer himself, all over the place.

It seems incredible, looking back, that we were genuine contenders for major honours for so long. Even Europe beckoned us. Nobody at Cold Blow Lane had ever thought in those terms before, not even in their wildest dreams. We continued to get rave reviews, and I had my share of those, but knowledgeable people were openly speculating about why we kept on winning. It was some time before the knockers began to concede that we weren't just long-ball hackers, that there had to be a little bit more to us. But after all those wet, cold Tuesday nights at the Den facing the likes of Lincoln, I still couldn't believe that we were even playing on the same pitch as people such as Mark Hughes, Bryan Robson, Paul McGrath, Steve Bruce and Jim Leighton, let alone being judged in the same terms. As the season went on, all of a sudden, after playing for the sheer enjoyment of it, we began to believe that we could actually go on to win the title. Ironically, it was, perhaps, the realisation that we could do it that finally stopped us from achieving our dream. With the benefit of hindsight, I can see that it was all a little too much for us. You have to have a certain amount of knowledge and experience to win the top league in English football. At certain places you have to be prepared to consolidate and settle for a draw. We never were.

Gradually, the feeling that perhaps we had gone as far as we could that year permeated the team. Perhaps the adrenaline had faded a bit; perhaps we were simply exhausted. It would have been great to have finished in the top three or four, but in the closing weeks of the season we were losing games we would have won earlier on. And once we started to struggle, there was no stopping the rot. It wasn't a bad season by any means, but we were disappointed nonetheless. After the way we had played through the dark days of midwinter, we honestly felt we were capable of finishing in at least the top three.

What a bunch of dreamers we were. We didn't know what it took to win that division or even what it was all about. Other clubs had launched themselves up the table on adrenaline in the past, and would do again. Yet the fact that we finished in a comfortable mid-table position made it a successful season, especially when you consider that people had been writing us off before it even began. I'd had a satisfactory year personally, scoring fifteen goals in all competitions. If I thought I should have done better, I at least knew my goals meant something in the great scheme of things. The season had been a thrilling experience, in spite of the slight disappointment at the end of it. We felt we knew where we had fallen down and how to get things right in 1989–90. In the close season we went on all sorts of trips, to Australia, Penang and Barbados, and had a great time. They are memories I wouldn't swap for anything.

Again we began the new season in good heart. We were all a year older and wiser, we thought, in the ways of First Division football, and we had pretty much the same team. And again we started off well, getting through the first five games unbeaten and topping the table in September. We were really enjoying ourselves. But coming up to Christmas it all began to go horribly wrong. I injured my ankle ligaments in a goalless draw against Queen's Park Rangers at Loftus Road on 25 November and missed the next six League games. Before long I was sitting in the stands watching my team-mates getting beaten in games we should have drawn at the very least. I came back into the side on 13 January and scored as a substitute at Nottingham Forest, but we still lost 3–1.

Don't get me wrong – I'm not saying that my absence was the reason we had done badly over Christmas and the New Year, because after I came back we went seventeen League games without a win. I scored a couple of goals in a 3–1 victory over Manchester City in the FA Cup, but we kept getting beaten in the League, and my ankle was still not quite right. I had to miss another five games in all, which didn't help. We had a couple of injuries to key players in that disastrous spell, but we couldn't honestly blame our poor record on that. If you're going to survive at the highest level in English football you have to have a squad that is strong enough in depth to take you through lean times. Ours wasn't. We just didn't have the back-up. The slide, when it came, was awful and irrevocable. Once we were into it there seemed absolutely nothing we could do to get ourselves out of it. My own form wasn't too clever, either – I scored only two League goals between the middle of January and the end of the season. Even now it isn't easy to put my finger on why we crashed so spectacularly It was a bit of inexperience, probably, plus a touch of naïveté, combined with the fact that losing is a habit that's easy to get into and the very devil to kick. It's a bit of a cliché, I know, but it's true nonetheless. When you go one down after ten minutes you think to yourself, 'Here we go again,' when, of course, you should be saying, 'Right, here's where we start winning this game.'

We were distraught, absolutely gutted. It was the end of our grand adventure; our flight at the top level had crashed pitifully to earth. It was probably the most disappointing period of my life to date, and it still figures high in the mercifully short list of sad times in my career. I so wanted to do well for Millwall, to give those rough-tongued, warm-hearted, salt-of-the-earth fans at the Den something to cheer about. Once again Tony Cascarino, my striking buddy, and I were pretty neck and neck in the goalscoring stakes when he was sold to Aston Villa for £1.5 million just before the transfer deadline. I suppose in a way that was the moment when the club conceded that they were going down. It was good business for Millwall, but it sent all the wrong messages to the fans and the team.

Even though our odyssey was over, there were still some outstanding memories for us to take back to the Second Division. Going to Manchester United was always a thrill, even though in that second season they simply murdered us 5–1. I scored the goal in that game, chasing a big, lofted ball and just beating Jim Leighton to it as he went to catch it, then flicking it into the empty net. It was nice to score against them; not so nice watching them net five against us without reply.

I can still remember the roar of the crowd at Old

Trafford, so much louder and more intense than anything I had ever heard before. When Mark Hughes scored one of his three goals that day the cacophony that greeted it was unbelievable. I remember thinking how great it would be to play in front of that every week, without even dreaming that one day I actually would. It was a frightening noise, but a wonderful noise, too. It was a daunting experience to go there as an opposition player. It still is.

I think it is significant about Millwall's two years in the First Division that, even in our first season when we were doing so well, we never really performed at our best against the best teams, the Manchester Uniteds, Liverpools, Tottenhams and Arsenals of this world. Being hard but honest, it underlined the fact that, no matter what the League table showed, we were always short of the highest class. It had been the experience of a lifetime playing against the greatest players and clubs in the land, but now it was back to reality.

Chapter Six

Out of the Promised Land

There was a strange mixture of emotions at the Den in the days and weeks that followed our relegation. We knew we had not been good enough in our second season of First Division football, and yet we still had faith in ourselves. We had been a good side when we went up, and although reason should have convinced us otherwise if we had really stopped to think about it, we felt we were still a decent outfit. After all, good sides don't become bad sides overnight, or even over two years. We were going back down with largely the same personnel that had taken us up, and we honestly felt we could challenge for a place in the top division again. And that is exactly what we did, although in true Millwall style, a crushing disappointment was to follow the euphoria.

John Docherty did not survive the drop. He was sacked a few weeks before the end of the season once relegation was assured, another victim, another unfortunate pushed off the managerial merry-go-round when things went wrong. I have never been able to completely come to terms with the compulsion of directors to blame the manager for absolutely everything that goes wrong. I know that nobody with more than half a working brain cell ever becomes a football manager in the belief that he has a job for life, but all too often directors take what I consider to be the easy way out, the perceived cure-all for a club's ills. I accept that a man who puts his head above the managerial parapet must do so in the knowledge that he might have it blown off; I acknowledge, too, that if you're going to pick up a handsome pay packet you have to shoulder the responsibility that goes with it and recognise that your salary has a built-in hedge against the consequent risk of dismissal.

But it's more complicated than that. For a start, the manager can only do his best with what he's got, and there is a strong chance that nobody else could have done any better in the same situation. The players, too, must hold up their hands and take their share of the blame. They can be coached to the hilt, prepared to the last detail by the man they call 'Boss', but when they trot on to that big, green, rectangular dancefloor they are the ones who must follow the right steps. If they fail, then they should be prepared to take some of the flak. No one man is responsible for making a team good or bad. But I don't suppose the situation will ever change; it is too firmly woven into the fabric of the game.

Finally, what of the directors themselves? Many men become directors of football clubs as a way of fulfilling their own secret dreams through others. Their love of the game should rarely be called into question. Indeed, the trouble with most of them is that they love the game a bit too much. They see in the players and the manager the people they would have liked to be and they get carried away with that dream. Many directors – most of them, probably – are successful in their business lives, and yet they routinely make the sort of decisions in the club boardroom that would result in a lynch mob being raised by shareholders of their companies.

I believe that, with very few exceptions, they should do what they're good at and leave the playing side of the club to the people who know what they're doing. If more of them applied the same rules to football as they do in business, football would be a stronger, healthier, more prosperous game than it already is. It doesn't apply to all directors, and I know that football is gradually becoming more businesslike, but there are still too many people dabbling in things they know little about.

None of that was much help to John Docherty. I was very sorry to see him go. He had led a team which, for a while, had proudly held their heads up and looked the First Division squarely in the eye. It didn't work out in the end, but it was a shame to see such a manifestly decent man sent packing. He went with the best wishes of his team ringing in his ears, and on a personal level he taught me a lot about the game which has stood me in good stead throughout my career.

The one serious error I think he did make was to bring Paul Goddard to Millwall from West Ham. He spent £800,000 on Goddard after we lost a couple of games early in the season, and it never really worked. For openers, none of the team thought we needed another striker. Millwall had an established forward pairing of Tony Cascarino and myself. We were effective both individually and as a two-man unit, and furthermore, we formed the right combination for the way our side played the game. Anybody coming into the Millwall forward line in those days had to have certain qualities, the most important of which was strength in the air. Docherty's style called for the long ball to be delivered to men who won it with their heads. Goddard was a clever, skilful centre forward, an England B cap and a player I had long admired, but what was the one weakness in his game? Dead right. He was not very good at all in the air.

To be blunt, there was not one player in the team who thought we needed Paul, great gifts though he undoubtedly possessed. Cascarino and Sheringham could deliver the goods, so Paul's arrival merely gave Docherty another problem. You can't spend the better part of £1 million on a player and then not put him on the park. But where was John going to play him? John's solution was to field Paul and me up front and put Tony on the left wing, and that completely spoiled the balance of the team. We were never the most sophisticated team in the world, but we did depend on having the right people to do certain jobs. With Paul in the team it just never gelled. It was unsettling that, having achieved some success playing in a certain way, we were now being asked to rip our game plan to bits and replace it with another one that wasn't going to work. Docherty, sad to say, never really figured out the answer to a problem he had created himself. Ultimately, it became just another nail in his own coffin.

During our two years in Division 1, a number of stories had circulated around the game, some of which even made the papers, suggesting that somebody or another was interested in buying me. They were never translated into positive action, and I never paid much heed to them until Cas was sold to Villa. It was only then, Tony's move coinciding as it did with the dramatic decline in the team's fortunes, that I began to wonder if there might, after all, be another turn in my career. But there was plenty of time for all that later. First there was a job to be done, namely to get Millwall back into the First Division, and we had a new manager to try to steer us there. The hardy perennial Bob Pearson was drafted into a caretaker role for a couple of months after Docherty was dismissed, but it was not long before he was replaced by a character who was as different in style and approach from John as it was possible to imagine.

We didn't get much chance to size up Bruce Rioch, the new man in charge, before the season ended because he was only there for our last game, but by the time we reported back for pre-season training in the summer of 1990 he had already made two significant changes. The first was selling Terry Hurlock to Rangers. I was proud to have played with Terry and very sorry to see him go. He went on to become Rangers' Player of the Year that season in their double-winning year. Secondly, he had brought in Steve Harrison as first-team coach. I went into the pre-season training session more than a little uncertain about my future. I thought there was every chance that the new regime would view me as being tainted by the club's lack of success the previous season. The new manager had already indicated that he wanted his own people with him by taking on Harrison, and I did wonder if the new broom might sweep me away like so much damaged goods.

But I need not have worried, because I got on with Bruce and Steve almost from the start. Bruce clearly had some regard for me, because he just about remoulded the whole team around me. His tactics were fairly simple: 'Get the ball to Teddy, let him move it out wide, give him the chance to get into the box and feed him when he arrives.' I liked that. It could be very good for me, I thought, and if it was good for me, it was likely to be good for the team as well. We had good wingers at the time – Jimmy Carter was a flier and Paul Stephenson was very capable on the other side. They were both clever, both intelligent, both good crossers who could get the ball into danger areas consistently well. It paid off handsomely.

Steve Harrison was good for me, too. He remains the funniest man I've ever met in the game. But to be completely honest, I have to say I didn't take to him at first. I'm a London boy through and through, and Steve was the first northerner I had really had anything to do with, and I remember wondering when we first met him if we would still be laughing at the same jokes in three weeks' time. But, strangely enough, the more he performed his party pieces, the funnier they became. He was very good for the team, not least because of the contrast he provided to Bruce. Bruce was very deep-thinking, a very strict disciplinarian, very serious, while Steve didn't seem to give a tinker's cuss for anything.

He would do things that in the retelling don't seem that funny – you had to be there to appreciate him. For example, we would be in an hotel on a Friday night before an away game, and he would go up to get his dinner and on the way back he'd trip, sending his meal everywhere. Staff would rush up to him from all over the place to make sure he was all right, and Steve would launch a stage wink in our direction as if to say, 'Got 'em again, lads.' He did that trick at almost every opportunity, and we, like a good audience, kept on laughing.

I remember staying at one hotel where the area we used for training was reached by walking down a 100-foot grass verge leading to a lake and then continuing for another 20 yards to the pitch. As we were all heading down the verge on the Saturday morning, Steve suddenly fell over and started rolling down the hill. We thought he'd have to stop rolling in a minute, but no, he just kept on tumbling, finally dribbling into the lake. We fell about.

You would think it would be difficult to take such a permanent clown seriously, but once the humorous stuff was out of the way, Steve proved he was a very good coach as well. He had an uncanny knack of getting inside players' minds. There is a lot of applied psychology in football, and Steve was brilliant at building up people's confidence. He laughed and joked with the best of them, but when he got down to work, he was one of the finest coaches I've ever had for getting situations and people right. Although he had been a left back himself, he obviously had a soft spot for strikers, because he put on some of the best shooting practices I've ever seen, so good that a lot of us would go back in the afternoons for another shooting session.

We started that first season back in the hurly-burly of Second Division football playing in a completely different style from the one that had seen us relegated. We had always been used to smashing the ball up long, but Bruce wanted quality balls so that the front players could get hold of it and control it. It was a total change, and one that we all responded to. If I had moved on after we were relegated, I might have ended up playing the Docherty way for the rest of my career. Instead Bruce insisted that we had enough good players to get the ball down, enjoy the game and play it how it should be played at the top level. He was a Second Division manager with First Division ideas, and that was no bad thing for every player on Millwall's books. All of a sudden, I was enjoying my football again: Bruce and Steve had been a real shot in the arm for my own game. Bruce was so committed to football, so straight-down-the-line, and so intense, you couldn't help but be affected by it.

Yet again I had a good manager at the right time. Talk about lucky Sheringham. Under almost every manager I've had, I've become a better player. To find now that the whole approach of the team was going to be geared to me was absolutely marvellous, and it was the best season I've ever had in terms of sheer goalscoring. I got thirty-eight in total, including thirty-three in the League – a healthy crop by anybody's standards, and one which earned me the Golden Boot as the Second Division's leading goalscorer. My biggest haul for a season up to then was the twenty-four I'd netted in our Second Division promotion year, 1987–8. Three years on, I was scoring like I had never done before. I did play well that season, although I say so myself, but I couldn't have done it without Steve Harrison's help. The way he worked me verged on the masterly.

I think if I'd been left to my own devices, once I beat my previous best tally I might have eased off a bit, content to have set a new personal record. But Steve wasn't prepared to let me stop there. He coached me using a very subtle technique that didn't fall far short of brainwashing. I would be sitting in the dressing room before a game and he would be alongside me, muttering, urging, cajoling, drilling his words quietly but insistently, repetitively, into my ear: 'Come on, I want another goal from you, and once you've got one I want two, come on, don't let it slip now. I want you buzzing, get up for it, there's another couple of goals here for you, look at the heights you can reach. I want you back in there, come on, give me another goal.' It was almost like a mantra. It got to the point where I could hardly hear what he was saying, but I knew without having to listen. When we got one game over, he would be on at me again immediately for the next one. It was incessant, but it was great. It was the kick up the backside I needed at that stage of my career. Everything was geared to me scoring goals, and it was coming off.

It was a memorable season for me, and almost a memorable one for the club. We were in a challenging position for most of it, and at one stage we had a good chance of gaining automatic promotion. We were undefeated in the first nine League games, in which I scored seven goals, a good enough return from the opening part of the season. I was feeling good and, like the rest of the lads, I honestly believed we were a top-class side playing in the wrong division. We played some good teams in that sequence, probably our best result being the 2–1 victory over Newcastle United at St James's Park. I got one of our goals against one of the great clubs in English football. They love their soccer on the banks of the Tyne – it really is a hotbed of the game up there. I can fully understand why players who've worn the famous black and white stripes always retain a soft spot for the club. You get the same sort of buzz when you pull on that magic red shirt at Manchester United.

The ninth and final game of a buoyant early-season period was a 4–1 thrashing we handed out to West Bromwich Albion at the Den. It remains crystal clear in my mind, because I scored a hat-trick, only the third of my career (I had bagged the first in a 4–0 home win over Huddersfield Town in my first full season of League football in 1986–7 and the second against West Brom again in a 4–1 victory at the Hawthorns the next year). After that we went off the boil a little bit, but kept the results ticking along. We had another decent run after Christmas, and in a spell of eight games I scored ten goals, including the first four-goal haul of my life when we beat Plymouth Argyle

4–1 in mid-February. Later in the season I got two more hat-tricks, scoring all the goals in a 3–1 win over Charlton Athletic and three in a 4–1 victory at Bristol City.

Towards the end of the season we had another powerful run and were a little unfortunate not to go straight back up. In the end we fell just short, but we had made the play-offs, and we were so confident that we thought we must prevail. We finished fifth in the League, but we reckoned we had got the best draw of the lot in Brighton. If we were guilty of anything, it was perhaps of being a bit overconfident. We thought we would walk it. We were wrong.

Brighton played really well in the first leg of the play-off at their Goldstone ground, winning 4–1. We were awful, and awfully ashamed, too. We knew the odds were stacked against us now, but we really gave it a go in the return at the Den. John McGinlay put us into the lead, the home crowd were really up for it and we did everything but score another two or three goals. It was not enough, and we did not even have the satisfaction of victory. In one of the most passionate nights of my footballing life, Brighton equalised and eventually won 2–1. What were to prove the last thirty minutes of my Millwall career were an awful anticlimax. They really brought it home to me what the club had meant to me. I'd had a great season personally, but I literally felt sick that we hadn't managed to regain for the club the place in the First Division we all felt it deserved.

There had been certain things that had discouraged me from the end of our second season of First Division football. For a start, I was good friends with Tony Cascarino, and as I've said, I didn't think he should have been sold when he was. I didn't feel it was a good time from the point of view of the club or the team, although it was a great move for him personally, and there was no way he was ever going to reject Villa's offer. It was talking with Cas about his move that made me begin to realise that I was not necessarily going to spend the rest of my career at the Den. He made me understand that playing for Millwall wasn't everything, that there might be something for me elsewhere. But before I could even begin to act on such selfish motives, I'd resolved to try to help the club get back where I felt they belonged.

Although we'd fallen at the final hurdle, part of me still wanted to have another crack at the job in 1991–2. I felt that if I spent another season at Millwall it would not be time wasted if we achieved our ambitions. On the other hand, I knew that if my career was going to progress, I should not spend another season in Division 2. During 1990–91 Steve Harrison had been working with Graham Taylor, the England manager at the time, and had told me that I was close to an England call-up. I knew Steve was telling me the truth, but I was still not confident enough in my own ability to believe that it was possible. Besides, I was only a Second Division player and there were a lot of First Division lads who I thought would come above me in the pecking order. On the other hand, Steve Bull of Wolves, also in Division 2, was getting the occasional place in the England line-up. But although I was higher in the scoring charts, Steve was more consistent. So an England place was still a long shot as far as I was concerned. It had not been top of my list of priorities at the time – I'd been concentrating on doing what was good for my club football career. If I got that right, and kept on scoring goals, other honours, such as a berth in the England team, would follow.

Now, however, I felt that perhaps the time had come

for me to part company with the club that had given me my chance in professional football.

I agonised over my decision for ages. My heart was telling me one thing and my head another, but in the end, I knew that, sadly, there was no choice. I had just turned twenty-five. I needed a higher standard of football if my career was going to progress, and I reasoned that if I stayed at Millwall I would have to get pretty close to my thirty-eight-goal haul again to stay in the hunt for an international cap.

I'd had a great time at the club and, my early hiccups with George Graham apart, I had enjoyed every moment of my years there. After all, without Millwall I might never have become a professional footballer in the first place. Even today, when I look back on my Millwall days, I can honestly say that they were brilliant. I'd had a very tough upbringing, but I'd needed it. It was character-building, too – you can't survive the stick I got from the fans in my early days without coming out of it a stronger person. They were hard people living in the unforgiving little world of south London, but they were warm, wonderful folk, and I loved them.

So, with hundreds of regrets, I was forced to tell the club that I felt I needed to move on – in spite of the very flattering offer of the best contract that had ever been offered to a Millwall player. And, bless their hearts, they did everything they could for me. I still like to think that the fans appreciated the fact that I had given good service to the club. I had been a loyal servant at the Den, and pretty effective in my own way – I had scored 111 goals for the club in all competitions in my eight years there.

As luck would have it, the first club to put in a concrete offer could not give me what I wanted most of all – First

Division football. Blackburn Rovers had tried and failed to sign Gary Lineker at the end of his distinguished Tottenham career. If I was their second choice after one of the most remarkable goalscorers in the history of English football, I considered it was only courteous at least to have a chat with their manager, Don Mackay. He told me how the multimillionaire Jack Walker had just taken over the club, and how ambitious he was to get it out of the Second Division. I was impressed, but in the end I felt there was very little point in leaving Millwall to go to another Second Division club, however big their aspirations. It has to be said that Blackburn had more money than Millwall would ever have, but there was no getting away from the fact that it could only be a sideways move for me. I was flattered by the fact that they were prepared to lay £2 million on the table for me and offer me good personal terms into the bargain, but I had to politely decline their generous offer.

Within a week, Nottingham Forest had put in a bid of £2 million. I immediately liked the idea of playing for Forest. There had been some loose talk of Tottenham or Chelsea being interested in me, but there had been nothing tangible from either of them to support such speculation. My main concern was to avoid the whole thing dragging on until the start of the next season. I knew if it did I might very well get caught up in the old Millwall emotional thing and end up not going anywhere. I thought about Clough and his track record; he had always had strong sides and his views on the game seemed to run along much the same lines as my own. My philosophy was to control the ball and keep it – something that had been drummed into me by my dad – and I believed that Clough thought that way, too.

Yes, this was more like it: I was wanted by an established First Division club with a good track record. I accepted their offer. And in doing so, I put myself into the hands of one of the most extraordinary characters I have ever met.

Chapter Seven

Clough the Unique

My first meeting with Brian Clough was a bizarre, almost surreal experience. In the company of Frank McLintock, who had once coached me and had now become my agent, I was being shown around the City Ground in Nottingham. I should have been in a state of sheer joy, but I was feeling slightly uneasy. I had signed for a First Division club for a serious amount of money, yet so far I hadn't met the manager. I wondered where he was, because I needed to talk to him.

Just then a familiar sound reached my ears. It was the celebrated nasal tones of the legendary Cloughie in the middle distance. As I turned a corner, he came through a door in front of me. I approached him, expecting, I suppose, some sort of warm greeting.

I didn't expect it for long. 'Ah, Edward,' he said as he walked up to me. I thought, oh no, please don't call me Edward. Tell me, please, that you're not going to call me Edward. The only person who'd ever called me Edward was my mum, when she caught me doing something naughty. I plucked up the courage to say, 'It's Teddy, Mr Clough. Only my mum calls me Edward.'

'Really, son?' he said. 'Well, it's nice to meet you, Edward.' First lesson learned. It was his way of introducing himself, of showing me straight away who was the boss around here. After that he rarely called me anything else but Edward. I decided not to correct him again.

Then I asked who'd be wearing the number 9 shirt, which I was keen to do as I'd always worn that number at Millwall. I wasn't thinking, really, because of course the man with the number 9 on his back at Forest was none other than the manager's son, Nigel, one of the star players. 'Just make sure you're wearing a shirt with a number between one and eleven on it, son,' he replied. So I took number 10, which I went on to become attached to.

He knew exactly what he was doing, and I give myself credit for realising it. Because this man who was an inextricable part of the folklore of the English game was a great psychologist. That was the reason why I enjoyed playing for him. Unlike most managers, he didn't set any great store by developing set pieces. His philosophy was a very simple one: 'There's only one ball, go and get into your areas and win it. Get the ball and pass it to a red shirt, turn, commit opponents, but above all keep the ball.' And that was it, really, and diametrically opposite to my early Millwall days of 'launch it, flip it and get on to the next one'. It was, however, very similar to Bruce Rioch's basic strategy, so the year I had spent with him, albeit at a lower level, was to stand me in very good stead under Clough.

There were some truly extraordinary players at Forest during my time there. Week in and week out, the out-standing member of the team was Des Walker, Stuart Pearce coming a close second. I had played against Des when we were kids, me for Beaumont and he for a club called Enfield Rangers. He had been a left-sided midfield player in those days, and not that good, to be honest. I think he was a bit like me, a late developer. And now we were to be team-mates.

I would say that Des was Man of the Match in 90 per cent of the games I played with him. He was just unbelievable, consistently head and shoulders above everybody else on the pitch. The crowd got it spot on. 'You'll never beat Des Walker,' they would sing, and ninety-nine times out of a hundred they were right. People just didn't get past him – he was quick, strong, lost no tackles, read the game like a master. At the time he was the best player I had ever had as a team-mate by a mile. If I had to pick a team from guys I have played alongside, Des in his prime would be my first choice.

Stuart was not far behind him. He never quite reached the same level as Dessie – who could? – but what he lacked in talent compared with Walker he made up for with complete concentration and total dedication. It was great to be part of a team that contained people like these two, who had represented England so many times. You couldn't help but respond to players like that.

I also enjoyed playing with Nigel Clough, who made up for the disadvantage of being the manager's son by being an outstanding footballer in his own right. He was very similar to me in many ways. He was a brave, clever player who was always prepared to receive the ball with his back to the goal and a hulking centre half breathing down his neck. He used to get whacked so many times by a Tony Adams or a Steve Bould or a Martin Keown, but he would always come back for more. Once you've been clattered as a centre forward, you can become very wary of taking the next ball because you don't know exactly what's coming up behind you and know that the chances are you will get thumped again.

But Nigel wouldn't flinch. He would receive that ball and, sure enough, he would be mugged again. And still he would come back for more. His game went beyond raw courage, though: his first touch was brilliant in that he could get the ball and turn in one go and lay other players on.

Paradoxically, the one thing to which I could never quite get attuned was Clough Senior's habit of basing everything around his son, although he was clever enough never to mention him by name. 'Get the ball and give it to the number nine,' he would say. I think that rankled a bit with a lot of the players, because we all felt we could play the game. All the same, Nigel was an incredible player, and when he went to Liverpool I'm sure most people thought his career would really take off. I think he was a bit overwhelmed at Anfield. At Forest he was one of three or four stars, whereas at Liverpool they all were. There were probably egos to match, too, and Nigel never had much inclination to push himself forward. I suppose you don't when you've got a dad like his.

And Brian Clough was an amazing man with equally amazing methods. We hardly ever trained in the strict sense of the word. His credo was that players should get as much rest as they could. Some days we would turn up for training and do just a ten-minute warm-up, led by Pearce (most clubs do at least half an hour). Then we'd run a couple of lengths of the training ground, set up for a five-a-side, kick off, somebody would score the first goal and Cloughie would stroll along with his walking stick and his dog and say, 'OK, that'll do you. Let's go.' We'd protest, but he'd insist that we saved all that energetic stuff for the game on Saturday. We'd say, 'All right, so can we do a bit of shooting practice?' but he'd get quite firm and virtually order us to go home and rest.

It was an interesting approach, to say the least, but it was never enough for me. Paul Hart, who was one of the club's coaches at the time, told me that in the days when he played for Cloughie he used to go off for runs on his own at night, just to satisfy himself that he'd worked up a sweat. I didn't go quite that far; in any case in the end I thought I really should go along with what the boss wanted. I don't know if it would have been much good to me in the long run, but I was playing for the man, he was my manager, he'd had a lot of success over the years and he certainly knew more than I did. So if that was what he wanted, it was only right that I gave it a go.

Match days were equally unreal. Cloughie would make a great production of putting a towel on the floor in the middle of the dressing room and planting a ball on it. 'There's the ball,' he'd say. 'Keep it. Play with it. Treasure it. Look after it, and if you do, it will come back to you. Keep the ball, remember. That's what you train all week for, to keep the ball. Not to give it away, not to kick it into the stands: keep it. The most you ever do is lend it to somebody else, and if you've cherished it while you've had it, it'll come back to you.'

To call his half-time advice a team talk would be to overstate the case by a factor of about a hundred. He didn't get the whole team together and tell us how we were going to change things in the second, what we'd been doing right and what we'd done wrong. He'd just sit in his favourite place inside the door and watch us come in and then, perhaps, decide that he wanted to have a word with one of us. If Archie Gemmill, another of the coaches, was talking to Roy Keane and Cloughie wanted to speak to Pearce, he would tell Archie to shut up, sit down, listen and learn something. He thought that if everybody paid attention to what he said to one player the whole team would learn more than they would from being told about their own individual games.

I scored my first goal for Forest against our local rivals, Notts County, in the third game of the season, then found the net eleven more times in the following twenty-one matches. After that I hit a barren spell. Five, six, seven games went by without my name making the scoreboard and there was some speculation that I might be dropped. I couldn't have complained if I had been, but Clough stuck with me through it all. Every week I'd look at the team sheet and half expect to be left out, or at least relegated to the substitutes' bench, but the demotion never came.

I eventually broke the spell with a goal in a 2–0 win over Hereford United in the FA Cup. I could have been forgiven for thinking that things would be all right now, but I made the mistake of basing my opinion on logic – you could forget that as far as the idiosyncratic Mr Clough was concerned. I suppose, having played for him for a while by then, I should have half expected it, but it still came as a shock when I discovered on the morning of the next match that I didn't figure anywhere in the team. It would be more accurate to say I was flabbergasted. He had kept faith with me all the time I hadn't been scoring, and now, when I had, he'd dropped me. I wasn't even a substitute.

I was still gazing, bewildered, at the team sheet when the man himself walked past. 'Son, do you want to sit on the bench with me today?' he said. Perhaps not surprisingly, I was a bit non-committal, so then he said, this time much more forcefully, 'Son, you *will* sit on the bench with me today.' As he intended it to be, just sitting there and listening to him for ninety minutes was an education.

Aged nine weeks, with my proud mum.

My love of fast red cars was to resurface later…

On holiday in 1969, aged three, with my brother Jimmy, six – and the ever-present football.

Posing bashfully for the camera with my dad in 1971.

Selwyn Primary football team 1976–7 with our haul of silverware: the Birmingham Cup, McEntee Cup, League Shield and Five-a-Side Shield. I'm in the centre of the middle row.

Aged fifteen (back row, fourth from right) with my team-mates at Monoux School.

All I ever wanted to do was play football, so it was a great thrill when I was offered an apprenticeship with Millwall. That's me in the Youth team, on the far left of the back row; Neil Ruddock is on the far right.

In action for Millwall: in 1988 against Nottingham Forest, the club I was to join three years later (right), and in my last match at the Den, the second leg of the play-off against Brighton and Hove Albion, which they won to deny Millwall a place in the First Division for 1991–2 (below). It was an awful anticlimax to my time at the club which gave me my big chance.

Back in Division 1 with Nottingham Forest under the incomparable Brian Clough (above). Duelling with Gary Mabbutt of Tottenham, the club I'd supported since childhood (left). My dream of playing for them was to be fulfilled a few months later.

Terry Venables (right), the man who brought me to White Hart Lane, with club chairman Alan Sugar in happier times.

With Terry's successor, Ossie Ardiles (below). For a striker, his tactics were gloriously liberating.

Ossie's Famous Five. From left to right: Nicky Barmby, Jürgen Klinsmann, Ilie Dumitrescu, Darren Anderton and me.

Eccentric goal celebrations number 1: marking Klinsmann's first for Tottenham with a communal dive in our first game of the 1994–5 season at Hillsborough.

MIRROR SYNDICATION INTERNATIONAL

Klinsmann congratulates me on another goal in that exhilarating season.

COLORSPORT

In combat with my old pal Neil 'Razor' Ruddock of Liverpool. Our paths have crossed again and again during our careers since we first played together in Millwall's Under-18 side.

A terrific moment: wearing the England shirt for the first time in the starting line-up for the World Cup qualifier against Poland in Katowice in 1993.

Another personal milestone: the first goal I scored on the hallowed turf of Wembley for my country, in the 3–1 victory over Switzerland in 1995.

COLORSPORT

COLORSPORT

Countdown to Euro '96. Climbing the Great Wall of China with 'Shaggy' Anderton (right), and flying the flag for England with coach Terry Venables and some of the lads (below).

Eccentric goal celebrations number 2: the Dentist's Chair revisited. Congratulating Gazza on his Euro '96 goal against Scotland with a re-enactment of the infamous incident.

The first of my two goals against Holland. Being made Man of the Match after that unbelievable game was the icing on the cake

Going out of the competition in the semi-finals after a penalty shoot-out with Germany gave a new meaning to the word 'gutted'.

another fast red car. This one –
my Ferrari 355 – is a bit of an
improvement on the model I had
as a toddler.

My son Charlie and I getting our
hands on the European Championship
trophy at last – though not quite in
the way I'd hoped.

Nicola and I unwind with my England team-mate Ian Wright and his wife,
Debbie.

Signing for the legendary Manchester United in 1997.

My first game for United was at White Hart Lane, where I took a fair bit of stick from the fans and managed to miss a penalty. But the important thing was that we won 2–0. Here I am congratulating Nicky Butt on his goal.

My header zips past Angelo Peruzzi to level the scores in our Champions' League match against Juventus at Old Trafford. It was my first goal in the competition, and the game, which we went on to win 3–2, was about as good a one as I have ever played in.

's always a pleasure to score against Arsenal, as I did with Manchester United
the 1997–8 season (top). On this occasion, however, I got into hot water for
issing the badge on my shirt after netting the first of my two goals in our 3–2
efeat (below).

The road to France and the 1998 World Cup. I head the ball into the net
for England's first goal in the qualifier against Georgia at Wembley (above).
Challenging for the ball in the big one against Italy in Rome (below left), and
enjoying a brief moment of jubilation after we ensured qualification before
being collared for a random drugs test.

ngland's SAS – Shearer and
heringham – training for the
g event.

One of the most harrowing events
of my life: reading out a statement to
the press after the Portugal incident.
David Davies of the FA looks on.

ur first match of France '98, against Tunisia. I nearly scored with this shot at
al from 30 yards.

Michael Owen comes on to replace me in the final minutes of our match with Tunisia. I felt I had done my bit, but little did I realise that my World Cup was almost over.

With Charlie at the World Cup final. Fate had decreed that I would have to watch the match from the stands, but I couldn't help thinking 'If only...'.

He never once addressed a remark to me personally, but I learned a tremendous amount that day about what he wanted from his forward players. In two simple actions – leaving me out, then making me sit with him – he taught me more than I would have ever picked up on the pitch in a dozen games. He hadn't told me he was dropping me, and he certainly hadn't told me why he was dropping me: it was very subtle, and very enlightening. It gave me an insight into what made this most singular of men tick. I was back in the team for the next game and scored a hat-trick against Crystal Palace in the League Cup.

We didn't pull up any trees in the League that year, finishing eighth, but we did do well in Cup football. We won the Zenith Data Systems Cup by beating Southampton 3–2. Admittedly this was not a desperately important competition, and the final did not mean a great deal, to be honest, but the match had a significance for me in that it was my first game at Wembley. In the Southampton side that day were Neil Ruddock and Terry Hurlock, both of whom were also making their first appearances at the grand old stadium. When we were all at Millwall we had dreamed about taking the club to Wembley. We hadn't managed that, but it was still nice for the three of us, the closest of close friends as well as opponents, to play at the national stadium for the first time together. It is an amazing place; I still love playing there. That day I tried very hard to savour the moment, because you never know when it's going to be your last game on the hallowed turf. You can't take anything for granted. There is an aura about the place that is indescribable; it's a wonderful pitch, wonderful atmosphere – just marvellous.

But we made it to Wembley again that season, to contest

the League Cup final with Manchester United. United won 1–0, and the result doesn't accurately portray their domination of the game. Brian McClair scored the only goal, but United would not have been flattered by four or five: they were simply a cut above us.

And we did well in the knock-out competition that really mattered. We wanted success in the FA Cup for ourselves and for the club, of course, but we wanted it, too, to give Brian Clough something he had never experienced – victory in an FA Cup final. Sadly, it didn't get that far. We played nicely in the earlier rounds, beating Wolves 1–0, Hereford 2–0 (the game that broke my goal famine) and Bristol 4–1 (I scored one in that tie, too). As each match came and went, so our confidence and expectations grew. We thought we were on to something good, so it came as a total shock to us when we went out 1–0 to Portsmouth in the quarter-finals.

We were really up for that game, but we were totally deflated when our goalkeeper made a mistake in the second minute. Mark Crossley came out for a corner, missed it and the ball was bundled into the net. We did everything but score after that, and we could have had about four goals, but try as we might we just couldn't breach their line. We couldn't blame Mark, because on another day he might have kept us in a game we deserved to lose. The defeat was down to all of us. It just went to show how in football, on one day you can make a dozen errors and get away with them, while on another you can make one and live to regret it. That game, incidentally, gave me my first sight of Darren Anderton, with whom I was one day to play at Tottenham. Even then, up against the mighty Stuart Pearce, he looked an outstanding prospect.

Those disappointments aside, it was for the most part a

happy season for me. I was playing for a firmly established First Division side who were capable on their day of beating anybody in the division. I had played with some pretty good people at Millwall in my eight years there, but the general level of ability at Forest was superior, and that was what I had been looking for.

As well as Walker, Pearce and Nigel Clough, I liked playing with Ian Woan. It's always a tremendous bonus to have a good left-sided attacking midfield player in your side, and Ian was a perfect example of the breed. He was a great, pinpoint-accurate passer of the ball, a dream to play with, and he made a good number of goals for me. I thought so much of him that when I was at Tottenham I tried to persuade every successive manager to sign him, but Terry Venables, Ossie Ardiles and Gerry Francis were not convinced. I must concede that Ian wasn't then, and isn't now, the hardest-working player by any stretch of the imagination – he'll willingly admit that himself – but every so often he puts a little spurt on. When he really exerts himself, he remains one of the most effective left-sided players in the country – as well as being a good friend and someone I enjoy taking money off on the golf course.

There were some great personalities in that side, but the biggest of them all was undoubtedly the manager. He was unique. He was capable of great kindness. A dustman could be made to feel like a lord by Cloughie. But he had the capacity for great cruelty, too, and he could bring someone down with a few vicious words. He had an aura about him, you could see it reflected in people's eyes when they were in his company. He was undoubtedly a great football manager who could speak with great eloquence about the game, but I didn't like the fact that when he took it into his head to do so he could inflict a fatal wound with his sharp tongue.

For what he achieved in the game, I think Cloughie deserved to be given a chance to manage England when he was in his prime, but I don't think he would have suited the mandarins at the FA as a figurehead. He was too irreverent, too full of his own ideas, too lacking in the powers of diplomacy, too outspoken for the people who run the English game. Regardless of how convinced you are that you're right, you have to know at what point to bite your tongue. Cloughie could never do that. I liked him for it; hundreds more hated him for the same reason.

By the time I went to Forest he had a bit of a reputation as a drinker, and it didn't take me long to find out about it. My first game for the club was a 2–1 win against Everton on a blazing hot day in August 1991. In the dressing room plastic beakers of isotonic drinks had been lined up for us to grab immediately after the match to quickly replace the fluids we had lost. I traipsed into the changing room, totally shattered, and grabbed the first beaker I saw. I took a long swig, and for the next ten seconds I couldn't breathe. It was a very large, barely diluted, vodka and orange. As I was struggling to catch my breath the manager walked in. 'I think I've just drunk your drink, Boss,' I gasped.

'My drink?' he said. 'What do you mean, my drink? It's not mine.'

No, Boss, I thought, of course it's not. The man who comes in to fill up the baths always brings a quadruple vodka and orange with him, doesn't he?

Throughout that season there was newspaper speculation that Tottenham were thinking of putting in a bid for me, but although it would have been great, I never really gave it much thought. I had signed a four-year contract with Forest, and I fully intended to see it out. I was reasonably happy there; I scored twenty-two goals, and

I would probably get more in my second season now that I had got used to the way the team played.

However, looking back, I don't think I ever quite settled down in Nottingham itself. I was a London boy used to the big-city life. You could drive into Nottingham and be out the other side in ten minutes. I was in an hotel for eight months, which wasn't the best home life for a professional athlete. I think it says a lot about my feelings about living in Nottingham that it was not until the last few months that I got a house to rent. There was never any question of buying somewhere up there; I just wasn't cut out to live in the provinces. Perhaps subconsciously I was telling myself and the rest of the world that although I might be here now, it wouldn't be for ever.

Another powerful factor in my wanting always to get back to London was that I missed my son, Charlie. I was still potty about Charlie and wanted to see him as often as I could. I spent an awful lot of time that year driving up and down the motorway to see him for a few precious hours. It had always been drummed into me by my dad that I must treasure my health and my time.

During the 1992–3 pre-season training period, the talk of Tottenham coming in for me resurfaced, and with renewed force. Throughout a trip to Ireland with the club rumours were circulating that Forest had accepted a £2 million offer for me from Terry Venables. They turned out to be true. Forest asked me if I would like to talk to Terry, and I said that I would, very much. I was being given the chance to join the club I would have given my eye teeth to play for, a club with one of the best coaches in the world. We duly met, and I thought we were a fair way down the road to clinching a deal when the transfer was called off, I think by Forest. As a lifelong Tottenham fan,

I was very disappointed, but I accepted that Forest were quite entitled to keep me there if they wanted to, and if so I would be happy with that.

The new season arrived, and it was a very big one for English football: it saw the launch of the FA Premiership. In the very first game I scored an absolute blinder that beat Liverpool 1–0 at the City Ground, cutting in from the left to beat David James and hammer home the sort of goal that George Graham would have delighted in. It was the first Premiership game to be shown live on Sky TV, and I'd scored: it would be an understatement to say I was pleased with myself. As we showered afterwards we were talking ourselves up a treat. We'd beaten Liverpool; perhaps there was something good coming for Nottingham Forest.

But the euphoria didn't last. Sheffield Wednesday beat us 2–0 at Hillsborough in the middle of the following week, and three days later Oldham thrashed us. I was substituted when we were 5–0 down and the lads fought back to 5–3. Suddenly, on the Sunday or Monday, the deal with Tottenham was rekindled, and off I went again to meet Terry Venables. This time it did go through. After all those years of admiring Tottenham Hotspur from afar, at last I was going to play for them.

To this day I don't really know why Forest agreed to sell me. Perhaps they felt I was homesick. Perhaps they thought that, even though I had scored my share of goals for them, I wasn't quite the finished article they'd been expecting when they bought me from Millwall. All I know is that I will look back on my year with Nottingham Forest with affection. And Brian Clough? Well, we had a strange, quirky relationship, but what an experience it was working with such a legend. And would I have missed it? Not on your life.

Chapter Eight

Bung in the Middle
of a Scandal

When I scored that goal against Liverpool on the first day of the FA Carling Premiership, heralded as a new dawn for English football, I experienced mixed emotions. I'm a goalscorer, a striker, a predator on the football field. It's what I do, so naturally I'm always happy to score a goal. But this one was different. I had almost achieved my lifetime's dream, to be signed by Tottenham, but it had been snatched away from me. With this goal, I thought, you are wed to Nottingham Forest, at least for the foreseeable future. And that would have been fine – I was plying my trade in what I still believe is the most competitive league in the world – but I'd had a glimpse of what might have been, and nothing quite compared with that.

And now, lo and behold, within the space of a week the Tottenham deal was all back on again. The red-letter day, 27 August 1992, started with Ronnie Fenton, Brian Clough's assistant manager, asking me if I was still interested in going to White Hart Lane. I couldn't get out of his office fast enough. If the clubs had agreed a deal, all I wanted was for Spurs to offer me a halfway decent contract. If they did, I would be a Tottenham player come hell or high water.

I met my agent, Frank McLintock, near White Hart Lane and we went into the ground together. I passed my medical with flying colours, and we talked a bit about personal terms. I was happy to accept their offer. By 4 pm I had signed my life over to Tottenham Hotspur Football Club. It was the happiest day of my professional life to date.

Next Frank and I had to go and meet Ronnie Fenton to hand over some medical papers that had to be sorted out so that I could be registered to play for Tottenham as soon as possible. We got the documents Forest needed and drove to meet Ronnie at an hotel in Luton, a convenient midway point between Tottenham and Nottingham. We had a meal in the hotel, then Frank handed over the forms to Ronnie, and we went back to Frank's local in Winchmore Hill for a celebratory drink. Little did I know that the events of those happy few hours were to erupt into a scandal that would send shock waves through the game – or for how long those shock waves would continue.

It was at that Luton meeting that a 'bung' was said to have been taken. The sum mentioned was £50,000, the money allegedly going to line the pockets of McLintock, Clough and Fenton for oiling the deal. I have been assured by everybody involved that no money exchanged hands then or at any time afterwards. I cannot personally swear to that, because I wasn't with the principal players in the deal every minute of the day or night. What I can say is that I never saw a penny change hands in any shape or form. And I will say that once again, just to make sure that nobody misunderstands me: I never saw money change hands, then or at any other time. I can put my hand on my heart and swear to that. Sorry – I know it would make for a juicier read if I said I witnessed large bundles of folding stuff being passed from one party to another, but I'm not going to lie. Certainly not for the sake of the headlines.

The accusations arose some time later, during the acrimonious and prolonged row between Tottenham chairman Alan Sugar and Terry Venables, a nasty, messy affair from which nobody emerged with much distinction. There was supposedly a sheet of accounts detailing a payment of £50,000 made by Venables to McLintock. That payment *was* made, but it was in settlement of consultancy services McLintock had performed for Tottenham over the previous six months. All three of the players in the piece, Clough, Fenton and McLintock, have denied time and again that any money was offered or received to facilitate my transfer. Clough has even gone into print to deny the charges in his autobiography.

I am sad that such allegations were made. Football doesn't need dirt or scandal or suggestions of impropriety – the hounds of the tabloid press make up enough as it is without people in the game giving them anything else to sink their fangs into. I am glad that, throughout it all, nobody ever claimed that I might personally have benefited from any such skulduggery. It was about me, but it didn't involve me.

One thing I do know, and that is that if there is enough mud flying around, and you happen to be standing a bit too close to the action, some of it will stick to you. To this day, it remains an uncomfortable phase in my life and I don't think I will ever be allowed to forget it. The affair hung over me for a long, long time. It was daunting to have to go in front of the inquiry that was set up and to be interrogated about what I did or did not do, what I did or did not see. Every time it was mentioned it was referred to as the 'Teddy Sheringham deal', even though it had nothing to do with me – I was just the piece of property that the argument was over. Nonetheless I was somehow tainted by it, and still, whenever the names of Clough or Venables come up, my name is the next one on people's lips. It shouldn't happen, it is a disgrace that it does happen, but there you are. It's a rough deal, to be honest. It could have been anybody, but it just happens to have been me. I have to live with it, but I don't have to like it. I prefer to think that the name of Teddy Sheringham stands for honour and honesty. That's the way I try to lead my life. In fact, it's that very honesty that has got me into trouble at times, but too bad, that's just the way I am. I'm not whining about it: I just don't think it's quite fair, that's all. End of subject.

Back to football. When Tottenham signed me, they had just lost 5–0 away to Leeds, and it was obvious that they needed an established, experienced hand to lead the forward line. Terry had brought in Dean Austin from Southend, Neil Ruddock had returned from Southampton, Darren Anderton had just been signed from Portsmouth, but in the manager's rebuilding plans I was the big signing of the summer at £2.1 million. I'd like to think that over the next five years I gave them value for money.

For me it was the realisation of a dream, a romance. It had a special feel to it, for there is an indefinable glamour that clings to Tottenham. When they were successful, they did things in a stylish way. In spite of Arsenal's subsequent golden period and Chelsea's resurgence under Gullit and

Vialli, I still see Tottenham as the biggest club in London, the one they all want to play for. If Tottenham had had the same success as Arsenal over the last decade, they would be a far bigger club than the boys from Highbury. Everybody talks about sleeping giants: Tottenham is just such a club. With a change in fortunes, they could still be the Manchester United of the south.

When I signed for the club, Terry Venables talked a lot to me about his grand plan for winning the Premiership and about the players he had and those he wanted. He had a good deal of faith in Darren Anderton, and he told me that I was the last piece in the jigsaw for the time being. The next season, he said, he was looking to buy another centre half, perhaps Des Walker, to play alongside Neil Ruddock, but for now things were developing nicely.

There were some fine players in the first Tottenham side I played in. Erik Thorstvedt – 'Erik the Viking', they called him – was in goal, but Ian Walker, later to become an England international, was the up-and-coming prospect. Austin was a very accomplished right back. For some reason he always got stick from the crowd, but I used to enjoy playing with him in the side. You always knew that Dean would give his all for the team without any thoughts of personal glory. Every club needs its Dean Austins, honest and straightforward.

Ruddock, of course, I'd been with at Millwall, so his qualities were well known to me. He had a sweet left foot – he was a centre half who could pass like a midfield player. Alongside him was Gary Mabbutt, who, although nearing the end of his career, still did a great job. His professionalism got him through a lot of potential trouble. Justin Edinburgh, who had been at the club for about a year when I arrived, was another Dean Austin at left back

– a very dependable, solid player, a typical good English defender.

Anderton took three or four months to settle in, but when he did he went from strength to strength. His quality shone out in everything he did. Even then it was obvious that he was England material. At full fitness, which he hasn't always enjoyed, his would be one of the first names I would write down if I were allowed to pick the England team. 'Shaggy' is just about the complete right-sided midfield player when he is functioning at his maximum efficiency.

David Howells in the centre of midfield was another 100-per-cent reliable performer. The number of bad games he had could be counted on the fingers of one hand. He was rarely outstanding, but he never, ever let us down, either, and he was good in the air. I didn't always see eye to eye with Vinny Samways off the pitch, but on it he was tremendous. He had the ability to control the ball in one touch and deliver it wherever you wanted it. He had great pace as well, and complemented my game brilliantly.

Nayim was at the club at that time, too. I thought he was a terrific player, a player of great skill and great vision. Remember that wonder goal he scored over David Seaman's head from the halfway line for Real Zaragoza against Arsenal in the Cup-Winners' Cup final at the Parc des Princes in 1995? Alongside me was Gordon Durie, who had fantastic running ability and could score a goal. Gordon had a few injuries that year, though, which gave a chance to the young Nicky Barmby, whose enthusiasm rubbed off on me. He wanted to get better, wanted to learn. Here was another England footballer in the making.

My first game for the club was a 1–1 draw at Ipswich, best remembered for our equaliser, which was bizarre, to say the least. Jason Cundy went in for a block tackle 5 yards into their half and the ball flew off his boot, over the head of the Ipswich goalkeeper, who was off his line, and into the net. But my home debut is the game that sticks in my mind most. It was the following Wednesday against Sheffield United at White Hart Lane, and I was fortunate enough to score in our 2–0 victory. It wasn't the greatest of goals, to be honest, but it was me who got the last touch before it went over the line, and that was good enough for me. It was a great moment, the first of many I was to experience over the next five years. Indeed, I had a pretty decent start to the season as far as goal scoring was concerned. I had nine before Christmas, a steady if not spectacular contribution. Then, in the New Year, I caught alight. The run started when I netted both goals in a 2–0 FA Cup victory over Norwich, and seven games later I had added another ten. I ended up with twenty-two League goals that season (twenty-nine counting Cup matches) and I won the Golden Boot for being the Premiership's leading goalscorer, two ahead of Les Ferdinand.

The lowest point of that season was our defeat by Arsenal in the semi-final of the FA Cup, which had to be staged at Wembley because no other ground would have been big enough to satisfy the demand for tickets. I still blame myself a bit for Arsenal's winning goal. I was supposed to be marking Tony Adams on the far post, but at the last minute Thorstvedt asked me to be the fourth man in the wall, so I had to go with the call even though I didn't think they would shoot from there. The effect of the move was to leave Tony a bit free, and he scored almost unchallenged with a downward header.

It was to be just about the last chance Terry Venables had to make an indelible mark at Tottenham. He had worked tirelessly to get the right blend at the club, not only on the pitch but off it as well. He recognised that it was important for people to gel as personalities, not just as footballers. You always felt that Terry's reasons for bringing people to the club went beyond their ability to play the game. They had to be able to fit into the grand plan that was to take Tottenham forward to greater things. As a person he was a delight to work for. He was always friendly and chirpy with everybody – except for one person, who I don't need to name. There was a great atmosphere at White Hart Lane under his stewardship. If he had been given the time, I am absolutely convinced he would have made Tottenham one of the great powers of English football once again.

But it was not to be. Just when things were beginning to come together, Terry was forced out. I'd had just one season under him, and it was a memorable one for a hundred different reasons. Despite his huge efforts, and ours, to make something truly worthwhile out of the club, he was not given the chance to bring his plans to fruition. I don't really know what went on in the boardroom at that time, but there was obviously a huge clash of personalities and there was only ever one man who was going to come out on top: the man with the money and the clout. The all-powerful Alan Sugar.

That first season at Tottenham was a special one for me on the personal front, too: it was during this time that I met my girlfriend, Nicola. We met through my team-mate Pat van den Hauwe, who was going out with Nicola's sister, Mandy Smith, once famously married to Bill Wyman of the Rolling Stones. I first noticed Nicola across a car park at White Hart Lane and was immediately struck by her. I asked Pat to introduce us, but he wasn't having any of it. He gave in when he and Mandy decided to get engaged. They had arranged a party to celebrate the event on Valentine's Day 1993, and he talked to Nicola, who agreed to meet me there if I scored a goal in our match that day against Wimbledon. I duly obliged, the introduction was made and things moved on from there. It was a turbulent relationship from the start. We were and still are madly in love with each other, but we have both created problems along the way, there have been splits and life has not always run smoothly for us.

Back at White Hart Lane, Venables was replaced by Ossie Ardiles, a rare man who transcended the antipathy still harboured by some English people for Argentinians in the years after the Falklands War. Ossie was universally liked throughout the English game for his modesty, his enormous skills as a footballer and his worth as a human being. At Tottenham he was still loved for the wonderful football he had played there alongside his compatriot Ricky Villa. Neither the staff nor the supporters wanted Venables to go, but if he had to, they couldn't have hoped for anybody much better than Ardiles to replace him.

The first season under Ossie, 1993–4, was a bitter-sweet one for me. The new manager's philosophy was simple – 'If they score three, we'll get four' – and, for a striker, gloriously liberating. The players had never heard anything remotely like Ossie's tactics in their lives.

'Keep the ball, play the ball,' he told us, 'and when it gets to Teddy up front, everybody fly forward to give him options – and that includes the full-backs.' In their world, if one went up, the other stayed back as security. It was kamikaze football, totally different from everything we had learned under Terry, and I think just about everybody was surprised when, at first, it worked.

I was in seventh heaven. I scored twelve goals in the first twelve games. Then it all crashed around my ears when I was injured against Manchester United. I was out of action for nearly five months, and while I was away, teams began to get the measure of Tottenham. Results started to go against us, and as I sat on the sidelines watching, frustrated, the season started to slip away from us at an ever-increasing rate. We lost and lost again, and before long losing became a way of life for us. From being one of the country's best sides in the autumn, by spring we were thanking our lucky stars that we weren't being relegated.

We all knew things could not go on like this. Something had to be done to strengthen the side for the following season, 1994–5. Ossie loved to attack, and wasn't about to compromise his deeply held principles, but at the same time he knew he had to do something drastic if Tottenham were to survive as a Premiership club and he was to keep his job. He waited until after the World Cup finals before he made his first move. One day he called me into his office to meet a new player and I was surprised to find Ilie Dumitrescu, who'd had such a great World Cup for Romania, sitting there. I was impressed, but I couldn't help thinking that it might be a bit difficult for him to play a role in a balanced side. I asked the manager where he was going to play, and he said we would sort something out.

The first training session Dumitrescu put in was unbelievable. Once he got the ball you never saw it again until he had bent it into the top corner of the net. We just watched, open-mouthed. We were aware that his arrival didn't make complete sense, but we knew for certain that this fellow would be loved by the Tottenham faithful. It looked like an inspired signing, but it was nothing compared to the next bombshell Ossie dropped on us.

A couple of days later he drew me aside and said that he was thinking of buying Jürgen Klinsmann, and that he wanted me to be the first to know. I was dumbstruck. Klinsmann was one of the greatest players in world football. Any club would have given anything to have him playing for them. Initially I couldn't believe it. Then something occurred to me. 'Hang on, Ossie. You've got me, Nicky Barmby, Darren Anderton and Dumitrescu. That's five players to play up front.'

'That's OK,' said Ossie calmly. 'We'll have five up front and five at the back.' I asked him how exactly he was going to achieve that.

'We'll sort something out. You're all quality players, there's a way to use you all.'

There's not a lot you can say to counter that sort of confidence, even when you're not quite sure whether the manager's gone off his trolley. I was astounded by Ossie's front. He was convinced that it would work. I didn't quite share his optimism, but I couldn't help but be entranced by the thought of what it would be like to play alongside the great Jürgen Klinsmann. It might work, it might not, but the experience could not possibly be less than interesting, of that I was quite sure.

The hype surrounding Tottenham even before the season started was incredible. I can remember the five us posing for a picture. Several of us expressed our misgivings, but Ossie airily waved all our protests aside. 'You're all good players,' he would say again. 'You can all fit in.' We would see.

Chapter Nine

The Famous Five – Ossie's Grand Folly

The first game of the season saw Ossie's grand plan for the Famous Five unveiled in all its glory. We were playing against Sheffield Wednesday, and the way it was to work went like this: Jürgen would play the furthest forward, 'Shaggy' Anderton would be on the right, I was going to play up front with Klinsmann with Barmby pushing forward from midfield, and the joker in the pack, Dumitrescu, would be out wide on the left.

This was hit or bust. We hit – just – beating Wednesday 4–3 at Hillsborough. Jürgen scored and so did I, but I ended up on the left of the midfield, largely because of the way Ilie wanted to play the game.

How do I best describe his performance that day? Well, he wasn't a defender, that was obvious – and that's being kind. It seemed that we were all running our socks off for him, because all he wanted to do was cut in from the left wing and bend the ball into the top right-hand corner. He tried that several times in the game, and continued to do so in the matches that followed. Sometimes the result was spectacular; more often than not, it wasn't. Ilie's attitude was: 'If it works, great. If it doesn't, so what?' He was a showboater, was Ilie, and it was all going to end in tears.

Klinsmann, meanwhile, lost no time in achieving the status of folk hero at Spurs. By the end of that game in Yorkshire, his place on the pedestal was assured among the Tottenham faithful. It was great to be involved with the first global superstar to play for the club in the modern era. He came in with such enthusiasm; we all wanted him to succeed. He had played for Inter Milan and then for Monaco, where he regularly appeared in front of crowds of 3,000 for one of Europe's leading sides. Coming from the relaxed atmosphere of the well-heeled Côte d'Azur, I don't think he quite realised how much passion there was in English Premiership football, but he quickly grew to love it. He integrated into the team very well, largely because of his tremendous ability but also because the players and the fans all wanted him to do well. And the love affair between Tottenham people and Klinsmann was resumed when he went back to play for the club again in the 1997–8 season.

We all knew Jürgen's reputation for diving at the right moment, so, in the dressing room before that first game at Sheffield Wednesday, we agreed on David Kerslake's suggestion that if Jürgen scored, we should all celebrate by joining him in a communal dive. When he did score, even Ian Walker in goal came upfield to throw himself on the deck with the rest of us. It was hilarious, but it was also a demonstration, however jokingly expressed, that this Tottenham side loved having Jürgen in its midst. Because it was an away game, a lot of Tottenham supporters missed that silly but magical moment live. Afterwards my son,

Charlie, said to me: 'Can you get Jürgen to do that dive again, Dad?' I laughed, but thinking about it, it didn't seem a bad idea – completely harmless, if a bit daft – to do a repeat performance for the White Hart Lane faithful. So I asked Jürgen to pull the stunt again if he scored against Everton in our first home game.

Of course he did score – twice, actually – in our 2–1 victory, and we all did the Klinsmann dive again. The crowd loved it. From that moment on he could do no wrong with the folk at White Hart Lane. However, that night sticks in my memory for quite another reason. Jürgen had scored both his goals when we were awarded a penalty. I was the appointed penalty-taker, but the crowd wanted Jürgen to take it to mark his home debut with a hat-trick. I was captain, and although I would have loved Jürgen to get his hat-trick, I was there to get the job done. I had been trained to be a good professional, it was a tight game and I felt I had to take the responsibility. As I walked up to place the ball on the spot I could hear the crowd chanting, 'Jürgen, Jürgen!', but I went ahead and took the kick anyway.

I missed. I was distracted by the wave of emotion coursing down from the terraces, I didn't concentrate on the job in hand and I blazed the shot high, wide and not so handsome into the crowd. I didn't know where to look, I was so embarrassed. Yet I still thought I had made the right decision, even if I had messed it up. I got a good deal of stick in the press over that – they said I didn't like the idea of Klinsmann being the top dog so soon after joining the club. That's rubbish. The only thing that would have pleased me more that seeing him score a hat-trick would have been setting him up for a fourth.

In September another Romanian World Cup star arrived

at the club. Gica Popescu was not as instantly popular as Dumitrescu and Klinsmann had been. For a start, he was nowhere near as flashy as either of them. He was no show-off, just a guy who was outstandingly good at his job. He was so gifted he could make anything look easy, the same sort of player as Gary Pallister has been for England and Manchester United, so quick in thought and deed that he sees situations before they occur and snuffs them out with supreme skill.

Yet the high-risk football we played under Ossie was bound to lead eventually to his departure from the club. The fans loved him in so many ways, and so did his players – he had the greatest faith that we could always score more goals than we would let in. But as a strategy for ensuring a healthy and prosperous life in the Premiership our game plan was an accident just waiting to happen.

Ossie finally went following a calamitous couple of results at the end of October: a 5–2 defeat by Manchester City at Maine Road and a 3–0 crash at Notts County in a League Cup game, a disgraceful performance that reflected no credit on either the manager or his players. It was to prove the last straw for the impatient and embattled Mr Sugar. Ossie's last game was against West Ham at White Hart Lane, for which he made me substitute in order to revise his pattern to incorporate Popescu as sweeper. I came on early in the second half and scored in an eventual 3–1 win. Everybody thought I should have stuck two fingers up at the manager that day for leaving me on the bench, but it wasn't like that at all. I wanted nothing more for this gentle, sincere man than that he should succeed. I knew what he was going through, and I would have loved to have seen him turn things round. But he had run out of time. The axe fell on Ossie the following Monday night.

Steve Perryman took over for one game, and then Gerry Francis arrived. Gerry was completely different from Ardiles in both style and approach. Himself a distinguished former son of Tottenham, he had a reputation for being a very organised, workmanlike manager. Wonderful though it had been to play for Ossie, organisation was what we needed at that precise moment. We were leaking worse than the *Titanic* and we needed somebody to come in and organise the back four to work as a unit.

Gerry's first game was against Aston Villa at home on 19 November. It was back-to-basics time, back to the Terry Venables way. Organisation, get the groundwork right, stem the haemorrhage of goals conceded, keep battling. We thought this was going to be the answer, the way Tottenham would get their credibility back. It was a minor heartbreak, that game. We were 3–1 down at half-time, fought back to 3–3 but were eventually defeated 4–3, a soul-destroying experience after we'd shown such tenacity. The result was the sort that had been common under Ossie Ardiles, but the way we went about our task that day was anything but Ossie's.

Our next game was a goalless draw with Chelsea at home, and insofar as we were managing to dam the flood of goals against us, it was a good result. I'll give Gerry his due: he didn't waste any time, he got to work on the defence straight away. We then drew 1–1 with Liverpool at Anfield and that was followed by a personal highlight of that season for me: the home game in December against Kevin Keegan's Newcastle. They had Ginola and Ferdinand, and were coming to give troubled Tottenham a hiding. They didn't. We beat them 4–2 – and I scored a hat-trick. My three goals were not only an achievement to be proud of, but also a timely one: when you have a new manager you need to make an impression on him pretty quickly.

Gerry's style, personal as well as professional, was dour in comparison to Ossie's. He was for ever telling us how much he had on his plate. I didn't want to know about his problems, and I used to ask him why he was telling us about them when we had enough of our own. I like managers who ask for your opinion and then listen to it, whether or not they actually act upon it. With Gerry, although he did ask for a view, I felt he never really took it on board.

However, we were gradually getting back our self-respect after making such a poor start to the season. We were playing catch-up pretty convincingly, and at last achieving some sort of consistency. We went on to register an unbeaten run of eleven games, yet that late purple patch did mask one or two deeper problems. For the third season we were in the care of a new manager, and that is unsettling for any group of players. Even though Gerry was getting things more organised, the club was in no danger of achieving anything more than respectability, and Dumitrescu had proved that he didn't have what it took to excel as a professional in the Premiership.

We now had the boat back on an even keel, but we knew we were not likely to make our mark on the Premiership that season, although we still had an outside chance of a European place. However, we genuinely felt we had a chance to go all the way in the FA Cup. After beating Sunderland 4–1 at Roker Park, we drew 1–1 with Southampton at home in the fifth round. Then came an extraordinary replay at the Dell. After only ten minutes we were 2–0 down. At half-time Gerry Francis had a flash of inspiration. He put on Ronny Rosenthal for the second half in a move that was to turn the game on its head.

Ronny scored two goals for us with amazing shots, but his third was the most spectacular of the lot. He simply turned the match around, but that was Ronny all over – he was either sublime or sublimely dreadful. On this occasion no defence in the world could have stopped him, and with further goals from Barmby, Anderton and yours truly we emerged the winners by 6–2.

We couldn't imagine a worse draw than the one we got in the quarter-finals. Liverpool away, enough to turn the legs to jelly. But we were on a high now, if only in the FA Cup, and so we were not unduly fazed by the prospect of the unbridled hostility of the Kop. We felt we could do it. We weren't yet the finished article in the League, but in Cup football we thought we had a chance to beat anybody in the land. Robbie Fowler scored for Liverpool early on, but before long Jürgen set me up with the chance to square the match, an opportunity I didn't waste. Come the second half we quite fancied our chances, although we would have gratefully settled for 1–1 and a chance to bring them back to our place.

And that looked like being the result until the dying minutes, when Anderton played the ball to me, I passed to Klinsmann and, with a minimum of fuss, he tucked it into the corner. The scenes of jubilation were amazing. We had stormed the Liverpool citadel. Even their fans cheered us off the pitch – there are no warmer-hearted foes in British football. My abiding memory of that game is of Jürgen only just managing to stop himself from throwing up, such was the emotion and effort he had put into the game. Say what you like about Jürgen Klinsmann, he was 100 per cent committed to the Tottenham cause in his short first spell at the club. Nobody could have asked more of him. That match exhausted us all mentally and physically, but we still managed to get a win and two draws in the three League matches that followed. We were being carried along by the euphoria of the Cup.

Having been put through the mincer in the quarter-final, we had to go through it all again in our semi-final, against the other Merseyside club, Everton. They weren't the side Liverpool were that season, but nonetheless it was going to be a highly charged occasion. For the players, FA Cup semi-finals are in many ways the most draining games of the lot. There is so much at stake: if you get to the final, you've got your match at Wembley, you've experienced the occasion, even if you lose. In the long term, the public at large might not remember who came second, but everybody at your club does. A defeat in the semi-finals is just the worst experience in football. Even your own fans pretty soon forget it when you get knocked out at that stage. We were determined that we were not going to be beaten in the last four for the second time in three years.

We were beaten. No, we were not just beaten, we were hammered, 4–1. We had to travel to Elland Road for a start, which we felt gave Everton an obvious advantage in terms of travelling time. We were also hit by an injury crisis and had to put out a team that had a distinctly patched-up look about it. We felt that, given a full squad to choose from, we might have had a real chance, but it was not to be. What made it even worse to bear was that Everton then won the Cup with a 1–0 victory over Manchester United.

It was a sad end to a season that had promised so much back in the late summer. In the space of ten months we had gone from the excitement of playing with some flamboyantly gifted footballers under Ossie Ardiles to the hard grind of being a worthy but slightly dull defensive outfit under Gerry Francis. Don't get me wrong. I know Gerry had to do what he did – we simply couldn't go on leaking goals at the back as we had been. If nothing else, Gerry made us much harder to beat and, to be fair to him, we only just missed out on a place in Europe. Our last five games in the League brought us two defeats and three draws. If we had turned two of those draws into wins, we would have been in Europe in 1995–6. All in all as the season sighed to an end, we felt that although under the new managerial regime we seemed to have spent 90 per cent of our time defending, we had at least consolidated, and had a chance to go one better the following year.

Yet somehow it all went wrong. For several weeks at the end of the season there was talk that Jürgen Klinsmann was going to leave. Dumitrescu had already been sold to West Ham and Popescu was muttering darkly about not liking the demands of English Premiership football. It was too physically demanding for him, he said, and in the end he was given the move he wanted. Barcelona got him in their sights and bagged their man. Gica was a player with great talent, an amazing player. I didn't want him to go, but I wished him well at his new club.

The departure of the Romanians was a shame, but the real tragedy for Tottenham was that Jürgen did go as well. We had become quite close, both on and off the field, and I fully understood his reasons for leaving. His contract contained a clause giving him the option of moving on at the end of his first year with us. In many ways his situation was similar to the one I'd been in at Nottingham Forest when Tottenham came in for me. The club Jürgen had always wanted to play for was Bayern Munich, and they were keen to have him. Bayern were the biggest club in Germany; no self-respecting German player would turn down the chance of joining them. If I had been in his shoes, I would have done exactly the same thing. We have stayed good friends, and he has been kind enough to say some complimentary things about the time he spent playing alongside me. In return, I'd just like to say that if I never play with a better footballer than Jürgen Klinsmann, I shall still have been a very lucky man.

After the departure of Klinsmann, Dumitrescu and Popescu, Nicky Barmby and I were given to understand that we would be playing together up front in 1995–6, a prospect that excited us both. We had played as a unit before and enjoyed it, and besides, we felt that if money was going to be spent, it did not need to be spent on strikers.

So what did Gerry do? He bought a striker. The club paid Crystal Palace £4.5 million for Chris Armstrong, lashed out another £4.5 million on Ruel Fox from Newcastle reserves, and then found a similar amount to bring Andy Sinton from Sheffield Wednesday, where he had been unable to command a regular first-team place. They were all worthy players, good Premiership material, but not the big names clubs like Chelsea and Arsenal had been signing, the people I and a few others thought were needed to give the club the kind of lift the arrival of the three foreign players had provided at the start of the previous season. It was another blow when Barmby joined the exodus. He kicked up something of a fuss following the arrival of Armstrong, and was sold to Middlesbrough. That meant four out, three in – and not one of them an improvement on what we'd had before.

So I went into my fourth season with Tottenham feeling a bit flat. At the end of the 1994–5 campaign we had felt we were not that far away from being a good side, but now it had been ripped apart. I am by no means denigrating the ability of the three incoming players, but not even they would claim that they could fill the boots of such men as Klinsmann, Popescu or even Dumitrescu, infuriating customer though he had been on more than one occasion.

Although I went into the new season believing that the club had lost ground on the playing side, it didn't show on the field. I scored eleven goals in the first ten games, so the goals were still coming regularly, even if the excitement wasn't there.

I had felt for about eighteen months that my career was going nowhere at Tottenham, but I comforted myself with the knowledge that I was playing for a club I loved. Sure, I was scoring goals, and we were in a respectable position in the League table, but I felt that there were cracks in the fabric of the team which were just being papered over. My frustration came to the surface on more than one occasion. I remember saying one day to Gerry, 'We're going nowhere. When are we going to get some quality in here, like we had last year?'

He didn't exactly encourage me with his reply. 'Well, I've bought Chris and Foxy, and I couldn't do much about Nicky and Jürgen going.' It was all very downbeat, very negative, very defensive. It was as if he knew that I was right, but couldn't allow himself to agree with me. As I've said, Gerry was the sort of manager who would bring his problems to the players, not the other way round. I rarely got anything but negative vibes from him. First it made me depressed; then it made me angry.

What was even more galling was that other London clubs were doing the business. Arsenal decided they needed to speculate to accumulate. They bought Dennis Bergkamp and spent £4.5 million on bringing David Platt back from Sampdoria in Italy's Serie A. Chelsea had Ruud Gullit and there was great excitement at Stamford Bridge. It seemed to me that they had seen what Tottenham had done to regenerate their team and their self-esteem and were following our example. Tottenham, apparently, were the only club who had not learned from what they themselves had started.

In spite of my feelings for Alan Sugar, I could partly understand why he felt the way he did. He had lost money on the two Romanians and the German. But he seemed either unable or unwilling to accept what had been gained in terms of excitement. If you look now at the three London clubs I've mentioned, Arsenal won the Double in 1997–8, and Chelsea won the FA Cup, the Coca-Cola Cup and the Cup-Winners' Cup. Tottenham? They're still playing catch-up.

My last season with the club, 1996–7, was in just about every way you care to mention my most miserable season in football. As I said earlier, literally dozens of fans approached me and urged me to do myself a favour and get away from the club. Their advice was born of the terrible frustration they felt. Like the players, the fans had seen the seeds of something worthwhile being sown in 1994–5. The club had been bubbling again, there was electricity in the air on match days. The team were unpredictable, probably a bit exasperating in some ways, but the White Hart Lane faithful at least had something to get excited about. We'd had some fantastic results in that one golden year.

After that Gerry Francis just kept telling me that he was on the brink of bringing in new players. 'We're looking at this one, Ted, and we're looking at that one,' he'd say.

'Just give us a chance, just be patient, I promise it will all happen, and you'll be happy with the outcome.' I liked what I was hearing, in spite of the fact that his words had proved totally empty before. I suppose it was because this was what I wanted to hear. I had no real reason to believe that there was a dog's chance of it ever coming true.

In spite of the way things turned out for me, I still feel a little sad that it didn't work out at Tottenham. I waited and waited. If we had ever got the kind of players who could make the side really tick, it might have made me happier – it might even have made me into a better footballer, because you can only improve in this maddening, wonderful game if you learn from those around you, and that includes other players as well as coaches and managers.

When things are going wrong for a side, it's very easy to hide. Some people I've played with – no names, no pack drill – have made an art form of giving nothing to the team and yet still managing to look as if they are playing OK. The man I'd always have in my team, even if he was a little less skilful than others, is the brave man, the one who wants the ball when the chips are stacked against him and his side. I like to think I never hid in that season of 1996–7, but there were never enough people showing themselves for the ball, and that meant me going deeper and deeper to look for it, and when I got it finding that there was nobody around me wanting it, nobody helping me out. It became totally soul-destroying, and it affected my game. I was injured more than usual that season, even though I still played over thirty games for Tottenham. The main proof of the way my season went, though, was my goalscoring record. I got only eight goals that season, easily the worst haul I'd had since I started playing League football regularly.

The funny thing is, in both of my last two seasons

for Spurs, we missed getting a European spot only by the narrowest of margins. Perhaps it was just as well, really, because there's absolutely no doubt at all that we didn't have a good enough side to have sustained a credible European campaign. The fact was that we got some respectable results in spite of ourselves. We were absolutely stretched to the limit more often than I care to think about. When good teams get in front, they keep the ball and make the other lot work for it, but that wasn't happening. We were perpetually hanging on by the skin of our teeth.

There were some humiliations along the way, too. I remember the jeers of the 'Gooners' on the terraces as Arsenal gave us a footballing lesson in a 3–1 defeat at Highbury. The following week we got hammered 6–1 by Bolton in the League Cup, a performance that for sheer awfulness was matched only by the 7–1 thrashing handed out to us by Kenny Dalglish's Newcastle in December at St James's Park.

I knew I couldn't wait any longer. By now I was a regular member in the England set-up, and I felt that if I carried on playing for such a patently unambitious club that might not last. No matter what personal standards you set for yourself, in the end you cannot help but be dragged down by the sort of dismal fare we were serving up to our long-suffering fans. I suppose, with hindsight, I could have forced the issue earlier, when the other three packed their bags. But deep down, in my heart of hearts, I didn't want to go anywhere else. After all, I am a Tottenham supporter myself, and always will be. I wanted to give Gerry Francis, and Alan Sugar, and Tottenham Hotspur, every chance I could.

It was the toughest decision I have ever had to make

in football, and although I know it was the right one, I will never forget what it was like to play for Tottenham Hotspur Football Club and how proud I felt to pull on the famous white shirt of the team I had supported as a kid.

Chapter Ten

England

I suppose it was something fairly basic that enabled me to become an international footballer. I wasn't the quickest thing on two feet, I didn't have the glamour that strikers are supposed to possess, but I could do one thing pretty well, and in a variety of ways: score goals.

When I was at Millwall I played for the England Under-17 side a few times and I once got a hat-trick for the Under-18s. I had only half a game for the Under-21s, a 1–1 draw with Switzerland. As a youngster I thought there was no chance of me getting a game for England youth sides in the face of so much high-class opposition from clubs such as Tottenham, Arsenal and Liverpool. But much to my surprise, they did call me up, and it was then that I first met up again with David Kerslake, with whom I had played under-11 football. Little did I know then that in a few years' time we'd be playing together at Tottenham.

The first inkling I got that a full cap might not be out of my reach was when Steve Harrison, Bruce Rioch's coach at Millwall, told me that England manager Graham Taylor was looking at me, as I recounted earlier. In a way, my suspicions that this would be a high mountain to climb from the foothills of Division 2 were proved correct, because I was a Premiership player with Tottenham before Taylor actually called me into his squad. I didn't get on the field the first time I pulled a full England shirt over my head: I was substitute for the World Cup qualifying game against Holland in 1993, a match England drew 2–2.

I shall never forget the moment when I was told I was to be in the starting line-up for the first time – a real England player. It was the day before the World Cup qualifier against Poland in Katowice in May, and Graham Taylor announced to the whole party that I was to make my debut in the team. There was a round of applause from the other players; I was quite emotional about it, although it wouldn't have done to have shown it. Footballers are a cruel bunch, and if I had cracked at that moment, I should never have been allowed to forget it.

It was a daunting prospect. Poland were no pushovers, and they were especially dangerous on their own territory. The details of that game will be for ever etched on my memory. We went a goal down after thirty-four minutes, Poland were flying and the home crowd were at our throats. It was only when Ian Wright came on with about six minutes left and scored that we managed to salvage a 1–1 draw.

I had an initial taste of Graham Taylor's oddball ideas back at our hotel after the game, when he went round asking us to give ourselves marks out of ten for our performances. I said, 'Well, six out of ten, could do better – but it was my debut.' Des Walker, a high-class international defender, was typically honest in giving himself four. Graham didn't say anything to encourage him, so that didn't do Dessie's confidence any good. Then he got to Ian Wright, who, equally typically, said: 'I give myself ten out of ten. I scored, I did my job. Definitely ten.' This characteristic piece of Wright self-confidence caused a ripple of laughter. But all this strange ritual did was reduce morale in the camp – and we had another World Cup game, against Norway in Oslo, coming up in four days' time. The experiment was never repeated.

It was before the Norway match that I had my first real misgivings about Taylor. We had played with a flat back four in Poland, and it had worked pretty well, but the day before the Norway game the manager got it into his head that we should play with three at the back. We were aghast, not at the players he picked there – Gary Pallister, Des Walker and Tony Adams – but at the formation he was asking them to play in. We hadn't worked on it at all, and the 2–0 defeat that followed was without much doubt the worst England performance in which I've ever been involved.

We returned to the dressing room at half-time a goal down, and the first thing Taylor did was to announce that I was being taken off. I was terribly upset. I thought, well, that's it, that's the end of my England career before it's even started. I felt, wrongly as it happens, that I was being made the scapegoat for the fact that very possibly England would be going out of the World Cup.

Graham Taylor was a law unto himself, a one-off. And a good thing, too, if you ask me. His philosophy was based on the long-ball game; along with Dave Bassett at Wimbledon, he was the originator of that style at the top level. He was preoccupied, unhealthily, I think, with statistics: he said that figures showed goals came because a defender gave the ball away with a bad clearance, somebody capitalised on it, got it, chipped it over the top, somebody else shot and scored. Two passes. Easy.

He believed, like Charles Hughes, the FA's long-time director of coaching, of whom he was a disciple, that because the number-crunchers showed that a certain percentage of goals were scored with two touches or fewer, the way to score goals was for players to get into their channels, get their head to the ball when it came through and shoot with their first touch. And that was the only way.

Statistics don't, in fact, show anything of the kind. And yet Taylor persisted with these tactics at international level against players and coaches who were far more tactically aware than he gave them credit for. Such simple strategies might work in some parts of English League football, but not in internationals. International football is about outwitting the opposition, not out-battering them, which was Taylor's way.

He was not good for England, nor, potentially, for English football. It is for that reason alone that I think it was probably for the best that England didn't qualify for the World Cup finals in 1994. If Taylor had got the side to the United States and they had done even moderately well, we might have been stuck with his philosophy for years. It would have been the worst thing that could have happened to the England team, and furthermore, it would have permeated through the English game as a whole. Instead he got the sack for not getting England into the finals, and it was a darned good job that he did.

Take this typical example of his methods. When Andy Gray was making his England debut in 1991 against Poland, we needed only to draw to ensure that we would qualify for the European Championship finals. Andy's first instruction from Graham was to get the ball back from the two centre forwards who were taking the kick-off and smash it as far as he could into the corner and out of play. 'I can't do that,' gasped Gray. 'The crowd will look at me and wonder what on earth I'm doing. Why are you telling me to do that?'

'Simple,' said Taylor. 'I want the ball as near to their goal-line as we can get it, so that when they take the throw-in, we'll have eleven men on the pitch to their ten and we can capitalise on the situation.' Bizarre, but true.

Taylor is still sticking to his funny ideas. I'm told that as recently as 1997–8 he took the Watford team out on to the pitch, pointed at twenty balls he'd put down in various positions and asked the players where they would play the ball from that position. And that, to my mind, just shows a total disregard for what the opposition might be doing. It would be all right if you were playing against eleven outfitters' dummies, but living, breathing people do tend to move about a bit.

As well as his quirky ideas, Taylor also had strange prejudices. I think most people would agree that Peter Beardsley is one of the great English players of modern times, and so is Chris Waddle. To think that world-class footballers such as these could possibly be kicked out of the England set-up is outrageous, but Taylor ousted both of them because they didn't happen to fit in with his thinking, such as it was. His ideas were too stereotyped, he didn't give players enough credit for the skills they had, and his tactical planning was hopelessly flawed. He did his best; but his best was, sadly, nowhere near good enough.

Not that I had to endure too much of the Taylor style. I was a sub for the World Cup qualifier in Holland, although I didn't get on to the pitch, and after that I was injured for the San Marino game that ended England's World Cup hopes for another four years. The long spell I had out the next season with that knee injury meant that I wasn't involved with an England party for another fifteen months. By that time Taylor had gone, to be replaced by Terry Venables, the man who had brought me to Tottenham.

Terry was, I think, the only legitimate candidate for the job, but there were reservations about him because of the allegations that were being hurled at him. Nonetheless, when it came down to what really mattered – the ability to develop strategy and tactics and to motivate players – he was the only man for the job. He had an edge of experience over other candidates who were mentioned, such as Kevin Keegan and Gerry Francis, and the charisma to deal with the media spotlight. He has many strengths, but I think the greatest of them are his attention to detail and the gift of getting over his ideas in an intelligent, coherent way. Another factor was that the public liked him. People naturally warm to Terry Venables.

Terry picked me for the first international I was fit for. He was a breath of fresh air, constantly trying to achieve a club-style set-up for the England squad. The major grouse of all the national managers I've worked with is that they don't see enough of their players, and it's a justified complaint. An England manager may not get his players together for two months sometimes, and it is difficult to imbue them with a club spirit, but that was what Terry wanted. So everything he did was geared around engendering a great team spirit for Euro '96. He was very loyal to his players, and even if they were going through tough times because of injury or a temporary loss of form, he would still get them involved in training sessions. He just wanted everybody that was in contention to get to know each other away from their club backgrounds. He refused to bow to media pressure and he would never discard a player after just one game.

Terry said he wanted great football from us, and he used the best footballers at his disposal to create a powerful backbone to the team. His key men were David Seaman, Paul Gascoigne, Tony Adams and Alan Shearer, a quartet that any national team manager in world football would be glad to have in his side.

Terry's philosophy, which I had relished since he was my club manager, sadly for such a short time, was to force the person you were playing against to make a decision while you yourself were asking him questions, such as: 'Can you mark me?' 'Can you tackle me?' 'Are you coming here, where I am?' Everything in my football today is geared to asking those questions. I set them; it is up to the other bloke to come up with the answers.

Terry gave me a lot of confidence as a player and continues to influence my game today. I remember once playing for Tottenham at home against Oldham, who had a big, blond centre half called Richard Jobson, who always had a good game against me. This time he was marking me out of it. He had outwitted me in the first half, and I noticed that he liked to play in the middle, so at half-time I said to Terry: 'Would it be all right if I go and play on the right wing for the second half and Darren Anderton comes in and plays alongside Nicky Barmby at centre forward so that he can use his pace against Jobson? Because if I go and stand on the right wing, Jobson's only mentality is to mark me.' Terry thought about this for a moment, then he said: 'Yeah, go and do it.' So I played on the right wing, and Richard didn't know what was going on. You could tell he wanted to mark me, and the whole game changed because of it. I had asked him the question, and he couldn't come up with the answer. It was Terry who had given me the confidence to try something that I thought would work on the pitch, and we ended up winning the game 4–1 with two goals from me and one from Shaggy.

Terry's days with England were wonderful, days when the England team reached for the stars and almost grabbed them. He was liked and respected by everybody with whom he came into contact. His players would have walked through brick walls and blazing infernos for him. He was that sort of man. To be perfectly honest, I don't really care about all the muck that's been thrown at him over the years. Alan Sugar – isn't it amazing how that man keeps coming back to haunt those with whom he's been in contact with over the years? – chucked more than most, but ask anybody who knows them both who they'd rather have had standing alongside them when the going got rough, and there will be only one answer: Terry Venables.

A lot of people might know what they want from the team they are managing, but to be successful you have to have a gift for being able to put it across and make it plain and simple, and not boring. The concentration span of your average footballer is not immense, so once you start babbling, what you are trying to convey loses its effect. You might be talking perfect sense, but if you can't get your players interested and absorbed, you've lost the plot. If you can put over a message that is short, sharp and to the point, you can get there. I've been with Terry when he has managed to get his point over to the one individual he was aiming at in a room of more than twenty people.

I would consider him a friend. I can just pick up the telephone and ring him even I haven't spoken to him for a while, as friends can, with no questions asked or expected. Terry has a tremendous warmth about him; I value him as a wise, wise mentor. One attribute I've always envied him is his ability to compartmentalise his life. He says that when he is on football business, he is on nothing but football business, but when he's away from it, he likes to look for other ways to keep himself busy. Some people just want to relax, to play snooker or golf, or read, or go to the cinema, or do one of a hundred other enjoyable but essentially undemanding things, when they're not on duty. That wouldn't be enough for Terry. He's a born entrepreneur, and he'd be off selling hats, or wigs, or something. It is partly that gift that has made him the success he has been in football.

It's amazing how some people will find something to whinge about, no matter what the situation. Take our programme of matches before the finals of the European Championship in 1996. As hosts we didn't have to qualify. Lucky old Venables, they said. Lucky old England, that they could indulge themselves in a series of preparatory and largely meaningless friendlies instead of slogging their way through a gruelling qualifying series. As if it were the fault of the coach and the players that England had been chosen by UEFA to stage the tournament that in our part of the world ranks second only to the World Cup. I sometimes wonder if some of them would have been happier if the finals had been held in Holland or somewhere, and if we'd needed to qualify and had failed to do so.

In fact it was not necessarily to our advantage that we played only friendlies leading up to the competition proper. England are still considered a prize scalp in the international game. After all, we *did* give football to the world, and no matter what the rankings said from time to time during the 1980s, other teams still desperately wanted to beat us. And with only friendlies on the agenda, we had no hard and fast way of gauging how competitive we would be when push came to shove in the hurly-burly of Euro '96. We felt that we were improving all the time, we firmly believed that we were becoming a side to be reckoned with, but we couldn't predict with any degree of certainty how we would fare when the action started in earnest. Added to that there would be extra pressure exerted on us by our own fans because we were playing at home, and therefore we simply couldn't afford not to be up for it from the first second of our first match. So no, we weren't lucky. We had to walk on to the Euro '96 stage without the benefit of a single dress rehearsal, and that's never easy.

I wasn't involved in the first match England played under Terry Venables, which was against Greece. Although I had returned to the Tottenham team after my long lay-off, I was still feeling my way a bit and wasn't really ready for England duty. I knew it, and so did Terry, but he had spoken to me and had said that as soon as he and I felt the time was right, he would have me back in the squad. So for the Greece game I was engaged to do a bit of punditry for Sky Sports. I really enjoyed watching that performance. Not because we beat them 5–0 – we'd been expected to win in any case – but because of the way we did it. We were playing great British football. I really believe that when the British style is played well, it can still beat the best sides in the world. It was a perfect start for England under Terry. So what if the opposition had not been of the highest class? We couldn't do any more than win well, and that's what we did.

I was looking forward to playing my part in this side.

Terry stuck to his word, and it happened in the very next game, against the United States, which was a significant one for me because it was the first time I played alongside Alan Shearer. Nobody knew it at the time, but it was to become a famous partnership: SAS – Shearer and Sheringham. He scored both goals in our 2–0 win, and I like to think I made a useful contribution to a very good performance against a team which had long since ceased to be a pushover in world football.

I was a substitute in the friendlies against Romania and Nigeria, but won a place in the starting line-up in the match against Uruguay at Wembley at the end of March 1995, which ended in a goalless draw. It was not such a convincing performance by the side as a whole, but the fact remained that, having played five matches under Venables, England had yet to be beaten. Speaking for myself, I felt I had played all right in the games in which I'd appeared, but I'm a goalscorer by nature and instinct, and I would not be satisfied until I got my name on the scoresheet for my country. Only then could I truly say that I had done my job. An England striker has not earned his spurs until he has struck for England.

In June we played host to Japan, Sweden and Brazil in the Umbro Cup, a friendly tournament which we used to test the team in a semi-competitive atmosphere against international competition. It was also a useful rehearsal for the country in the elements of hosting an international football tournament. I was substitute against the talented and surprisingly lively Japan side at Wembley on 3 June, and again played reasonably well when I came off the bench to make my contribution to a hard-fought 2–1 victory. Darren Anderton, my Spurs team-mate, scored three minutes into the second half after exchanging passes

159

with Alan Shearer, then Japan deservedly equalised. We won through a penalty after John Scales had a shot handled on the line. But I was troubled by a niggling worry: I had now played in seven England games, either as a substitute or as a member of the starting line-up, and still I had not broken my goalscoring duck.

Five days later I put that right in our match against Sweden at Elland Road, the first international not to be played at Wembley. But not before I became the subject of the crowd's derision. I deserved it, too – I missed the sitter to end them all. We were a goal down when my big chance came. It was a perfect cross from the right and I remember thinking that the goalkeeper was going to expect me to put my header in at the far left corner, so instead I went for the near post. And flicked it wide. It was one of those misses that make you wish the ground would open up and swallow you, red face and all. I had so much time to score, perhaps too much. It was a goal that my mum could have scored, to be honest, and my mum, for all her brilliance as a mother, is no international striker. The jeers and catcalls rang round the ground. 'Stupid southerner,' they yelled. 'Can't score for toffee.' Or perhaps slightly stronger words to that effect.

Ten minutes later I silenced the fans. It was a sweet moment, a moment to die for, a moment when I proved I could keep my head in international football and score when the chance was on. My goal made it 1–1, and although the Swedes played outstandingly to take a 3–1 lead, we pulled it back to 3–3 with goals from David Platt and Darren Anderton. There were amazing scenes after our fightback. Anybody would have thought that we'd just won the World Cup. It was great to be a part of that. I reasoned that I had made a decent fist of my international career so far. I could have done with a few more goals, but I could draw consolation from the fact that Terry was prepared to accommodate my style of play. He had taken on board the fact that I wasn't your average forward, and that I could make a contribution playing in the way I had made my own. It involved me going deeper than an out-and-out striker and trying to provide an intelligent link between midfield and front line while at the same time being able to move into threatening positions if the situation called for it. And the strategy does work: for most of my career at the highest level I have played deeper than some of my contemporaries, but I have still scored more than my share of goals.

We needed to beat Brazil in our last game to win the tournament, but we found ourselves on the wrong end of a 3–1 hammering, the first defeat for a Venables England side. I started that match and watched in admiration as Graeme Le Saux gave us the lead with a magnificent volley from outside the penalty area. But it was the last time we really threatened their goal. We performed well enough in the first half, but Brazil were fantastic in the last thirty minutes, both individually and as a team. They absolutely took over and played us off the park. It was a chastening experience, but in its own way a valuable one. It told us that we were not yet a complete side. We still had a lot to learn, but we felt that with Terry Venables at the helm we were capable of transforming ourselves into a power in world football once again after too many years in the wilderness – a period during which the national side had been dubbed by one of the country's most distinguished tabloid newspapers 'Taylor's Turnips'. That was one occasion when the *Sun* was distressingly close to the mark in their assessment.

The Umbro Cup was a worthwhile exercise. It was no easy ride. Every game we played was part of the learning curve. If you didn't learn from playing at Wembley in front of 80,000 baying fans – every one of whom was simultaneously looking for a world-class performance and waiting for the team to fall flat on their faces – you were never going to learn anything.

I couldn't wait for the real action of Euro '96, when everybody would be performing under the most intense pressure and the really good players would make their mark. Having said that, when you play for England, wherever you play and whoever the opposition, it's always a massive stage. At your club the fans and the local press have a view, but when you appear in an England shirt every football-lover in the country is looking at you. It doesn't matter what club you're with, every football fan in England has an opinion of you. And they are fully entitled to hold that opinion – if they didn't, it would mean that they didn't care – but it doesn't make life easy for the players. If you do well, there is no spectator in world football who will give you more praise; if you don't, they make their feelings known loud and clear, as they are perfectly justified in doing.

I love playing for my country and it's great to be in a side full of the best players that English football has to offer. The knowledge that on a particular day somebody rates you as one of the eleven best players in England is something to be proud of. Nobody can ever take it away from you. The buzz is tremendous. But I'm not a Stuart Pearce. I don't wear my patriotism on my sleeve like he did. It was fine for him, because that was the way he was, but it's not my style. That doesn't mean that I care any less than Stuart did. I would die for England. Playing for the nation was the dream that consumed me when I was a kid, and I feel privileged that I've been able to make it come true. You want to be remembered not only by your contemporaries, but by future generations, and the only way truly to achieve that is to play international football and make a success of it. I've had a marvellous living out of the game and it has given me things and taken me to places I could never have imagined when I was an eight-year-old playing for Selwyn Primary School. It is my England career that has brought me all that.

After the Umbro Cup, our programme of friendlies continued with substitute appearances for me in the goalless draws against Colombia at Wembley and Norway in Oslo. They were not the best performances in the history of England football, to be honest, but at least we were proving that we were a difficult side to beat. We had a coherent defensive pattern which we managed to maintain in those games. Terry was moulding England in the same way as he had moulded Tottenham in his early days at White Hart Lane. Flair was all very well, and there was always a place for it in Venables teams, but first came organisation. At Tottenham, Ossie Ardiles, to his cost, was living proof that nobody achieves lasting success by simply relying on a team to score more goals than it concedes. To be sure, Terry Venables' England teams had to start getting some goals, but the first objective in any football match has to be not to let them in. We had achieved that – now for the next step.

It came in the friendly we played against Switzerland in November 1995. I was in the starting line-up, and after we took the lead through an own goal I scored the second in our eventual 3–1 victory. A header from the right wing, it was, and it was the better of the two international goals

I had now netted. It was my first for England at Wembley, which made it very special, and it was good enough to be shown occasionally on television even today. Steve Stone scored the third from point-blank range after the Swiss goalkeeper dropped the ball on the line. I went home that night feeling quietly satisfied with myself. It was another challenge taken on and overcome.

We played three more games in the winter of 1995 and spring of 1996, drawing 1–1 with Portugal, beating Bulgaria 1–0, a result which does not reflect our superiority in the encounter, and a drawing 0–0 with Croatia in April. I should have scored in the last ten minutes of that match when Steve McManaman hit the post and I failed to convert the rebound. I cursed to myself, because the talented Croatians had begun to flag a little in the closing stages. Strikers don't like missing chances, especially easy ones like that.

Our last home game before the European Championship started in June was on 18 May 1996 against Hungary. We played some brilliant football on our way to a 3–0 victory. I set up Anderton for the first goal, Platt netted the second and 'Shaggy' Anderton got another to wrap up an easy win. It was a rousing end to a preparatory campaign that had brought us closer together as a team. Terry deserves a lot of praise for creating that unity. We were becoming the 'club' side he had said he wanted to build when he had taken over as England coach in 1993. We were evolving into the footballing equivalent of the Three Musketeers – 'All for one, and one for all'. It was a good feeling. If only we had known what trouble that very camaraderie was going to bring.

Chapter Eleven

The Dentist's Chair
and All That

We were aghast when we heard where we were going after we completed our pre-tournament schedule of home games. We were to be sent halfway round the world to play just a couple of matches – almost as far away as you can get without starting to come back again. We were going to the Far East, for God's sake, and we weren't the only ones who were asking why it was necessary for the squad to travel such a distance. The public and the media were equally dismayed. It was a bad idea, they said, on top of a gruelling domestic programme, for us to have to face an energy-sapping journey to the other side of the planet.

As a breed, professional footballers like nothing better than a good whinge. Of course, the reality is that we have a terrific life, playing a game we love for wages to die for. The average man in the street would give his eye teeth for the smallest taste of what we enjoy on a regular basis. This England team was no exception to the general rule. We did have a moan; we were tired, we said. Why did we have to go all that way to play two meaningless matches? We could do that without leaving Europe, couldn't we?

It was only when Terry explained his reasons for wanting to take us to the Far East that we began to see the common sense behind his plan. He wanted to get us well away from England, where the pressures of Euro '96 were already beginning to build to a tremendous level. If we'd stayed nearer home we would have been unable to avoid getting caught up in the whole merry-go-round of hype. There would be newspaper stories every day, and, knowing certain sections of the press as we all did, the yarns they came up with were bound to become more fantastic by the day. In the end we happily went along with the idea, accepting that it had a lot to commend it. If we'd realised that there is nowhere in the world far enough away to distance us from sensationalised stories, we might have had second thoughts.

Instead, off we went to China, where we were to meet the national team, and Hong Kong, where we were going to play a select XI made up of local players and a few British professionals imported to give the game a slightly more competitive edge. It was very humid in both places, but that was no bad thing since we were preparing to play at Wembley in the height of the English summer. The long flight was as boring and tiring as we had foreseen, but once we got to China we stayed in a nice hotel and were looked after very well by our hosts. In our free time we played cards, got to know each other a little better and even went to visit the Great Wall of China. I'm not a great sightseer, but I must admit that was an amazing experience.

Both legs of the trip went very well and I remember thinking that this side was developing a team spirit that I had never experienced before in an England squad. Terry and his aides played their part in that, but I also think there was a great will among the players to make the team a success. We grew more and more confident that we could do really well in Euro '96, and we came to appreciate that Terry's strategy had been a sound one. We were happy and raring to go. We had about ten days left before we played our first game in the tournament and getting two decent results helped our morale, too. We couldn't see anything on the horizon that might upset things now.

After the Hong Kong match Terry told us to go out and enjoy ourselves for one last night. It was going to be our final opportunity to let our hair down as a group, have a few beers and unwind before we went home and got down to our last-minute preparations. There was an extra reason for celebrating, too: it was Paul Gascoigne's birthday. So we went to a club in Hong Kong called the China Jump and the evening developed into one of those daft nights which professional footballers very occasionally get involved in. We spend a lot of our lives denying ourselves that one extra drink, one more laugh or one last prank, so when we get the chance to have fun with official approval, as we did then, we grab it with both hands.

The evening started innocently enough. We had one or two drinks and then somebody suggested we try a concoction called a Flaming Lamborghini in honour of Gazza's birthday. Several of them went down, and it was after this that things started to get a bit silly. The level of hilarity rose when Robbie Fowler, chatting to a girl in the bar, was overheard by Gazza – or so Gazza claimed – to utter the immortal line: 'Do you come here often?'

Then somebody's shirt got ripped, and before long, everybody was tearing everybody else's shirts to shreds.

We were all wearing tracksuit bottoms and Umbro T-shirts, so it wasn't difficult to pull the shirts off each other's backs – it wasn't as if we were wearing dress shirts or anything.

Bryan Robson was our chaperone that night. He'd been sent out with us by Terry to make sure we were all OK, and he was about twenty yards away from where the high jinks were going on. Some of us decided that Robbo shouldn't be allowed to escape, so we went over to where he was standing, chatting and sipping a beer. As usual, Bryan was well turned out – nice shirt, nice pair of trousers – but we didn't see that as any reason why he should be treated as a special case.

Robbo, however, was clearly not all that impressed with our game. It wasn't until his shirt was in pieces that he revealed it was a Versace number his wife had bought him. I remember there was also a pair of outsized boxing gloves hanging up in the bar, and we were slogging each other with those. I suppose the alarm bells should have rung when a couple of people took pictures of us with our shirts hanging off our backs, but we were on a lads' night out, enjoying ourselves. It didn't enter our minds that major trouble might come from all this.

And it might easily have ended there if somebody hadn't noticed a chair over by the dancefloor which they called the Dentist's Chair. The idea was that you sat in this chair and two barmen would come over and pour three bottles of different spirits down your neck. We had noticed the horseplay going on round this contraption and decided to have a go ourselves. There were four of us, I think – myself, Gazza, Robbie Fowler and Steve McManaman. It was, in all honesty, pretty innocent, just one of the silly things that happen when a bunch of blokes – or, dare I say it, girls – have a night out together.

Unfortunately, the photographs that were taken of us found their way into the hands of the newspapers and we were crucified in the press. It was just my bad luck that the all-important picture was taken when I was sitting in the Dentist's Chair. And the hullabaloo didn't end there. Next came allegations that we'd had a riotous plane trip home the following day and had broken two televisions in the process. Terry's team were branded a disgrace. We ended up having about £500 stopped out of our pay for the alleged damage to the plane. We had had the first-class cabin on the Boeing 747 to ourselves. For the first five or six hours we'd had a big card game, along with one or two beers to help us get to sleep when the time came. Things never got close to getting out of hand. Sure, we all had a few drinks, but it was nothing like the night before. In fact I wasn't aware of anything untoward happening on that flight until these claims were published the day after we got home. Even now I don't know what it was all about, and I don't think anyone in the team knew anything about the televisions that were supposed to have been broken. The whole episode was overplayed by the press, but people always prefer to think the worst of professional sportsmen. Looking back, I can see that it was a bit foolish to have got so carried away in the China Jump, but even so it was never more than skylarking.

When we got back to England and started work on our final preparations, we weren't allowed to let the incidents in Hong Kong and on the plane prey on our minds. The horseplay, real or alleged, was over and done with. Now it was time for action.

Our first game in the tournament was against the Swiss,

and I shall never forget as long as I live the sense of expectancy before the game, the long walk out through the famous Wembley tunnel, the explosion of affection and support that hit us when we entered the stadium. So it was a shame that the game itself was a bit of an anticlimax. Alan Shearer gave us the lead, his first goal in a spell of fourteen England matches, but the determined Swiss outfit equalised through Turkyilmaz's penalty near the end after Stuart Pearce was adjudged to have handled the ball. It was a hard decision, we felt, but the 1–1 draw was probably a fair result – we never played as well in that game as we were capable of playing. I went out on the Saturday night with my girlfriend and another couple to a club-restaurant called Faces, where we had a meal and a moderate amount to drink to go with our food. Somebody spotted me, and yet again, the press made a big deal of it, claiming I'd been out getting drunk surrounded by four blondes. I have to say it hurts a bit when people say outrageous things like that without knowing the score. It was a totally innocent night out with another couple, but I was made to look like a complete villain. Fast-forward to the early summer of 1998, and another piece of press mischief was to prove much more damaging.

The next match on the agenda was the Scotland game, and there was the level of hype that we all expect when these two old foes meet each other. It was seven years since England and Scotland had played each other and eleven since Scotland had defeated us. People still said that Scottish players were more committed to playing for their country than we were, and that they loved nothing more than to beat England. Terry made sure we played that card to our advantage.

Scotland probably shaded the first half, but we raised

our tempo in the second and became stronger and stronger the longer the match went on. Shearer scored the first goal from a Gary Neville cross and we celebrated like mad. Scotland, though now being comprehensively outplayed, had a chance to equalise from the penalty spot after the referee decided that Adams had tripped Gordon Durie. Gary McAllister, their skipper, was given the task, but was left with his head in his hands when David Seaman second-guessed him and pushed his kick over the bar. The gods were with us, we thought. The ball had moved fractionally as McAllister ran up to take the kick. He could have taken that penalty on another ten different occasions and scored every time, so we celebrated quietly.

Much more exuberant was the reception that greeted that wonderful, magical goal from Gazza, which sealed our 2–0 victory. Gascoigne left Colin Hendry for dead as he advanced into the Scotland penalty area and rounded off the job with a marvellous volley past Andy Goram. We gave the crowd a repeat of the Dentist's Chair routine, as Paul lay flat on the ground by the Scotland goal and the rest of us squirted water from a plastic bottle into his open mouth. Some people thought that this was in slightly bad taste after the flak that had been hurled at us, but we were so high on adrenaline from Paul's moment of sheer genius that we automatically accepted his invitation to re-enact our moment of folly in steamy Hong Kong a fortnight before.

Our next game was against Holland, and it was a vitally important one. As both sides had identical records – won one, drawn one – the result would determine who went back to Wembley for the quarter-finals. There was some speculation that we might settle on a nice, comfortable 0–0 draw, but neither we nor the Dutch were up for anything like that. A draw might have denied us the chance to play in the last eight at Wembley and if we had lost we could have been out of the competition altogether. A win, however, would give us everything we wanted and ensure the departure of the Scots at the same time.

It was an unbelievable match, without a doubt the most tense I had ever experienced with England. We were magnificent that night, utterly magnificent. People didn't think an England team could play the sort of football we produced, and we proved all the knockers wrong. This was international football of the highest class you could imagine, and we were the ones who were playing it. After a nervous start by both sides, we took the lead when I picked the ball up and flicked it to Steve McManaman. Steve passed to Paul Ince, who tried to take it on but was brought crashing to the ground as he moved into the penalty area. Penalty. Shearer scored with a minimum of fuss to make it 1–0. We were on our way.

The score stayed that way until after half-time. We came out for the second half brimful of confidence, and before long we were 2–0 ahead. It was a thrill for me to score that goal, a header thumped home from a Gascoigne corner. By now we were totally in command, and could easily have been four goals up. Our self-belief was sky-high, and it showed in our football as we passed and interpassed, never letting the control slip for a moment. Afterwards it was said that this it was the best British football seen for thirty years and I must admit that it felt a bit special. The Dutch were a good side, there's no doubt about that, but they couldn't live with us on that Tuesday night in June 1996.

The Dutch were beginning to look a bit ragged by the time Gazza and I combined to give Shearer the opportunity to score the third goal – but not as ragged as they looked after I got our fourth. Darren Anderton cut in and fired in a shot that took a bit of deflection, and I was in the right place at the right time to follow up and hammer it past Van der Sar in the Dutch goal and into the net. The euphoria was unbelievable, the buzz around the ground amazing. It will live with me for ever. The only slight dampener on the occasion was that, because Alan Shearer was already carrying a booking and I had got a yellow card for a tackle in the first half, Terry Venables took us both off to save us for the quarter-final. It was a sensible decision, the only one he could have made in the circumstances, but it was a little disappointing to miss the chance to complete our hat-tricks and not to have been on the field when the final whistle blew.

The Dutch knew full well that they had been thrashed, but to be fair to them, they never stopped trying and they eventually got a goal to make sure they stayed in the competition. For us, meanwhile, it was the climax we had all been waiting for, the perfect performance at the right moment. For me personally it was a great night, and as good a game as I had ever appeared in at any level. The whole occasion – beating the fancied Dutch side, playing at Wembley, scoring two goals and, just as a bonus, being named as Man of the Match as well – was just beautiful. What an unforgettable event. I'm told that in Trafalgar Square that night there were thousands of England fans celebrating and singing and chanting my name. As we went back to our hotel the road was lined with supporters waving banners and cheering, and I remember holding the telephone to the window of my hotel room and telling my girlfriend to listen to the songs of the crowds outside.

We all felt like having a party that night, but there were to be no drinks for us. We still had a job to do only

four days later. We had to consciously bring ourselves
down from the euphoria and knuckle down to plotting
our strategy for dealing with the talented Spanish side
in the quarter-finals.

Terry Venables, who knew the Spain coach from his
days at Barcelona, told us that he never played five at
the back, so we formulated our game plan accordingly.
But as soon as the game started, lo and behold, for the
first time in history they were playing five at the back.
We'd been expected to beat the Spanish, but at the end
of extra time in the goalless draw, they were doing to us
what we had done to Holland only four days before. By
that time, Terry had substituted me and I wasn't on the
field for the penalty shoot-out. Alan Shearer took the first
one and scored, and I remember that Spain missed one and
had one saved, but I think that what sticks in everybody's
mind from that match is Stuart Pearce's penalty.

The thoughts of every English supporter in the crowd
that day were with Stuart when he marched up to take his
spot-kick. Stuart, you'll remember, had missed his penalty
when we were beaten by the Germans in the World Cup
semi-final in Italy in 1990, and I don't think there was
an English person on or off the pitch who didn't admire
his bottle in putting himself in the firing line again. You
could hear the whispers going round the stadium – and
the whispers of 80,000 people can be pretty deafening.
It was typical of Stuart, who is as strong a character as
I've ever played with, that he didn't think twice about
taking the penalty, but his reaction when he scored, all
screaming defiance and courage, was wonderful to see. Six
years of pain had been wiped from his memory at a stroke.
I rejoiced for the team, and for myself, and for the whole
country, but I also rejoiced for Stuart. He never once let

England down in his distinguished international career. I make no apologies for being an unreserved Stuart Pearce fan. It seems incredible to me that there were people who criticised him for his emotional response to scoring that goal. He was way over the top, said the carpers; he was an embarrassment as he strutted away from the penalty spot, eyes blazing. Embarrassing? Why? Because he was proud of the three lions on his England shirt? Because he had exorcised a bad memory? Because he saw it as a chance to make amends to his country for an occasion when, as he saw it, he had let it down? Rubbish. Complete and utter rot. Stuart Pearce was, and still is, an exemplary professional footballer. He is a man to look up to. So why should we be embarrassed by him? Instead, we should be proud of him, and be glad that there are such men who will give their all in the colours of their country.

Pearce's penalty was the single most emotional moment of the whole match, but when all had been done and dusted, it was just a job of work that had to be done. We couldn't afford to relax, for we were men on a mission, and we had to play the mighty Germans in the last four. If the expectations of the country had been big before the Holland game, in the build-up to our confrontation with Germany they were absolutely enormous. The hopes of every single football-loving person in the land were piled on our shoulders. We knew the Germans were good – bloody good – and that they were above all efficient. They had skill in abundance, more than people gave them credit for, actually; they had organisation; they had the knack of peaking at the right time in the competitions that mattered. Most dangerous of all, they were our bogey team. They had got ample revenge for their defeat by England in the World Cup final of 1966. They had beaten us 3–2 in the World

Cup in 1970, and eventually put us out on penalties in the semi-final in 1990.

In the days leading up to the game, we worked constantly at areas where we would need to counter their strengths and capitalise on their weaknesses, while developing a strategy of our own which we hoped would give them problems. The prize that awaited the winning team was enormous. The feeling that the side which beat the Germans would win the championship was inescapable. We believed that we were the masters of our own destiny and we thought that fate owed us one. We had come so far, and we were not going to go down without putting up the fight of our lives.

We had a dream start when Alan Shearer gave us the lead in the first few minutes, but within a quarter of an hour Stefan Kuntz had equalised. Game on. Both sides had chances, but that night, memorable and turbulent though it was, was never one for inspired football in the ninety minutes of regular time. Perhaps there was too much at stake for that. When full-time arrived the score was still locked at 1–1. Now we were into thirty minutes of 'golden goal' time, in which the first team to score would win the game.

Strangely, it was only then that both sides came completely out of their shells. Some wonderful football was played in that half-hour, probably the best of the entire competition. Both teams had chances – Darren Anderton was denied the winning goal by a post and, even more agonisingly, Gazza came within a whisker of scoring the winner when he slid in unmarked on the far post and just missed pushing a low cross-shot from Shearer into the net. Indeed, he's become almost as well known for that miss as he is for the spectacular goals he has scored. We could have won the game in that spell – we played enough good football to have done so, but, to be fair to them, so did the Germans. It was spine-tingling, pulsating stuff.

For the second game in succession, the contest went to penalties, and the tension was almost too much to bear. It fell to me to take our fifth penalty to put us 5–4 up. On that short walk from the centre circle to the penalty area I seemed to be moving in slow motion. If someone had told me it had taken me twenty minutes I would almost have believed them. It is a huge relief to put away such an important penalty – you are desperate not to let your side down. My shot went in, thank God, but in the end the coveted place in the final was decided by an England miss. And the man who missed, with the score standing at 5–5, was Gareth Southgate.

I will never forget the look of terrible agony on Gareth's face when his kick was saved to give Germany a 6–5 victory on penalties; I will never forget the numb feeling that spread throughout the wonderful grey bowl of Wembley; I will never forget Terry Venables being the first man at Gareth's side, cradling his face in his hands and trying to console him. I will never forget the emptiness we all felt deep inside at the realisation that our great adventure had come to an end. It was a terrible yet wonderful night for English football. We had taken on the best and had got within one dead-ball kick of beating them, but now we were out.

I felt miserable for myself, for the team, for the whole country, but most of all I felt miserable for Gareth, as honest a soul as ever laced up a pair of football boots. It was somehow not right that the responsibility for the success or failure of an entire footballing nation should be placed on the shoulders of one, fallible human being.

Back in the dressing room you could have heard a pin drop. Nobody could think of anything to say to comfort Gareth. Eventually, Tony Adams made a move towards the shower and, in his own inimitable way, called over his shoulder: 'Well, it was a fucking awful penalty, Gareth.' Everyone burst out laughing in spite of their misery, and the ice was broken.

I know that the penalty shoot-out is now the accepted way of settling deadlocks, and I suppose it is the only way – at least the outcome is settled by footballing skill. I just don't think failure should ever be blamed on an individual. Football is a team game, and it is somehow wrong that, ultimately, it should become a one-on-one contest between penalty-taker and goalkeeper, each of whom will become either hero or villain in the space of a few, torturous seconds.

Yet however sorry we felt for ourselves, the man we felt most sorry for was Terry Venables. He had put his heart and soul into leading England to triumph, and now he had to leave us in defeat. We didn't want him to go, because we felt that he was still the best man for the job, but the faceless men at Lancaster Gate had stipulated that Euro '96 would be his first and only chance to win something significant for the country.

Let it be said here and now that the players would have moved heaven and earth to keep him. Before Euro '96 started Paul Gascoigne went on national television to plead with Terry to stay, and with those who employed him to keep him on, after the competition was over. Paul was speaking from the heart that day, and his appeal was quiet and eloquent. I can tell you that every man jack of us was totally behind him as he voiced his support for the best coach, the best manager, the best motivator and the best mentor that any team, or any individual in it, could hope for. Gascoigne's plea fell on deaf ears. Terry knew that his reign was going to end with this one grand effort, and the men who walked the corridors of power at Lancaster Gate were in no hurry to keep him. I mean no disrespect to Glenn Hoddle, who took Terry's place, but there is not one footballer in the land, from the humblest Third Division journeyman to Premiership star, who wanted El Tel to go.

Several people were mentioned as possible successors. Jimmy Armfield, who had been retained by the FA to head-hunt a replacement for Graham Taylor and had done such a great job in coming up with Terry, was entrusted with the task again. Armfield was exactly the right man to do it. He is a respected former international who keeps in close touch with the game through his connections with BBC Radio 5 Live. I understand that Alex Ferguson was offered the job but preferred to remain with Manchester United. Besides, can you imagine what it would mean to certain people on both sides of the border if a Scot were to be appointed to manage England? Other names that were bandied about included Kevin Keegan, two Francises (Gerry and Trevor), Bryan Robson and Howard Wilkinson.

In the end, Armfield went with Glenn Hoddle, and in my opinion, he was the right person for the job. He had a certain charisma created by his marvellous ability as a footballer, he was well versed in the ways of continental football from his days playing under Arsène Wenger at Monaco, he had proved he could do the business at club level with Swindon and Chelsea and he would be respected by England footballers. Nevertheless, it was a tough decision for Glenn to make. He was painstakingly assembling a fine side at Chelsea, and would have retained the respect of English football-lovers in and out of the game even if he had opted to turn down the chance to coach the national side. By accepting it he was, after all, potentially on a hiding to nothing. It is typical of the man, a man of strong beliefs, undoubted loyalty to his players and an iron-hard will, that he took up the challenge. If anybody could take on the Terry Venables mantle, it was Glenn Hoddle. He would have to make some unpalatable and potentially damaging decisions before he led us into the World Cup in France in 1998, but never at any time did he shirk his responsibilities. If Terry had to go, Glenn was going to be an admirable replacement.

Chapter Twelve

World Cup Here We Come

Glenn Hoddle was a wise, witty and wonderful footballer. I used to watch him play for Tottenham in the days of his youth and my infancy and marvelled at what he could do with a ball. To a young lad he was a complete player, and there were plenty of people a good deal older than me who thought he was sensational as well. And yet, in spite of winning fifty-three caps for England, he never became firmly established in the side. His football was too pretty, people said; he used to flit round the edges of a match; he wasn't the sort to get his boot in when it mattered. But to those who looked for higher things than the sticking in of boots – and I count myself as one of them – he was a player in a million.

I was pleased when the FA showed enough vision to pick Glenn as England coach. He liked creative players, I felt, and that meant I might have half a chance in his sides. I wasn't counting my chickens, but I thought if I maintained the decent standard I had set for myself in my England career to date, I might impress him enough to be included in his plans.

In many ways, Glenn inherited a tougher job than Venables did. Terry had had only friendlies to contend with in the run-up to Euro '96, whereas Hoddle had to launch his England side almost immediately into a campaign to re-establish its credibility in the world order. We had failed to earn a ticket to the World Cup finals in the United States in 1994, and neither the footballing public nor the ever-critical media was going to be content with anything less than qualification in some style for France in 1998. Furthermore, Glenn had no time to bed down his ideas and plans – his first game in charge was a World Cup qualifier.

We were to play in Group 2 with Poland, Georgia, Italy and Moldova, and even if on paper Moldova, and to a lesser extent Georgia, were unlikely to cause us too many problems, success could not be taken for granted. There is no such thing as a foregone conclusion in international football these days, now that standards have improved so much all over the world. And both of the other two countries, Poland and Italy, had given us headaches in the past. For our first game, away to Moldova in Chisinau, I was injured, but the boys did a good job in the little republic which had been an independent country for only five years. Nicky Barmby, Paul Gascoigne and Alan Shearer scored our goals, and we were up and running.

I was with the squad for the second game, at home to Poland in October 1996, but not in the side. I had injured my thigh playing for Tottenham, and although I had been back in the Spurs team for a couple of games, Glenn felt that I was not yet ready for the rigours of international football. If I were a selfish so-and-so, I would have been pleased that I was not playing in that match, because in the first half we were terrible – and this was against a Polish side which was said to have been torn apart by internal strife. They certainly showed no signs of it in that first half. Baluszynski and Warzycha set up an opening for Marek Citko to clout the ball past David Seaman and Poland took the lead after just seven minutes. They continued to be a real handful for the rest of the half.

Yet the strange thing was, we led 2–1 at half-time without ever finding our rhythm. Thank heavens for Alan Shearer, who scored both our goals. The first was set up by David Beckham, who hit a long cross. Shearer beat Polish goalkeeper Wozniak to the ball and it was 1–1 after twenty-five minutes – more than we deserved, quite honestly. Twelve minutes later, Shearer and Les Ferdinand, who was playing alongside him in my absence, combined well to give Shearer the second goal. A lot of the credit for that must go to Ferdinand, who was marvellously unselfish in shielding the ball until the moment was right to give Shearer the short, scoring pass.

Glenn gave the boys a right rollocking at half-time. They were not working hard enough in midfield, he said. It was not what he expected from an England side, especially after the good performances they had put in during Euro '96 and in the game against Moldova. We breathed a collective sigh of relief at the end of that match. We had not played well, but at least we had got the right result, which is, I suppose, the sign of a good side. Golfers always say that you can tell a good player by the fact that he doesn't play particularly well but still shoots a 68. The same goes for football. Even so, we had cause to be thankful for the winning start for Hoddle's England, and now we had to begin playing like a side that was capable of holding up its head in the best company.

The game in which we did so was against Georgia in

Tblisi in November. We knew the Georgians had some good players, and we had particular respect for George Kinkladze, who had been producing some spectacular stuff for Manchester City. Well, we won 2–0 and we looked the part. We were composed and skilful from defence through the midfield to the front, where I played alongside Ferdinand in the absence of the injured Shearer. I gave us the lead after a quarter of an hour when Gascoigne fed Ferdinand, and Les, unselfishly again, saw me moving into space on the right channel and put me through to score with a shot that came off a defender and went past the goalkeeper, Zoidze, after Murtaz Shelia failed with an attempted interception. Gazza and I then set up a deserved goal for Les before half-time. If you look back to the qualifying campaign, Ferdinand had several really good moments in various games. Don't let anybody tell you that he shouldn't have got into Glenn's final twenty-two for France. He is always prepared to forget about personal glory in the interests of the side.

In the second half we just shut them out. It was a good, professional performance in which we scored our goals at the right time and then didn't give the opposition a chance to get back into the game. I think Georgia got only one shot on target in the whole match. Above all, we had emerged as a classy side capable of playing top-quality football and we knew that both Italy and Poland now had to go to Georgia looking for a win.

That was our last World Cup fixture of 1996. We had made a good start – played three, won three, 9 points out of 9 – but we were all well aware that the first match of 1997 would be against Italy, at Wembley, on 12 February. That was a date that was stamped on our minds. It was like a League programme in some ways: you have to clean up against the weaker sides, because you never know what might happen against the powerful ones.

And Italy were certainly one of those. By the time we met them it was already established that we were the only two teams capable of qualifying for France. The match was a huge occasion, played in front of a Wembley crowd filled with vocal Englishmen and just about every Italian waiter in the land, and although I was injured for the game, I lived every moment for the England boys. I was watching from the stands with Nicola, and it was a lot worse having to sit there, helpless, to be perfectly honest. If you are not on the field you have no chance of even trying to influence the outcome. And I was not the only injured player for England's biggest match to date under Glenn Hoddle. David Seaman and Tony Adams had also had to pull out, and so two vertebrae in what Hoddle was already calling the backbone of his side were not on the field.

We knew we could not give the Italians half a chance, because they were so clinical in their finishing. You also had to be aware of their ability to hit you on the counter, and it was from just such a move that the all-important goal came. Matt Le Tissier was caught in possession and the ball was threaded through to Gianfranco Zola, the little maestro who was the idol of the crowd at Chelsea. You can't give Zola those sort of openings and hope to get away with it, and sure enough Franco made us pay that night as he cut into the penalty area and slotted a low deflected shot off Sol Campbell – who nearly got it – past Ian Walker, my Tottenham team-mate, on the near post. Afterwards Walker took a lot of stick for failing to save that goal, which I felt was unwarranted.

The England manager tried everything. He put on Ferdinand, Paul Merson and Ian Wright for Le Tissier,

McManaman and Batty, but not even fresh legs were able to help us. We were disappointed, but we knew that we had by no means reached the end of the road yet.

We had to wait two and a half months for our opportunity to put ourselves back on course for the World Cup, and we succeeded in doing so in our home game against Georgia. In the meantime we got back into the winning habit with a 2–0 victory in a friendly against Mexico, the first opportunity Glenn Hoddle had to field a side in a match whose result would have no wider significance. We took the lead when Rob Lee, who had been brought into midfield, put me through, I cut into the box and when I was halted the ball bounced into Paul Ince's path. Ince shaped to shoot, but was scythed down. I scored from the penalty spot. Alan Shearer was missing for this game, and in his absence it was Robbie Fowler, my striking partner for the night, who scored our second after substitute Ian Wright's header from a Le Saux cross was beaten away by the goalkeeper to Robbie's feet. Fowler doesn't miss chances like that. It was a powerful and committed performance and the confidence was clearly seeping back to the side. We felt more and more that the away match against Italy would settle the group, and our belief that we could do the job in Rome in October grew stronger.

The home World Cup qualifier against Georgia saw the return of myself and Alan Shearer as an attacking unit. SAS were back, and although the performance of our side was workmanlike rather than inspired. The first half was coming to an end when we broke the deadlock. Graeme Le Saux made the opening with one of his surging runs from left wing back and slipped the ball to Shearer, who sent in a thundering cross. I managed to get in front of my marker – I think it was Shelia again – and headed the ball home. It was a moment to savour, a moment when, after a series of niggling injuries, I felt at last that I was back as a card-carrying member of the England side. It felt good to score that goal, and it felt almost as good when, in the very last minute of the game, I pushed the ball back from an indirect free kick for Alan to batter it in. SAS had come, had seen and had conquered.

In the midst of my traumas with Alan Sugar at Tottenham, on 24 May, we dismissed South Africa 2–1 with goals from Rob Lee and Ian Wright. But much more important was the game exactly a week later, against Poland in Katowice. Italy might have been the make-or-break game in the group, but first we had to dismantle the tough, uncompromising Poles in their own backyard. A win here would ensure that we could do no worse than earn a place in the World Cup qualifying play-offs. The Poles, who still had an outside chance of qualifying themselves if they beat us, didn't make it easy for us but, again, it was a victory for England. Alan scored the first goal after five minutes, after Paul Ince set him up with a marvellous run. It was a fine defensive performance in which we gave Poland hardly a sight of our goal. I put the finishing touches to a move sparked off by Rob Lee in the last minute. We could even afford to miss a penalty. The culprit? Amazingly, it was Alan Shearer. I felt I played my part that day, not only in scoring what was potentially a vital goal but also in helping the team to keep their shape in the face of some heavy provocation by Poland.

A few weeks of welcome rest and relaxation beckoned, but first came Le Tournoi, the four-nation tournament in France involving the hosts, ourselves, Brazil – and Italy. It might have been only a friendly tournament, but the way things went might nevertheless be significant to the wider picture of the World Cup. Our first match was against Italy. This was our chance to set ourselves against them. If we did well – or even beat them for the first time in twenty years – it would give us a tremendous psychological advantage for the big night ahead in October.

We won, famously and brilliantly, by 2–0, against almost the same side that had beaten us at Wembley in February – only Maldini was missing. Ian Wright, who had probably his best game in an England shirt, scored after twenty-five minutes and combined with Paul Scholes for the latter's goal, two minutes before half-time. It taught us that we could beat these Italians, and it proved to them that we had more than a couple of decent strikers in England. Now we were level-pegging: in the previous four months we had won one match each. We couldn't wait for the decider; Italy, on the other hand, or so it seemed to me, were less enthusiastic at the prospect.

The big battle was over, but the next, against France, was also important in the context of the World Cup. The French hadn't been beaten on their own soil for three years, and not at home by England in forty-eight. Our performance lacked a little of the fluency we'd shown against Italy, but yet again we proved that if we had to be neat, purposeful and compact rather than blindingly brilliant, we could do that, too. There were chances at both ends throughout the match and David Seaman had to pull a magnificent save out of the hat to beat away a superb effort by Pierre Laigle. We didn't make the breakthrough until the last five minutes, when the French goalkeeper dropped my cross and Shearer was, as ever, on the spot to drive home the winner. We deserved to beat France, I think, and, what's more, we had won the tournament, irrespective of the result against Brazil.

It was just as well, because the Brazilians beat us 1–0 at Parc des Princes. Paul Ince tested the Brazilian goalkeeper with a searing shot in the first period, but we didn't really get into the match until the second half. There was a strong conviction that one goal would probably settle it, and so it proved. The goal eventually came when Leonardo pushed the ball through to Romario, who moved in on Seaman and slipped the ball past him. We were disappointed, of course we were, but nevertheless we felt we had proved a thing or two to some people – not least to Cesare Maldini, the Italian coach, and his squad. Ronaldo, said to be the best player in the world, appeared against us in that last game, and although Sol Campbell made a fine job of man-marking him, he showed his quality time and again. He is an awesome player in an awesome team, although I'm still sure that if we played to our strengths of organisation, courage and spirit we could give Brazil more than a fair run for their money.

We went our different ways after that, to concentrate on the new season in the Premiership. Within the next couple of weeks I was to become a Manchester United player. I was thrilled about that, but I had international duties on my mind as well as I went through pre-season training at Old Trafford. As we embarked on the 1997–8 season, the moment of truth was approaching on the world stage too. Before Italy took over the thoughts of the England squad, we had one other small matter to be disposed of. Moldova were our visitors on 10 September at Wembley and, although I was unfit, I went along to the game with the team. Alan Shearer was out, too, having just started his long lay-off after picking up an injury in a pre-season match with Newcastle, and Ian Wright and Les Ferdinand had come into the side in our places.

Only a week or so after the tragic loss of Diana, Princess of Wales, it was a moving night at Wembley. During the playing of the national anthem there was an eerie silence in the stadium. The feeling in the England camp before the game was that we wanted to put on a special show in memory of a great lady whose death had affected everybody in the country. I'm glad that the team were able to do so. Paul Gascoigne was magnificent, and proved what a wonderfully dominating player he can be. He totally ran the game, nudging and grafting in midfield and leaving the gallant but outclassed Moldovans to chase his shadow for ninety solid minutes. They simply couldn't handle him – but I don't think any team in world football could have done that night.

Paul Scholes gave us the lead when he headed home powerfully from a David Beckham cross, and within a minute of the second half England were two up. Wright fed Gascoigne, who drew the Moldova defence before returning the ball for Wright to provide the finishing touch. Gascoigne hit the post shortly afterwards, and then went one better as he collected Wright's pass and scored. Three-nil now, but England were not resting on their laurels. Stan Collymore came on to replace Ferdinand and set up Wright to score our fourth goal in the ninetieth minute.

We couldn't have hoped for a better game. We had won 4–0, but in a way the most important result of the night came from Tblisi, where Italy could not manage more than a goalless draw with Georgia. Short of Georgia actually winning the match, it couldn't have gone better for us. Now we could go to Rome on 11 October in the knowledge that a draw would bring us automatic qualification for the World Cup finals, whereas Italy needed a win. Their result in Georgia had underlined how well we had played there, and they had only been able to draw in Poland as well. Our confidence grew as the match got closer. If we were disciplined and kept our shape, we could go through with a draw. And they had to win. We kept repeating this mantra to ourselves in the countdown to the game.

Another factor in our favour was the discontent in the Italian camp. The players were beginning to become irritated by what they saw as Cesare Maldini's indecision in terms of both his personnel and the formation he was going to use. Zola would be in the team, then out, and the same went for del Piero, Inzaghi, Casiraghi and Ravanelli. Glenn Hoddle knew our best line-up, whereas Maldini was still groping round for a solution. And Maldini had no choice but to press for goals. Italian football has traditionally been based on watertight defence: soak up the pressure, break the hearts and the resolve of the opposition and, only when you have done that, let the attacking midfield players and hugely skilled strikers express themselves. The Italians play that way in Serie A and in international football. It was against their nature to throw everything into attack, but this time they had no alternative. They had to take chances, and I must admit it was nice to be going there to cause them concern and dismay.

It was a monumental performance by England on that memorable Saturday, a display of power and commitment and discipline, the national side's finest showing for years, Euro '96 included, because of the prize at stake. We had no intention of missing out on the World Cup finals again, and I don't think Glenn Hoddle or anybody else in England could have faulted us for the way we played. Everybody contributed to the best 0–0 draw in the history of England football. Tony Adams, Gareth Southgate and

Sol Campbell were majestic across the back, David Batty and Paul Ince – who had to go off to have stitches in a head wound and returned with a bandage round his head and his shirt tinged pink with the blood he had spilled for his country – were immovable in the centre of midfield, and I supported Ian Wright. And missed a goal, a miss that almost led to a winner for Italy.

It was in the last minutes of the game that Wright went round goalkeeper Peruzzi and hit in a shot from an acute angle which hit the post and came back to me. A hundred and one thoughts flashed through my mind as that ball bounced into my path. Should I do what George Graham had told me to do all those years ago and smash it, or should I try to stroke it in? It came a little too quickly to allow me to try for the goal, so I tried to go round somebody to give myself a chance of scoring calmly. But the ball was nicked off my toe.

The Italians moved the ball swiftly up the left wing and a cross saw Christian Vieri's header go just wide. Having almost scored at the other end, I was powerless to do anything to help prevent them from scoring. My heart was in my mouth at that moment. If we had let one in as a direct consequence of my failure to take the chance, I would never have forgiven myself.

A few minutes later the final whistle blew. We had done it. We were there. France, here we come. The scenes of jubilation were incredible; everybody was hugging and kissing and there were more than a few tears as well. Glenn Hoddle said that he was proud of us, and that everybody in England should be, too. Although I say so myself, I had to agree with him. I had never played in a side so totally focused on what they had to do in a particular match. It's another memory I'll carry with me for the rest of my life. The England fans that day were absolutely fantastic. They loved every minute of the game, but their Italian counterparts grew more and more restless as it wore on. They were pretty vocal in their criticism of Maldini, especially when he replaced Zola with del Piero with twenty-five minutes left.

As we celebrated afterwards a small note of farce crept into proceedings. Leaving the pitch, Gareth Southgate and I were collared by FIFA officials to go and take a random drugs test, for which you have to provide a urine sample. So while the rest of the lads were whooping it up in the dressing room, we had to go back and perform. And we couldn't. What with all the adrenaline that had been pumping round our bodies and all the fluid we had lost in blood and sweat, we just couldn't deliver. We tried water. Nothing. We tried orange juice. Nothing. We tried tea. Still nothing.

The two Italians who were chosen were Benarrivo, the substitute, and Albertini. Benarrivo was the first to oblige, so he was allowed to rejoin his team-mates. Albertini made a valiant effort, but all he could manage was about an inch and a half, and you are supposed to supply the testers with about three inches. Poor chap – I did feel a bit sorry for him. It was unfortunate for us two as well, but at least we'd secured our place in the finals. There was Albertini, trying to come to terms with the fact that the Italians were not yet out of the woods, and he couldn't even join his colleagues in their moment of disillusionment.

Then Gazza poked his head round the door. 'Have you got no beers, lads?' he asked. We asked him where he thought we were going to get a beer when we'd only just come off the pitch. 'Hang on a minute, I used to play here,' he said. 'We used to keep some beers round the back.' He disappeared and returned shortly afterwards with three bottles of Italian lager. Gareth and I soon had the tops off ours, clinked them together in mutual congratulation and got them to within about two centimetres of our lips before an official came in and told us hastily that we couldn't drink beer as it might corrupt the sample. So near and yet so far. A beer might have helped to solve the problem, too. As it was, Gazza had to take the beer back to the dressing room and we were left with nothing stronger than orange juice, tea and water. I think it was not until about an hour and a half later that Gareth managed to provide enough of a sample to satisfy the drugs testers. It took me thirty minutes more. Gareth couldn't prevent himself from having a good laugh at my expense.

As a result of all that messing around, I never got to join the rest of the lads in their moment of triumph. The other boys are probably still telling stories about that marvellous night, but I can't – I was stuck in a back room somewhere trying to pass water.

Even though we had qualified, there was still plenty left to do before we took on Tunisia, Romania and Colombia in Group G in Marseilles, Toulouse and Lens respectively in the summer of 1998. Glenn Hoddle probably had a fair idea about who he'd be choosing to form his squad for France, but now that the most vital job was done, he had a sprinkling of friendly internationals in which to settle on the twenty-two good men and true who would carry the hopes of England in arguably the most important World Cup campaign for the country in twenty years or more. Our reputation had been hugely enhanced by our performance in the qualifying competition. Now we had to go not one, but several steps further. The whole of footballing England expected – and we were in no mood to let them down.

Our programme of friendlies revealed that, although we were a coming side, we were still not quite there. On 15 November, the same night that other countries were slugging it out for the few places left in the World Cup finals, we beat Cameroon 2–0 with goals from Robbie Fowler and Paul Scholes, and although I did not play in that game I started the match against the in-form Chilean side at Wembley in February. I was taken off with twenty-five minutes to go to be replaced by Alan Shearer, who was making his comeback for England after that pre-season injury. They beat us 2–0, both goals coming from the irrepressible Marcelo Salas. One of them was an absolute gem – he took a through ball on his thigh and volleyed it past Nigel Martyn – and the other a penalty.

We were given a bit of a lesson that night, and we did not exactly cover ourselves with glory, either, in a messy 1–1 draw away to Switzerland. I was a substitute, coming on to replace young Michael Owen, but I couldn't do much to help to dig us out of the mess that we had got ourselves into. We got our act together against Portugal in April, but only after escaping scot-free from a first half in which Portugal hammered us. If they'd had a striker of Alan Shearer's quality in that game, we would have been dead and buried by half-time, so many chances did they make. We improved vastly in the second half, and I returned to scoring mode when I ran on to a through ball, waited until the goalkeeper had committed himself to coming out to narrow the angle, then lifted it over him and into the net. It felt good to be back in the side, and it felt even better to get back on the scoresheet in a 3–0 victory. Personally, I had been going through a bad patch for Manchester United, and had even been dropped from the side, so it was nice to put in a decent performance again.

After seventy-three minutes I was replaced by the young man who was to play a huge role in my own immediate future. Michael Owen had a couple of chances in the latter stages of the match and looked a lively customer, and we all knew that he could play the game, even at the tender age of eighteen. He was definitely one to watch, not least for his confidence, mastery of the all-important first touch and blistering pace.

That said, there are always a host of good forwards around and at least one waiting in the wings – a Les Ferdinand, a Stan Collymore, a Robbie Fowler or an Ian Wright. Michael Owen was just one more. Although I recognised his huge talents, I still felt confident and comfortable with my position. All through the long and arduous qualifying programme, if I had been fit, I had played. Although Alan Shearer was always the perfect diplomat when asked who he would rather partner, I don't think I'm being conceited in saying that it was generally accepted that of all the leading strikers in the country, Alan preferred to have me alongside him. I liked to think – and I still do, in spite of all that happened subsequently – that I had the ability to bring the best out of England's premier striker.

We had played magnificently to qualify for the World Cup and had had our moments in our pre-France warm-ups. Nevertheless I must admit that there were a few alarm bells ringing. We had been outplayed on the night by Chile, and although we had produced some good football in the second half against Portugal we had been guilty of a few worrying slips before half-time. We could still do well in France, we felt, but we would have to buckle down if we were to make a lasting impression against the best sides in the world.

Chapter Thirteen

Old Trafford Dreams

When I had signed for Tottenham Hotspur in 1992 it was the fulfilment of a dream, albeit a romantic one. They were my team, the team in which my heroes had played. It was *Boys' Own* stuff, the classic story of the kid who grew up on the other side of the footballing tracks coming to play for the club he had idolised as a youngster.

Manchester United were different. They were a club that occupied a unique place in the universal community of football; a club 98 per cent of whose fans, it was said, would never see them play; a club whose fame transcended national boundaries; a club whose name was known and venerated from Acapulco to Adelaide, from Zagreb to Zanzibar. A world club, a club for the world. Munich '58, the Busby Babes, George Best, Bobby Charlton, Denis Law; the stuff of legends. And I was going to play for them.

In the days when Millwall were in the old First Division it gave everybody in the first team at the Den a particular buzz to go to Manchester United. Sure, there were other big games in a season, but there was nothing quite like playing in front of the Old Trafford faithful. That great stadium, where the ghosts of glories past still walked, if only in the minds of their thousands of lifelong supporters, was like a cathedral that held a special place in the hearts and minds of football-lovers everywhere. And this was to be my home ground.

Things had happened so fast when I returned from that holiday in the United States that I was still slightly dizzy when I reported for training at my new club. We did not have long to think about things, because almost immediately we were off on a pre-season tour of the Far East. David Beckham and Gary Neville had both, like me, been with England at Le Tournoi in France, and they were given permission to miss the Far East jaunt, but Alex Ferguson wanted me to go along to give me a chance to get to know the rest of the lads in the squad. I could understand his point of view perfectly. An important season was just around the corner, and it was obviously essential that I acclimatised before we got into the serious stuff. My new boss also discussed with me what he perceived as my role in the side. He was anxious, first and foremost, that I should not go too deep to seek out the ball. He'd had a problem with Eric Cantona in that respect, he said. Cantona had sometimes come into deeper positions than he would have liked, and he did not want the same thing to happen with me.

I knew what the manager was saying to me, and again he had a point, but it was something that I did not quite agree with. I have never thought of myself as a direct replacement for anybody, so I did not have Cantona and his game on my mind at any time. I succeeded Gary Lineker when I joined Tottenham, and, I suppose, took Peter Beardsley's place in the England set-up, but I like to think I brought different qualities of my own to those sides. That doesn't mean I don't respect what Lineker or Beardsley were, because they were both great players. I'm sure they could do things I can't, but by the same token maybe I can do things they might not have been able to do. However, because I was the sort of player I was, the feeling among Manchester United fans was that I was stepping into Cantona's shoes, and that's the sort of pressure you can do without in your early days with a new club. I couldn't understand that. Funnily enough, Les Ferdinand, who arrived at White Hart Lane after my departure, found himself in a similar situation.

I don't think anybody would disagree that Cantona's was a unique talent. Like Chris Waddle and Paul Gascoigne, he was the kind of player people would go a long way to watch and pay good money to do so. He scored some outstanding goals, some of which were absolutely unbelievable. When he was on song, some of the things he did were majestic. If I managed to achieve half what he had, I'd be pleased. But that was him; this was me. I was not the second Eric Cantona, I was the first Teddy Sheringham, and I felt that, if things went well for me and the team, I could help to carry forward the success the club had achieved in the previous five years.

Some players might have found it difficult to come into this set-up, but I was lucky in that I already knew Gary Pallister, the Neville brothers, Paul Scholes, Nicky Butt, Andy Cole and David Beckham from England squads, and I had played at Forest with Roy Keane. So it was not as though a sea of unfamiliar faces greeted me when I walked through the door. In fact the whole first-team squad made me feel pretty much at home from the start, and I must admit that the Far East trip was useful on that score. At home, when you finish training you all go your separate ways, whereas on tour you're with the rest of the team all the time, which helps a lot when you're settling into a new club.

When we got back, I couldn't wait for the 1997–8 season to start. Pre-season had gone well, I was bedding in nicely and the whole side felt that we were on the brink of another big year. We had a Premiership title to defend and the Champions' League beckoned. Our first big game was the season-opening Charity Shield against Chelsea, the FA Cup-winners, at Wembley. I had played for five years for Tottenham without winning a thing, and now I had a chance to put a medal in the trophy cabinet in the first competitive game I played for United. It was a good and surprisingly competitive match. Mark Hughes gave Chelsea the lead and Ronnie Johnsen equalised for us, then we won on penalties. I had been substituted about fifteen minutes before full-time, so I wasn't on the field for the penalty shoot-out.

One game, and already I had a medal. This was good. I liked this a lot. I remember big Peter Schmeichel taking the mickey out of me afterwards. 'Look at Teddy,' he said. 'He's got a medal at last. It's your first, isn't it, Ted?' I joined in the laughter. It didn't mean that much to the others, to be honest – they'd won bigger things than an FA Charity Shield gong. But Peter was right, it was my first medal, and it was something nobody would ever be able to take away from me.

That Wembley date was a week before the beginning of the Premiership season, and our first game was against none other than Tottenham Hotspur at White Hart Lane. Talk about a baptism of fire. There was a heck of a lot of space in the newspapers devoted to my return to the club, having left on such acrimonious terms with the chairman, but I can put my hand on my heart and say that to me it was just another match, and one we were expected to win. Even so, it did feel slightly funny to run on to that familiar pitch at White Hart Lane to face the very same people who, only a few weeks before, I had anticipated playing alongside.

It was a sultry August day and the reception I got from the Tottenham fans was as hot as the weather. Some of them called me a Judas, and that hurt a little, I suppose, but at the same time I could understand their feelings. After all, I had been one of their bigger players, and now here I was running out with the opposition in the opening match of the season. I knew from my last few months at the club that a lot of them were not happy with the way things were going there, which probably made my departure a bigger blow. When I came on to the field a few people applauded me; then the applause and the jeers got to about fifty-fifty. Before long the whole of the home crowd was baying for my blood. But that's football. You have to be prepared to accept that sort of thing and not crumble under the pressure. I had been brought up in a hard school at Millwall, so nothing was going to get to me now.

The funny thing is, a lot of Tottenham fans have spoken to me since about that day, and almost to a man they've said something along the lines of, 'Ted, I've got to apologise for all the Tottenham fans that day. It wasn't me – I was there, but I promise you it wasn't me.' I must say it sounded to me like about 30,000 fans were all singing the same song. So I'm sure even those who apologised were joining in with the rest at the time. Perhaps afterwards they felt a bit sorry for me. Well, I can tell them all that they did not get me down. It's all part of football, and the Tottenham crowd were just practising a bit of gamesmanship to make their team win.

They didn't. We did, 2–0, with a Nicky Butt goal and an own goal. I didn't get on the scoresheet, but I had a chance when we were awarded a penalty in the second half when the score was still 0–0. I missed it. Now, that *did* get to me. I had taken many a penalty against my old mate Ian Walker in training, so he knew where I liked to put them and I knew where he liked to dive, and there was a bit of bluff and double-bluff going on out there. When I strode up, I had decided exactly where I was going to put the ball: low to his right. I overdid it, pulling it a bit too much to his right, and the ball thumped against the base of the post and came straight back to me. Even then I did the wrong thing. I knew I couldn't have another go at it, and I didn't think any of the other lads were coming up behind me, so I just hoofed it away.

Needless to say I got even more stick for that – I bet Alan Sugar was jumping up and down in glee in the stands when I missed that penalty, happy as a sandboy. If so I was happier: we had got over the first hurdle, and even though I'd thrown away the chance to score my first goal for Manchester United, we'd done the important thing and won the game.

The atmosphere surrounding us in those early days of the season was one of expectancy. We had a marvellous record to maintain, and for a club such as Manchester United, there is only one way to do that, which is to win even bigger prizes. To some clubs success might mean doing well in the League, to others taking a meaningful stab at the FA Cup, but at Old Trafford it had to be both of those, and more. For us, it was to be the year we made a major thrust into Europe. The Champions' League had to be our major objective. We had done Cups, we had done the League, now we wanted to conquer Europe as well. Only at Manchester United is it a realistic aim to attack on three fronts, and we felt that such a target was well within our capabilities.

Our first home game was three days later, against Southampton. It was my first real taste of playing in the red Manchester United shirt at Old Trafford. It was a big moment, and lots of my friends and family were there to see me pass this new milestone in my career. That match taught me a lot about how opponents react when they come to Old Trafford. Southampton were to develop into a decent Premiership team during the season, but that day they were content to try to survive. They hardly got out of their half until David Beckham, who had come on as a substitute early on, scored the winner late in the game. Then the Saints did come out of their shell a bit, but by that stage they had no choice if they were going to salvage anything from the match.

Andy Cole was injured in the early part of the season, so I played my first few games alongside Jordi Cruyff. My contribution against Leicester was useful rather than inspired, except when I managed to miss a glaring open goal. In the first half Paul Scholes had a header parried by the goalkeeper, and as the ball came back to me I saw the keeper go down again. I thought he had a fifty-fifty chance of getting a hand to it, so I tried to put it just a little bit wider, and hit the post from about 3 yards out. There were a few howls of frustration from the crowd, and I felt a bit silly. I couldn't imagine how I had failed to tuck it away – it had been easier to score than to miss.

In the White Hart Lane game Tottenham had at least

tried to take the battle to us, but our next away match, at Leicester, gave notice of how most home sides would be playing against us. We had about 70 per cent of the play, but they just piled all eleven men behind the ball and defied us to get through. We got stronger and stronger as the game went on, but for all our superior class, we couldn't get past the solid wall of defenders. The Leicester fans were ecstatic with the goalless draw. Of course, they'd have preferred to have won, but a point against the mighty Manchester United was next door to a victory. It was something I had to come to terms with; I knew we were a good side, and we would win more than we'd lose, even against opponents hell-bent on nothing more ambitious than defence in numbers.

There was one small black moment at Leicester. In the second half I went for a cross and took a kick in the ribs. They got progressively more painful over the next few days and I had a lot of trouble sleeping, but I kept quiet because we had a big game in the middle of the following week against Everton and I did not want to be missing out on something like that so early in the season. I'm glad I did. I played against Everton even though my ribs were still killing me, and had my second red-letter day with Manchester United: I scored my first goal for the club in a 2–0 victory. We absolutely ripped Everton apart that night, and the main architect of our success was Ryan Giggs, who was simply on fire. It was Giggs who made my goal. I got the ball in the centre circle and played it to him on the left, then arrived late on the cross and hit it with my left foot. It took a bit of a deflection, to be honest, but there was no chance of me not claiming that one.

Barry Nevill, my agent, brought my son Charlie to the game, and it was nice that he was there to see me score my first goal for the club. But the look of confusion on his face when I ran over to him was a picture. Poor old Charlie was in a bit of a quandary. He'd always been a Tottenham fan, and for the first few weeks of the season, when anyone asked him if he was a Manchester United supporter now, he remained adamant, like all loyal fans should be, that Tottenham were still the team for him. However, by the time he'd been to Old Trafford a few times and seen the likes of Beckham, Giggs, Scholes and Butt in action, I think he was won over by the way we played.

The day I finally realised that he'd become a United fan was when we went shopping for the away kit for him. At Tottenham, Charlie had always had the shirt with 'Sheringham' and the number 10 on the back. As soon as I got to Manchester United I bought him the Sheringham home kit as before. However, when he came with me to get the away strip he said he wanted the Beckham number 7 shirt. Beckham was his hero; I was only his dad. There's not a lot you can say to that.

Talking of shirts, that number 10 has served me well over the years. I was 10 at Tottenham and was lucky enough to get the same number for England. At Millwall, however, I'd been number 9, so when I went to Forest I asked Brian Clough if I could have it there. But Cloughie's son Nigel had had the 9 for years, and Clough Senior wasn't about to change that now. 'Just make sure you're in the first eleven, son,' he said. 'Don't worry about what number you are.' There was no answer to that. So number 10 I became, and that's where I've stayed ever since.

At Manchester United, David Beckham had worn the number 10 shirt since his first year in the side. However, I'd heard that he wanted the number 7 to follow in the footsteps of Bryan Robson and Eric Cantona, so I asked

Alex Ferguson if I could have 10. Alex knew that Beckham was anxious to wear number 7, so he said I could have 10 if I wanted. I'd have been delighted to have worn any old number, to be honest, but it was still nice to be able to keep the one with which I'd come to be associated.

Back on the field, our next match was a 3–0 victory over Coventry. I had a bit of a tussle with a Coventry defender and had more pain in my ribs as I went down. I got through the game, but afterwards I decided that I couldn't keep quiet about the problem any longer. So when I joined the England party for the World Cup qualifying game against Moldova I told the doctors about it. They sent me for a scan, and back came the report – two cracked ribs. That meant I missed the England game and also Manchester United's 2–1 home victory over West Ham. And next on the agenda was the club's first Champions League match, away to Kosice. I wasn't anywhere near fit for that, and Alex Ferguson knew it, but he had no choice but to put me on the subs' bench. The squad was shorn of strikers and he needed cover in case Andy Cole, who had by now returned to the side, was injured.

I'm quite glad that I wasn't required that night, because I wouldn't have been able to move about too freely, but we played brilliantly against admittedly mediocre opposition and won 3–0. Kosice weren't a strong side, but there's no such thing as easy ride in Europe these days, and you can slip up in these games if you're not careful.

I was still not 100 per cent fit for the match against Bolton that followed the European trip, but I went as a spectator. Once again we had the lion's share of the play – I'd say about 90 per cent – but were held to a goalless draw, and once again, I couldn't believe how overjoyed the opposing fans were to get a draw against us at home.

It was a situation we were to encounter time and time again during the season. I had more or less recovered from my injury in time for the Chelsea game at home, and I came on for about the last fifteen minutes when we were 2–1 down. I was feeling only the occasional small twinge from the ribs now, and was able to move about quite freely. Ole Gunnar Solskjaer also came on as a late substitute, replacing Paul Scholes, and, in the last few minutes of the match, equalised with a wonder goal – which Ole is always likely to do.

We had remained undefeated in our first eight Premiership games of the season, but that run came to an end in the ninth, against Leeds at Elland Road. They nicked a goal and then defended it in depth, and even though we put them under a lot of pressure we could not break down George Graham's well-drilled side. No team coached by Graham will ever be easy to beat, and he had made his mark on a Leeds side that had previously had a habit of leaking goals.

Our defeat was not the only gloomy note in that game. Even more important than losing the 3 points was losing Roy Keane: he snapped his knee cruciate ligament, an injury that was to put him out for the rest of the season. It was the first major casualty of our campaign, and it was an important one, because Roy was one of the players around whom our side and our playing style was built. He is an inspirational player, so he is valuable not only for what he does himself but also for what he brings out of others, and his long-term absence was going to be a huge blow.

Roy would be sadly missed, especially as coming up four days later was our Champions' League match at home to Juventus, the biggest one in the group, no question, and one that in some quarters we were not expected to win.

Ronnie Johnsen came into Keane's place to give the side that certain bite in central midfield. I had heard from the other players about European nights at Old Trafford and how incredible the atmosphere was. They had not exaggerated. When we walked out on to the pitch just before the game the air was electric. Unbelievable.

Juve had beaten Manchester United twice in the previous year, and we knew we had to prevent them from getting off to a good start. So you can imagine how we felt when Alessandro del Piero gave them the lead in the first minute of the game. We were stunned, shocked beyond belief. It was a setback that would take some recovering from. In the light of that, I'm proud to have been a part of a performance which showed the rest of Europe that our club, and English football, did not know when it was beaten. We played the game of our lives, and it was my first goal for the club in European competition that got us back into contention. I passed to ball out to Giggs on the left and kept going after I'd delivered the pass. Giggs attacked the full-back, put in a fantastic low, raking cross to the far post and I came in, rose above everybody and headed the ball down into the far corner of the net. The roar from the crowd was frightening; I don't think Juventus knew what had hit them.

The Old Trafford faithful could have been forgiven for becoming a little blasé about watching their team winning everything in the League. They're used to it, so they don't see a Premiership victory as anything out of the ordinary. This, though, was different. For a start, it was unusual for us to be the underdogs. and now we were looking the better side. The fans sensed that they might be watching something very special. And indeed they were, as they knew for certain when Paul Scholes scored our second and Ryan Giggs the third. This was about as good as it got, as good a game as I had ever played in, certainly on a par with some of England's best performances in Euro '96. Even the small element of anticlimax introduced by Zinedine Zidane in the last minute, when he got a goal from a free kick for Juventus to narrow the gap to 3–2, could not dampen our spirits. We had still come through a torrid test of our skill and our courage, and it convinced us that we could go a very long way in Europe in 1997–8.

Three days later I scored in our 2–0 victory over Crystal Palace, and then we drew – again – at Derby, 2–2. We felt we would do pretty well to get a point there, but we could have had more if I hadn't missed another penalty after Giggs was brought down by the goalkeeper. I honestly thought that I couldn't hit a penalty any more sweetly. It was going about two inches inside the post when the keeper flung himself across, got his fingertips to it and nudged it on to the upright and away. Two taken and two missed: I was heading for relegation in the penalty-taking stakes. Fortunately, I went some way towards redeeming myself by scoring with a good header in the second half, and Andy Cole made it two near the end.

Our next European encounter was against Feyenoord at home. They were tough opposition, but we were too good for them on the night, producing another exciting and competent display to beat them 2–1. We were cruising now in this competition: played three, won three. Paul Scholes scored one of our goals and the other was a penalty converted by Denis Irwin. It looked like I was out of a job. I think that game saw the best front six we played all season. Cole and I were up front, Giggs on the left and Beckham on the right, and Butt and Scholes combined superbly in central midfield. It was a formation that could accommodate all attacking situations and most defensive ones, too. We did not often get the chance to play exactly that six; if we had I think the team might have achieved even more. The game three days later against Barnsley gave me a small foretaste of what was in store for me. Alex Ferguson made me a substitute. I did not fully understand his reasons, and asked him if he would explain them to me. He said that he wanted to play Cole and Solskjaer up front, as they needed match practice together. I was not at all happy with that, and said so, but I had to accept it. What made it doubly unfortunate for me was that, on the basis of the season they'd had so far, any striker worth his salt could hope to get a goal or two against the Barnsley defence.

Ours did, too. Cole got a hat-trick, Giggs two and Scholes one, and there was even a goal for Karel Poborsky, making a rare appearance from the subs' bench. I was glad that we won, of course, but less pleased that I had not been allowed to play a part in our biggest win of the season. Whether or not I should have been left out for that game, I was back in for the next one, scoring a couple of goals in the 6–1 drubbing of Sheffield Wednesday. Despite our hatful of goals, I didn't feel the balance was right. In the absence of Giggs we played three in midfield and three of us – myself, Cole and Solskjaer – up front.

Next we went to Feyenoord and dispatched them 3–1, Andy Cole scoring his second hat-trick in three games. The next game was a 3–2 defeat at the hands of Arsenal in the Premiership on 9 November. I got a load of criticism for kissing the United badge on my shirt at Highbury. It was said that, as a former Tottenham player, I was inciting the crowd. Not true. It was just a reflexive expression of my delight: although we were beaten that day, it was a good one for me on a personal level. I got both our goals against Arsenal, and all Tottenham fans will know what I'm talking about when I say that scoring twice against the Gunners was a special pleasure.

David Beckham came on to replace Gary Neville, scoring two goals in our 5–2 win at Wimbledon. Ronnie Johnsen played in place of the injured Scholes in a comprehensive 3–0 home win over Kosice in the Champions' League at the end of November, but the basic shape of our front six was still there. I feel even now that we were at our most balanced when Cole, myself, Giggs, Beckham, Butt and Scholes were together on the field. That period was also my most fruitful spell of the season individually. I scored eight goals in nine games and felt that I was really doing my bit towards showing the whole of the Premiership and also a good part of Europe that this Manchester United side were as good as any in the club's recent history. We felt buoyant and confident that we were going to have a glorious season. If we had known what was to come, perhaps we wouldn't have been quite so optimistic.

Chapter Fourteen

The Three That Got Away

Our last fixture of the year in the Champions' League phase of the European Cup was a big one – the away match to Juventus on 10 December. Andy Cole was on the substitutes' bench and I started the game with Solskjaer as my partner. We played some excellent football that night and did just about everything but score, especially when Cole came off the bench to replace Solskjaer in the second half. It was not, by any means, our best display in Europe during the season, and we were beaten 1–0 in front of 47,000 baying Italian fans. Those of us who had played against Italy in the all-important World Cup qualifier in Rome in October knew that performing in front of a hostile Italian audience could be a daunting experience and how easy it would be to freeze. We didn't do that, but Juventus still won like the champions they are; they had the art of winning, rather than merely of playing brilliantly, off to a tee. We all learned something that night, and we did have the considerable satisfaction of knowing that, in spite of the defeat, we were in the quarter-finals of the European Cup, where our rivals over two legs would be Monaco.

That was something to give our fans. To reach the last eight of the biggest competition in Europe was an achievement in itself, but we were determined that it wasn't going to stop there. If we could have played those two games immediately, I'm convinced that we would have gone on to the semi-finals, so well were we functioning as a team at the time. As it was, we were not due to meet Monaco until March, by which time the Manchester United side that met the French champions would be a very different one, in attitude and confidence if not in personnel.

But at the end of 1997 our confidence was sky-high; we honestly felt that there wasn't a team in the country that could live with us. That belief was borne out, by and large, by the results, too, but there was an important little spell ahead of us. If we were to keep our advantage, it was vital that we maintained our form through this.

The Christmas period is always a testing time for clubs, for a variety of reasons. Games pile in on each other and the strength of a club's first-team squad is quite often a telling factor. As for the players themselves, they can never enjoy Christmas in the same way others can. Keep off the drink, eat sensibly, don't do anything silly. Some I've known over the years have whinged a bit about the sacrifices they have to make over the festive season, but it's all part of playing football for a living. You're a professional entertainer as well as a professional athlete, and if people want to watch you over their holiday, they've a right to expect to be able to do so. The fans pay your wages and it's up to you to put on a show for them.

Four days before Christmas we went to Newcastle, who were already demonstrating that they were not the power they had been in recent years. We beat them 1–0 with a goal from Andy Cole, a former Newcastle favourite, who scored again when we defeated Everton 2–0 at home on Boxing Day, along with Henning Berg. I did not play in that game – the boss was trying to rotate his leading players a bit and I was given a rest on the subs' bench, but I came back into the side three days after Christmas, when we went to Coventry. Gordon Strachan had really turned round the fortunes of the Sky Blues after taking sole charge of the club when Ron Atkinson left. For some years Coventry had been the whipping boys of the Premiership, but now Strachan's powers of organisation were transforming them into a more than useful side.

They played well that day, beating us 3–2 in a real ding-dong affair. Alex Ferguson played Solskjaer, Cole and me in the same team, and Ole and I scored our goals. We did not play that badly – they were just the better side on the day. Obviously, we were not pleased to have dropped three points, but the defeat hardly dented our confidence. We were still at the top of the table, and nobody looked capable of knocking us off our perch.

As we looked ahead to the New Year, I think everybody at the club, from chief executive to manager to players to office staff to tea lady, felt we were destined for great things. We were good, very good, and we thought nothing or nobody could stop us. The year we were leaving behind had been good enough for the greatest club in the land, but we believed we had the ability, and the desire, to make 1998 even better. It was, if you like, a feeling of power, and it was a fantastic feeling. It was in this spirit that we produced what I reckon was our finest performance of the season. We were going well in the League, but on the fourth day of the New Year we had another challenge. It was FA Cup third round day, and fate had determined that we would visit Chelsea, the holders.

At that time Ruud Gullit was still in charge at Stamford Bridge, and under the command of the charismatic Dutchman, Chelsea had proved themselves a fine, competitive side. They had the defensive soundness of the likes of Sinclair, Duberry and Leboeuf, the midfield dynamism of Di Matteo and Petrescu and a front three of Vialli, Zola and Mark Hughes. It was a combination other managers would have given their eye teeth for. Not only were there outstanding individuals in the side, but Gullit had forged a unit that was greater than the sum of its individual parts, and one which would go on to win the European Cup-Winners' Cup. And we absolutely slaughtered them.

I don't know what perfection in football is. I've never played in a game in which my team, or our opponents for that matter, were perfect. Football, by its very nature, is an imperfect art. But that day Manchester United provided the closest thing I've ever known to the perfect performance. We were blindingly, staggeringly brilliant, and I don't think anybody, whether they were fortunate enough to have been at Stamford Bridge, or whether they saw the game later that night on *Match of the Day* on BBC1, will ever forget it.

Chelsea, of course, were no mugs, but for seventy minutes they were reduced to chasing the red shadows from Manchester as we played some marvellous, one-touch football. It was one of those days when you almost didn't have to look up before passing, because you knew somebody would be there. The Chelsea crowd are a hard old mob to win over, but even they knew they were witnessing something special. Almost unhindered, we built up a 5–0 lead with two goals from Beckham, two from Cole and one from me. Poor old Chelsea had been quite fancied to complete a successful defence of the Cup, but here they were being given a total football lesson. They didn't know what had hit them.

To be fair to them, they tried to make a game of it throughout, and even scored three goals in the closing stages to restore some respectability to the result. So at least they were able to walk off at the end with their heads up. Deep down, though, they knew they had been on the receiving end of a king-sized mauling. We wouldn't have been flattered by a 5–0 victory; they were by a 5–3 defeat.

We had gone into the game as the bookies' favourites to win the Cup and also to do the Cup and Premiership double. We were even a pretty short price for the treble of Cup, Premiership and European Cup. Now some bookmakers stopped taking money on us. As it transpired, they should have kept their books open. If they had, they would have made a tidy few bob by season's end. You couldn't have blamed them at the time, though. There was no side in the country that could stop us, and not even a surprise 1–0 defeat by Southampton at the Dell in mid-January was enough to cause anything but the faintest of alarm bells to ring. We were still upbeat, still confident.

We weren't to know that by then our best times in the League were already behind us. We had played some superb football to get to the top of the tree, but it was never to touch the same heights again. I missed the Southampton game with a hamstring injury and was disappointed to watch the lads being shaded by the Saints, but as I looked back to the first half of the season, I felt that I had played my part in the team's success. I had made a slightly slow start, which could be explained by the fact that I was in my first season with the club, but I had blossomed to score eleven League and Cup goals. That sense of satisfaction was to be short-lived. I was to score only three more goals as I, together with the whole side, hit a wall we found impossible to surmount.

The hamstring had not improved a lot by the time we entertained Walsall in the fourth round of the FA Cup at home, so I didn't play, but I can't imagine I was much missed so total was our domination of a Walsall side who were brave in defeat but, frankly, not in the same class as us. I was fit enough to be on the bench for the League game against Martin O'Neill's Leicester, and came on to replace Henning Berg, but I could do little to prevent our second 1–0 reverse in successive Premiership games.

We were a slightly subdued band as we sat in the dressing room after that game. It was the first time in the season we had been beaten in two League matches running, and we could not figure out why. The manager was, rightly, less than pleased with us, and told us so, but we didn't really need telling. We knew that we had not done ourselves justice; we had let ourselves down, and the club and the fans too. We just had not clicked somehow. It was almost beyond explanation, but there had to be an answer. Maybe we were a little tired, but even if we were that would have been more of an excuse than a valid reason. We had do something about the situation, and fast. Having been untouchable at the top of the table, we were now very much aware that there was – in spite of what everybody, including the bookies and the football writers, had been saying – another club in the Championship race. Arsenal were playing some confident, dominating football, and they weren't giving goals away. We could not afford to take our eyes off them. It was time to pull up the socks, grit the teeth and all that stuff.

In spite of our resolve in the wake of the Leicester defeat, our next result was not all that clever, either. We were held to a 1–1 draw by Bolton at Old Trafford – another inexplicable outcome. We had class, we were bristling with internationals, and earlier in the season we had beaten far better sides than this Bolton outfit, whose main attribute was courage and dogged determination. We played the better football, but that was only to be expected. What was not as easily understood was that we had nonetheless dropped a couple of points and had bagged only 1 out of the last possible 9. We still topped the table, but our position was no longer unassailable. Suddenly we were looking vulnerable.

Immediately after that came a disappointing 1–1 draw with Barnsley in the fifth round of the FA Cup. I scored my first goal for getting on for six weeks, but that small personal achievement counted for little in the context of a lacklustre performance by the team.

A potential Championship-winning side would have snapped out of it and fought back like tigers after that miserable little run, and in the space of the next eleven days we looked as if we were actually going to do so. We beat Villa 2–0 in midweek (goalscorers Beckham and Giggs, nothing for Sheringham), accounted for Derby 2–0 on the Saturday (Irwin penalty, Giggs, nothing for Sheringham again), and the following Saturday shaded Chelsea 1–0 (Phil Neville, once more zilch for Sheringham). I was becoming increasingly frustrated by my dwindling goal tally, but the interests of the team came first. Certainly, against Chelsea we had produced nothing like the football we had played against them only a few weeks before in the

FA Cup, but hey, so what, we had won, hadn't we? And we were leading by 9 points again.

But the gloom and despondency were not over. In the week between the Derby and Chelsea fixtures our dream of the elusive treble came to an end when we were knocked out of the FA Cup 3–2 by Barnsley in the replay. If Alex Ferguson had been asked before a ball was kicked in anger back in August where his priorities lay in the coming season, in all probability he would have put the European Cup just ahead of a successful defence of the Premiership title with the FA Cup a clear third. Personally, I didn't consider any one of those that much more important than another. The reason I had become so thoroughly disillusioned at Tottenham was that they hadn't looked likely to win anything. I wanted away for the good of my career, and uppermost in my mind was the desire to win cups and medals. I wanted a significant achievement in domestic football to be put against my name, and now one of my chances to do that had disappeared.

I hate to wallow in clichés, but I really did feel gutted after Barnsley beat us. For some reason best known to himself, the manager left me out of the starting line-up, preferring instead to play Erik Nevland, the young Norwegian. It was obvious from pretty early on that Erik's inclusion in the team was not going to work, so I was brought into the action quite swiftly, but, even though I scored one of our goals, my main emotion after we lost to an inferior side who were superior on the night was one of overwhelming disappointment. I still felt that Manchester United were the best team in the country, but it was becoming increasingly clear that something was going seriously wrong.

I said that tiredness is really only an excuse, but I do

think that fatigue had something to do with it: attacking on three fronts for as long as we did is bound to take its toll. The true winners are the sides who can overcome that, either with superior will or superior strength in depth, and there was an uncomfortable feeling that we were proving agonisingly short in both departments.

There is nothing worse than playing in a side who have achieved a lot but whose grip on things is beginning to loosen. I had experienced a similar situation much earlier in my career with Millwall, when we slid from being First Division title contenders to mid-table obscurity. This time, however, the stakes were very much higher. We were going for victory in one of the toughest leagues in the world and trying to win the major European competition as well. It was unthinkable that we would fail on both fronts.

The first leg of our European Cup quarter-final in Monaco was a strange experience. It is well known that land in the tiny principality on the south coast of France is at a premium, but nothing can prepare you for playing football on what is effectively the fifth floor of a multi-storey car park. The club is housed in a complex that includes the car park, offices, shops, an Olympic-class swimming pool and a multi-use sports hall. It's a pretty good way to make the most of limited space, but the pitch that sits on top of the lot has a bone-hard playing surface that does nothing to promote good football.

Let's not beat about the bush as regards the 0–0 draw that ensued that night in early March. It was a dull, boring game which wasn't a particularly good advertisement for English or French football. Having said that, although it's always nice to nick an away goal in a two-leg tie, if you can't manage that, a goalless draw is the next best thing. We didn't play well in that compact, immaculate little ground, but we felt we'd done a reasonable job.

There was a hangover from that game, however, and it was to lead us into another of those frustrating and dispiriting little runs like the one we'd experienced in January. Sheffield Wednesday beat us 2–0 on 7 March, four days later we could do no better than draw 1–1 at West Ham and then, in a real crunch match, Arsenal beat us 1–0 at Old Trafford on the following Saturday to complete another spell in which we earned only 1 point out of a possible 9. We had the points under our belt, but Arsenal had the games in hand. It's always said that having the points is more valuable, because the others don't know what they are going to earn from the matches yet to be played, but the way Arsenal were performing, you couldn't honestly see them letting too much slip. This was getting serious.

The return leg against Monaco came four days later, and somehow we had to get ourselves back up for it. It wasn't the best way to prepare for an important European Cup tie, but we were stuck with it and had to make the best job we could of it. I still think that if we'd had Ryan Giggs and Gary Pallister in our side on the fateful night of 18 March we would have beaten Monaco. I've already said how highly I rate Pally, and nobody will need me to tell them what a wonderful player Ryan is. I'm not knocking anybody who came into their places for the second-leg match, but nevertheless I'd maintain that their absence made the difference between us winning and going out on the away goals rule after a 1–1 draw.

We got off to the worst possible start, whereas for Monaco it could hardly have been bettered. David Trezeguet, the twenty-year-old French international, gave them the lead early on with a shot that was later calculated to have gone into the net at 96mph. Raimond van der Gouw was deputising for Peter Schmeichel, who had pulled a hamstring against Arsenal, but not even the Great Dane would have had much of a chance against that. What a blow. The game had been going for only six minutes and already Monaco had pulled off one of their prime objectives – they had scored the magic away goal. Ole Gunnar Solskjaer eventually pulled one back for us, but although we gave them a bit of a battering in the latter stages of the game we were held at bay by a commanding Monaco defence.

It's in games like this that the big money you're playing for becomes an irrelevance. Sure, we all like the wonderful lifestyle that playing football for a top club gives us, but when it comes to the crunch, matches such as the Monaco one are about pride and a sense of achievement. When, in spite of your best efforts, it all comes to nothing, it's totally crushing. Before you ever become a professional footballer you're somebody who plays the game because he loves it. The man who plays the game only because he happens to be rather good at it is going to get nowhere fast. He might make a few bob out of it, but he will never reach the heights, because he doesn't have the passion, he doesn't really care whether he wins the major medal or the important cup or the big league. In football, if you're interested in your bank balance to the exclusion of everything else, you're never going to be truly fulfilled.

So all of us in the Manchester United side that night were completely and utterly drained by our departure from the competition; absolutely wiped out by it. As for me, I don't think I'd ever been so dejected in my professional life. I'd achieved good things with England and been a successful player at the top level for a number of years, but ultimately what you want for yourself is achieved only by a whole team. Collectively we had failed, so we had failed individually as well. It was something of a relief to me to be able to escape from the club pressure for a few days by joining the England squad for the World Cup warm-up game against Switzerland. Immediately that game was over I rejoined United, but I had to sit out the match against Wimbledon ten days after the Monaco defeat because I was on a one-match suspension for getting five bookings through the season. I wasn't happy to be forcibly excluded at such a vital stage, but I reckoned I would probably get back into the side for the match at Blackburn, which was the first of a vital six-match run-in to the end of the season. I was wrong. I was dropped unceremoniously.

Now I was really unhappy. It was the first time I had suffered the indignity of being dropped for no apparent reason. I went to see the manager to ask him why. Alex Ferguson told me that he thought my performances had dipped in the previous month or so and he wanted to get somebody running against Colin Hendry. Hendry wasn't as quick as he had been in the past, the manager said. He felt Hendry's legs were going a bit, and he believed that Ole Gunnar Solskjaer would exploit this weakness better.

I told the boss frankly that I couldn't accept that. I thought that Hendry was still a major stumbling block. You had to move him first so that other people could get in behind him, rather than making somebody run at him. Ferguson replied that he had made his decision and he was going to stick with it. I argued that what he was saying now didn't make sense to me. He had said in the previous three or four weeks that the reason we hadn't been doing so well was that the team that had played so well for him in October, November and December had not been available. 'Now you've got us all fit, and yet you're still not playing the formation you said the club has missed,' I said. The manager was unmoved. He told me again that he thought my performance levels had gone down lately, and that I wasn't going to play. I didn't like it, and said so, but I had to accept it.

Alex Ferguson himself does not get all that involved in the nitty-gritty of coaching. He tends to leave that to his assistant, who does everything very short and sharp to keep everybody on their toes. Until the 1998–9 season, when he left to manage Blackburn, the boss's number two was Brian Kidd. At the height of the season, Brian's style was just right. You don't want to be slogging your insides out for three or four hours a day – it wears you out. You need to be saving your legs and your energy. Where Alex really comes into his own is just before a game. He will get the first-team group together and go through what the opposition is good at and what their weaknesses are. There was a famous story about the legendary Bill Shankly, who used to tell his players at Liverpool that yes, United had Best, Law and Charlton, but if his boys couldn't beat three players they needed their backsides kicking, because the rest were rubbish (except he didn't say rubbish). Alex Ferguson is a bit like that. He's as clever at picking a good player and finding the right characters to get together in a team as anybody I've ever met. Obviously, I wasn't happy when I was left out, but the boss always had the courage of his convictions, and I respected him for that.

Against Blackburn we started very poorly. We went 1–0 down and the formation the manager had put out – Beckham, Scholes, Cole, Solskjaer and Giggs in, with Sheringham and Butt on the bench – was just not working.

Nicky and I talked about it in the first half, and agreed that there must be a chance that we would both get on for the second. He did, I didn't. At half-time the boss said that there had been no fluency in our football. He took Solskjaer off and put Nicky on to drop into midfield, with Scholes moving up more as an out-and-out striker. Naturally, I felt I should have been put on the field as well, because the tactical plan was just not coming off, but the manager insisted that was how it was going to be. However, he asked me to keep warmed up, as he had it in mind to put me on after ten minutes of the second half.

Fortunately for the team, Alex Ferguson's switch worked. We scored within five minutes of the restart to make it 1–1 with a good goal from Cole, then stretched our lead to 3–1 with further strikes from Scholes and Beckham. There was no way I was going to get on after that. It goes without saying that I was delighted for the team and the club, but personally, I was at an extremely low ebb.

Next came a home game against Liverpool. The boss couldn't very well change a winning team, so he started with the formation he had finished with at Blackburn. I felt a bit sorry for Ole Gunnar Solskjaer in this game. In the previous match he had been in the starting line-up; this time he was not even a substitute. I spoke to him about it, and he was very down, which I could understand. I was disappointed myself not to be playing, but as the team had got a good result without me, I had to acknowledge that the manager's decision had been fully justified. At least I was on the bench, so I had a chance of being involved at one stage or another.

We got off to a flying start, Ronnie Johnsen giving us the lead with a super goal. Then Michael Owen scored an equaliser before being sent off for an atrocious tackle on Ronnie, who had to be carried off, his season over. Young Michael had already been booked for a foul on Peter Schmeichel and could have been cautioned for one or two other fouls. He really put himself about in that game, and it was obvious from very early on that he might be heading for trouble. Anyway, he went, and Liverpool probably felt that he had done his bit in scoring the goal.

I had come on for Phil Neville with about twenty minutes to go, and we threw everything forward, but could not score the second goal we felt we deserved. Since Wenger's Arsenal were still doing well, a draw was very disappointing, and I felt that Liverpool saw it as something of an achievement to have made life difficult for us. Everybody wants to put a spanner in Manchester United's works, and Liverpool probably went away from that game satisfied that they had done a good job on us. We were still 9 points ahead, but Arsenal, threateningly, still had three games in hand, and they were continuing to play some excellent football. They could not be relied on to drop points.

The writing was on the wall. Before long we were only 6 points to the good and they had four matches in hand. To keep ahead we needed them to lose a couple, but they didn't look likely to do so.

Meanwhile, we drew our next game 1–1 at home with Newcastle, a game that should have been won yet one that would have been lost had Solskjaer not made a huge personal sacrifice in the interests of the team. Newcastle had taken the lead before we had equalised through David Beckham, and we were still at 1–1 as the game entered its final five minutes. We were throwing everybody forward. Suddenly, Rob Lee made a run for goal and Solskjaer, who was, strangely, the only player in our half, brought him down with a blatant professional foul. Ole started walking before the referee even got to him – he knew he was going to be sent off. It was the only thing he could have done, and the whole team thanked him for it. He was wrong as far as the laws went, and we all knew that, but the point that might yet win us the Premiership had been at stake.

Because we all recognised what Ole had done for the team, we were a bit surprised when the manager weighed into him afterwards. Ferguson told Ole that he must never do anything like that again. If we'd had eleven men on the field, we might still have got a winner, because there was no guarantee that Lee would have scored. We were astonished. Ole had been totally unselfish. At the moment the crisis occurred, he had had only the interests of the team at heart. He did not stop to think that the tackle he launched on Lee would get him suspended. It might not have suited the purists, but Ole's action that day – the consequent suspension ended his season – helped us to salvage that point.

But 1 point was not really enough. Arsenal were cruising, winning 3–1, 4–1 and 5–0. They had not always been the most prolific goalscoring side, but they certainly never seemed to let any in. You had to give them credit for maintaining their form. They were playing well and winning consistently when the pressure was on, much as we had performed in October and November, destroying everybody they came up against and growing in confidence with every game.

Still, while there was life there was hope. We went to Crystal Palace and beat them 3–0, then accounted for Leeds 3–0, and finished the season with a 2–0 victory over relegated Barnsley – a game in which I scored my first goal for the club for two and a half months. It gave me little satisfaction, for by then Arsenal had won the Premiership.

They did so only by a point, and then lost to Liverpool and Aston Villa in the last week of the season, but if they'd had to grind out a couple of good results against those two sides, I think they would probably have managed it.

If I was looking for excuses, I could point to injuries to key players in the second half of the season, but Wenger, too, had his fitness problems down at Highbury: Bergkamp, so influential, so skilful, had just picked up the injury that was eventually to delay his appearance in Holland's colours in the World Cup finals; Adams and Ian Wright were out of action for some time. In the end Arsenal simply stood the pace better than us. But I do think that the fact that we were going for wins in three very different competitions left us spread very thin at crucial moments.

In general, you have to say that the season went pretty well for us, in spite of the fact that the highest position we achieved in anything was second. When we were playing so brilliantly early in the season, it was a joy to be involved. It was football you usually experience only in your happiest dreams. So all in all, I relished my first season with Manchester United.

One thing that did disappoint me was the way the crowd lashed into me towards the end of the season. I don't think they ever really appreciated what I was doing for the team, but having said that, theirs was an attitude that I wanted to turn around. There was no way in the world I was going to be defeatist about it. I had something to prove, and I wouldn't rest until I had the fans on my side. The key to discovering whether you're doing things more or less right is the other players' response to you. I always say the definition of a good player is someone the others want in their team. In a season in which I played OK sometimes and not so well on other occasions, I don't think I had the full respect of the other players. You feel it; you don't have to be told. It was something I knew I had to work at. If you're playing for Manchester United you have to realise that the expectations are very high, and if I'm honest, I don't think I quite came up to scratch in my first season there. I did some good things, but I could do very much better.

I still have a lot to offer at the top of the game, I'm confident of that. I still have belief in my ability; even though I'm thirty-three, I'm far from done for. I feel I still have a few good years left in me at the highest level, because I've never been a player who relies on pace to get me through. And I think I'm tough enough mentally. I won't let stick from the terraces get me down. It's taken me a long time to get to the pinnacle of my profession, and I've no intention of letting it all slip through my fingers now.

Meanwhile, what of our dream treble of Premiership, FA Cup and European Cup? That season it probably was never quite on, really. If we had done everything we wanted to do, we would probably have been facing five games in the last week of the season. The way the game is set up in England, the side that wins the Premiership and the European Cup in the same year has to be some team. Come to think of it, the English team which wins only the European Cup will have achieved something pretty phenomenal. You also have to bear in mind that the FA Cup is a very big deal in England, much bigger than its equivalents are in the rest of continental Europe. If you're going to maintain interest in all three, your club is going to have to play getting on for sixty games a season, and to perform at your best throughout you are going to need a huge squad of top-class players that can be juggled around without diluting the strength of the side. It is these difficulties which made our 1999 treble such a remarkable achievement.

Back in 1998, as my first season's experience of playing for a club whose ambition extended beyond its national boundaries drew to a close at Barnsley on that balmy Sunday afternoon in May, there was much occupying my thoughts. There were still big fish to fry with England. The world and its footballers awaited; I was looking forward to joining them in combat. As our League season ended I still did not know for sure if I would be given the opportunity to do so. For a few mad, sad days at the beginning of June it looked possible that I would be presented with the chance and then risk having it taken away from me.

Chapter Fifteen

Dreams and Nightmares

It was tough to pick myself up from the crushing disappointment at the end of my first season with Manchester United. What had started so brightly, so promisingly, had finished with the whole club experiencing the hollow feeling that comes when hopes and dreams turn to disillusionment. But although one door had closed on us with a resounding crash, I and eight of my team-mates had to forget United for a while and start preparing for an even bigger challenge – the World Cup finals.

Some of my colleagues who would almost certainly be playing in France had been told by Alex Ferguson that with the title won and lost, they could have a week off up to and including the final game of the season against Barnsley. Paul Scholes, David Beckham, Ole Gunnar Solskjaer and Phil Neville were excused from that game, but Peter Schmeichel, Ronnie Johnsen, Gary Neville, Nicky Butt and I were made to play. The boss told me that I was experienced enough to play through it, which I couldn't completely understand. Like the rest of the team, I'd had a hard season, and felt that a week off would have benefited me, but after putting my case to him, I accepted his decision. In my book, what the manager says goes, even if you don't particularly like it at the time, so I played on without further objection. Not, I have to say, that it made a blind bit of difference one way or the other.

While Schmeichel, Johnsen and Solskjaer waited for the call from their respective countries, Scholes, Butt, Beckham, the Nevilles and I were named in Glenn Hoddle's twenty-nine-man squad to spend a week in the five-star luxury of the La Manga resort in south-east Spain, from where we were to travel to compete in a couple of games in a little tournament in Morocco and, most crucially of all, to play and train our hearts out in a bid to convince Glenn that we were the people he needed to defend the honour of our country in France.

But there were a few little preliminaries to be negotiated first. They started with the final friendly match before our departure for Spain. The last time England fans saw us in action before France '98 was in a game against Saudi Arabia, World Cup finalists like ourselves. The game was at Wembley and therefore not a truly accurate test, because you can never compare playing in your own national stadium with wandering around a big country such as France like a bunch of footballing gypsies and facing some of the best footballers in the world everywhere you go.

In a way the Saudi match was a disappointing one, because it ended in a goalless draw. We would have liked to have given our fans something better to remember us by as they said their farewells to us and wished us good luck in the battles ahead. Yet in another respect the match provided valuable practice for us. Every area in the world has its own way of playing the game, and the Saudis were a typical Arabian side – full of speed, good technique, great on the ball but perhaps lacking a bit in the finer points of teamwork. They played some very good football individually, but when it came to stringing together moves involving several players they were found wanting at times. They love their football in that part of the world, and what they love most of all is to be dazzled by skill on the ball. Saudi Arabia were a side which reflected that preference.

That said, they still managed to hold us at bay for ninety minutes, so these standard-bearers for a still-emerging sport in their region could hold their heads up against a side who were ranked in the top ten in world football. I played for sixty-one minutes, until I was replaced by Ian Wright, and I thought they were a plucky outfit. Although confronted by superior opponents in terms of individual skill and, most of all, organisation, they would not give in. It was a decent rehearsal for what we might expect from Tunisia in our first game in the finals, and although we didn't score any goals, we opened them up a few times. OK, so we were expected to win and put on a good show to prove to the country that we were fit and up to the job of winning the Jules Rimet Trophy, but although we didn't produce the final breakthrough and convert our superiority into goals, there were some positive lessons to be learned from the match.

Then it was off to La Manga. In my experience the choice of training camp says a lot about the preferences of the manager. Glenn loved his golf, and La Manga had three championship-standard golf courses, a five-star hotel, the Principe Felipe, and, as an added extra, several football pitches in absolutely perfect condition. If Glenn had had the opportunity to custom-build a place to take his players, he couldn't have come up with anything more perfect.

Like most of the other players, I thought the resort was pretty special, too. It suited me down to the ground – great golf, wonderful hotel, beautiful surroundings, superb football facilities. As a professional footballer who also happens to be a golf nut, I couldn't possibly have asked for more.

The golf at La Manga was something else. We played full rounds twice, and we also had the chance to get out several times to play nine holes in the cool of the evening. It was not long before we put together a group that became a regular four-ball. I was initially picked to play with Shearer against Scholes and Owen, and the four of us had some really tight games – I think we ended up winning one match each and battling it out for four draws.

The whole experience was a good one for the squad. The manager was very relaxed throughout and that rubbed off on us. I felt it was a very worthwhile exercise. From the manager's point of view it gave him the chance to get to know the team a little better, look at how they ticked as a unit, and so on. For us players, the trip was a welcome opportunity to learn about each other, whether we were playing golf, training or simply socialising with each other. On the face of it, it might not seem important whether or not we got along as human beings, but my own experience tells me otherwise. If you gel with somebody off the field, the chances are that you might click on it, too.

Yet it was in same ways a strange time, because although we grew closer together as a group, we were all acutely aware that, no matter how mutually supportive we were, we were also doing our best to prove to the manager that we were better than the players with whom we were vying for places in our specialised positions. It's a weird feeling, believe me, knowing that, although the man alongside you might be a good friend, you are working your socks off to present a better case for inclusion than his, and vice versa. So it was a time for togetherness, sure, but it was also a time when competition was at its most intense.

And when the final decisions were made as to who was staying and who was heading for an early flight home, those of us who were selected felt enormous sympathy for the players Glenn was rejecting. Yet at the some time we were tremendously relieved. If you have any sort of feeling for your fellow professionals, people you've played alongside in any number of battles, you do bleed a little with them even in your own moment of elation. It was not quite dog-eat-dog, but in the end you have to think of yourself in these situations. Nonetheless, the day it happened, the beauty of La Manga faded into insignificance. Even in our happiness, all we could think of were those poor lads along the corridor who were packing their things and getting ready to fly home.

Until then it was never far from our thoughts that at the end of our time in Spain the twenty-nine-strong squad was going to be reduced to twenty-two. However, our prime aim in that week was to work on our strategy for beating Tunisia in our first game in France. It gave us a chance to knit together a few more things before the big kick-off. We knew it was going to be hot in Marseilles, where the World Cup match was to be played, and we knew the way we wanted to go about beating Tunisia was to aim to retain possession in the middle of the field and then hit them with fast counter-attacks. The temperature in La Manga helped us to acclimatise to the heat, and our two trips to North Africa were also useful in that respect.

I was left out for the game against Morocco, as were Paul Scholes, David Beckham and Alan Shearer, but that was far from being bad news. All that proved was that it was likely that Glenn's starting line-up was beginning to take shape. He gave a chance to the likes of Ian Wright and Dion Dublin and put Owen on the bench. The match, played in strength-sapping humidity, was a real test of fitness, and the baying of the capacity home crowd for our blood got us used to a hostile atmosphere as well. Owen it was who came off the bench and scored the goal in our 1–0 win – another reminder to the manager that he was around, on form and looking dangerous.

There were people at home, most notably in certain sections of the tabloid press, who criticised our participation in the Moroccan mini-tournament. I thought it was pretty good, all in all. We did not have to face the prospect of long flights – we were back at our Spanish retreat in under two hours after the games.

Among the many positive aspects of that week, two clouds emerged during training. First, Ian Wright, whose fitness had been in question for some time, finally fell out of contention with a hamstring injury picked up against the host country, Morocco. We were all disappointed that Ian was going to miss out on what would almost certainly have been his last chance to play in the World Cup finals. I've got a lot of time for Ian – he's a bubbly character whose infectious love of football rubs off on everybody around him. I was sad for him. He's one of those people who make football the great game it is, still bouncing with enthusiasm as he moves further and further into his thirties.

The other blow was Paul Gascoigne's fitness. I did think he looked a yard short of full fitness at certain times, and in the 0–0 draw against Belgium that ended our participation in the Moroccan tournament (and in which Shearer, Owen and I did not feature), he wasn't at his best, to be honest.

But it was not much worse than that. I didn't really read too much into it – I'd seen Gazza lose a stone in weight and get his pace back in a week to ten days, and I saw no reason why he shouldn't do so again. He still had a part to play, I thought, and it might well prove to be a pivotal one. Gazza is the sort of person who can turn a game in a split-second of vision, and because of that I felt he still had a place in the set-up even if he wasn't going to be an automatic starter in every game. Paul can achieve in ten minutes what others can't do in ten matches.

In private, I thought a lot about my own chances in that week. In spite of Michael Owen's performance against Morocco and a lot of speculation back home, I still felt comfortable that I would be playing in the first game in France. I had been a professional footballer for fifteen years, and knew that, if selected, all I could do was go out, do my best and accept the consequences if things didn't go well. I'd had my share of disappointments during those fifteen years, but I'd learned to weather them. If you were picked, you had to tell yourself that you were in the team on merit and try to do the job to the best of your ability. For all those reasons I didn't see Michael as a threat and, furthermore, I didn't think Hoddle would put him and Shearer together because they were too similar. If only I'd known.

While all this was going on, crunch time was getting closer and closer. We trained with our usual intensity on the Saturday, and in the evening we were allowed our first drink of the week. We went into the Piano Bar, which they cut off from prying eyes with sheets over the windows, and had a sing-song with Brian Chapman, the highly talented resident singer-pianist. We all had a few beers that night, but nobody got silly – with the exception of Gazza. Whether he sensed something from Glenn's attitude to his fitness and was trying to drown his sorrows, I don't know, but whatever the case, he got pretty drunk that night. I wondered that evening, and not for the first time, whether Paul might have a bigger problem with alcohol than even he cares to admit.

The next day we had another round of golf, but our minds were not really on the game, because afterwards we were due to go one by one, at five-minute intervals, according to the time we had teed off, to see the manager and be told whether we were going to France or not. A certain amount of ribbing went on as the interviews got underway. When David Seaman, who was a dead cert for the squad, came out we were all leaping about as we congratulated him. It was a bit silly, I suppose, but it was a way of relieving the tension that was mounting as each player went in and re-emerged either elated or numb with despair.

Although naturally I was thinking first and foremost about my own chances during those terrible few hours, my thoughts were with some of the other lads as well. I had grown quite friendly with Dion Dublin and Paul Merson, and they, along with my old friend and former team-mate Darren Anderton, were all on the verge of selection. Privately I couldn't believe that Glenn would go into the finals without Shaggy's great talents. The only element of doubt was his fitness, for he hadn't had the happiest of times with Tottenham during the season. Phil Neville was very confident before his interview because John Gorman, Glenn's assistant, had given him to understand that he had no need to worry and that he would be all right. So when he was left out his disappointment was all the greater – he was really down, he really couldn't take it in. Having had his hopes built up, it was a huge blow to him.

While all this was going on the odd whisper started to circulate. There was going to be a shock, went the murmurings, and it possibly involved Gazza being sent home. Even so, when it happened, nobody could quite believe it. He was such a big player, one of the most influential England footballers for years. Surely he couldn't be rejected? After all, this was a man who could turn a match in a moment of inspiration – remember his breathtaking goal against Scotland in Euro '96, when he made a highly talented player in Colin Hendry look like an untried novice? We had all seen his performances during the week, and wondered, but we still couldn't take it on board that England would be going into France '98 without him.

Yet now I look back on it, I think Paul himself was half expecting the axe. Rather unwisely, he'd had a few beers during our golf game, and then downed a few more after he'd finished, and I've got to admit that he was quite the worse for wear when he went in to see Glenn for the crucial conversation that put an end to his World Cup dream. Whether his condition that afternoon was the final proof that Glenn needed, I don't know. I shouldn't think so for a moment – I imagine the manager's mind was made up long before Gazza made the long, awful walk into his room.

The scenes that followed were horrible. Paul went into his bedroom and Paul Ince went in to talk to him, but he was inconsolable. He was simply devastated, screaming at the manager in a drunken state and losing control of his feelings. I couldn't say I knew exactly how he felt, because by this time I'd been told I was in the final twenty-two, but having known Paul for a number of years, and understanding what playing football for England means to him, I had a pretty good idea.

There were disappointments for some of the others, too. Ian Walker, who had been a valued team-mate at Spurs, was in tears; Nicky Butt had not been confident of being in the final twenty-two, so although he was upset, he wasn't completely in pieces.

Gascoigne, on the other hand, certainly was. If more or less anyone else had made the scene he made that afternoon, everyone would have been surprised. But Paul is a passionate person, perhaps too passionate for his own good sometimes, and throughout his England career he had spilled tears for his country – everyone remembers his crumpled-up face back in 1990 when a badly timed booking meant that he would miss the World Cup semi-final against West Germany. I for one have never forgotten it.

Paul Gascoigne is a unique player with unique talents. So often in his career he has been worth the price of an admission ticket on his own. Now we would be going into the finals of a World Cup without him – and even more tragically for him, it might prove to have been his last chance for a crack at the ultimate prize. I suppose, if you were being hard, you could say he had brought his misfortunes on himself – Paul is nothing less than a genius, and genuises don't always play by the same rules that apply to other people. All I can say is that on that afternoon in sunny Spain in the early summer of 1998, the twenty-two who were left, including the man who got a place at Gazza's expense, whoever he was, were in a state of shock.

Within an hour of the fateful decisions having been made, the disappointed ones – Gazza, Phil Neville, Dion Dublin, Nicky Butt, Ian Walker and Andy Hinchcliffe – were on a private jet back to England, there to mourn in whatever way they chose. It must have been terrible for them: going to the World Cup finals is the pinnacle of any player's career. I would have liked to have been able to have had a word with them, although I have no idea what I could or would have said. But neither I nor the rest of the boys had that opportunity. They were gone that quickly. Gone, but not forgotten.

The rest of us were left with conflicting emotions. We were pleased for ourselves – who wouldn't be? – but at the same time we felt slightly diminished. We had been twenty-nine tightly knit people. Then twenty-eight, when Ian Wright fell by the wayside, and twenty-seven when Andy Hinchcliffe was stricken by injury. We had lost another five of our number. We had always known that was the way it had to be, and that there would be grief as well as happiness in La Manga, but it didn't make it any easier to accept. We were determined to do well in the days and weeks that lay ahead – for ourselves, for our manager and for our country, but in addition each of us, I think, would also be doing it for those who had failed, albeit gloriously.

For some there would be another chance, whereas for others, this disappointment would almost certainly spell the end of their England careers. Even as the news was somehow being leaked to the English press that evening, Paul Gascoigne must have wondered as he flew home, tear-stained and unhappy, whether his colourful past had finally caught up with him. A fool to himself? Perhaps. The best player of his generation? Probably. A wonderful, flawed one-off destined never to fulfil his capacity for genius? Certainly. Whether England could afford to be without him in France, I wasn't so sure. Time would tell.

The next day, after Glenn Hoddle had finally confirmed

to the world and his wife that Gascoigne had been sent home, the squad returned to England. From Luton Airport we went our separate ways, with instructions to report back to Burnham Beeches the following Friday. We were reminded that between now and then we were still to consider ourselves on England duty, and warned to be careful, because the tabloids would be keeping close tabs on us. There's nobody in the world who has a sharper nose for the slightest whiff of scandal than the English tabloid hack, so we had to watch our every move, whatever we chose to do with our little break. Enjoy yourselves by all means, Hoddle said, but remember they're out there looking for you. I fully intended to be careful. I hadn't got this far only to mess it all up now, I told myself. If only I'd listened.

Chapter Sixteen

Portuguese Follies

I had been determined not to take it for granted that I would be in the England squad. It is never a good idea to build up your hopes about anything, no matter how confident you might be that it is going to come your way. So I did nothing about planning a break before the World Cup until I had been formally told that I would be going to France. Once Glenn had given me the good news, I rang some of my friends and asked them if they fancied a few days golfing in the Algarve, where we could play every day, perhaps have a few beers and feel the sun on our backs. I was keen to be out of England if I could, to get away from the intense media pressure and fall-out from Gascoigne's omission from the squad.

I met my friends at an airfield near Southend, where we boarded a private jet I'd hired to take us to Portugal, and we arrived at our hotel at about midnight on the Monday. We were back again on the Thursday evening of that week, but in those three days I got myself involved in an incident that was to throw my precious place in the England squad into jeopardy.

I was playing golf at Penina on my last afternoon in the Algarve when Barry Nevill, my agent and friend, rang and asked me what I'd been playing at. Barry is a very calm individual who doesn't get rattled easily, but clearly something was wrong: I could tell from his voice that he was seriously worried. In the next few minutes I found out why. Barry had just received a telephone call from a reporter on the *Sun*, who told him that a big story, accompanied by a huge picture, was to be splashed across several pages of his paper the next day alleging that I had been caught, with a cigarette in my mouth, in a nightclub at 6.30 in the morning with a blonde girl perched on a stool next to me. He asked Barry if he had any comment to make. Barry had given a noncommittal answer, then immediately rang me and demanded to know if there was any substance to the story. He didn't pull his punches. If it was accurate, he said, he would have a real job trying to defend me.

It began to dawn on me what had happened. I explained the situation to Barry, and I could hear the relief in his voice when I told him exactly what had gone on. Barry knows me as well as anybody, and he knows that I never tell him anything but the truth. However, that didn't mean that I was in the clear. Convincing him was not the point; the paper had a picture that appeared, on the face of it, to incriminate me. I decided to ring Glenn Hoddle to warn him about what was happening, but I could only get hold of Peter Taylor, so I put him in the picture and asked him to let the manager know.

When I got home and looked at the photograph in question, I could see what all the fuss had been about. They say a picture is worth a thousand words. In this case those thousand words were a pack of lies, but they were plausible enough. The papers had really gone to town on the story, and had even recycled the photographs taken of that group of England players, including me, in the notorious Dentist's Chair in Hong Kong before Euro '96.

I'm glad to have the chance to put the record straight now. This is what actually happened. When my friends and I arrived in Portugal we went straight to bed and got up at about midday the next day. We spent the afternoon lazing by the hotel swimming pool, drinking Coca-Cola, having a few laughs and playing Scrabble. Even though I was on holiday I was trying to be responsible. I knew it would be silly to walk round a golf course in the hottest part of the day, so we didn't start any of our games until the late afternoon. My friends and I are all mad keen on the game, so we stayed on the course until the sun was going down.

We then went back and showered and changed, and went out to have a meal at about midnight, going on to a club at about 2 a.m. It is true that we stayed at the club pretty late, but it was just a case of being in a different time frame. We would have been up for the same amount of time if we'd gone to bed at eleven o'clock on the Monday night, played golf during the day, then eaten and done our modest bit of clubbing in the evening. In any case, our first game in the World Cup was two weeks away. I did not for a moment feel that I was putting my fitness in jeopardy by enjoying a few bottles of beer with my friends, providing I didn't go silly. And I didn't go silly, in spite of the way things looked in that photograph.

It was alleged in the newspapers that we had been drinking since the early evening. Not so. In the early evening we were still well into our game of golf, and there was no beer-drinking while we were playing. Quite apart from the fact that we wouldn't have been so stupid as to knock back cans of lager on a hot golf course, we all take the game too seriously to spoil it by drinking alcohol while we are playing. Coca-Cola was the strongest thing that passed our lips as we played some of the great courses lining that stretch of the Algarve coast.

When the incriminating photograph was taken I was talking to a girl in the nightclub. I had already posed willingly for lots of pictures with holidaymakers in the Karaoke Bar, and there were any number of witnesses who could confirm that at no time was I was even close to being drunk. The girl I was chatting to had a cigarette in her hand and was about to light it. Her friend said she would like a shot of us, so I said, 'OK, give me a fag, then,' and stuck it, unlit, into my mouth to pose for the picture. I think I was trying to put the cigarette in her ear. Silly? Childish? Pointless? Even worse, dangerous? I plead guilty to all four. But at no time did I even try to light the cigarette. I have always been a non-smoker – I'm dead against the habit, actually – and I was hardly likely to start smoking now. I was acting like a kid, but I was playing it strictly for the laughs. I did have a few glasses of beer, but not that many. The people who were quoted in the paper as saying that I was stumbling about the place and knocking over tables were, I'm sorry to say, very much mistaken – and that's being polite. I did see a couple of reporters in the hotel trying to drum up a story, but I wasn't worried as there wasn't much of a story to be had.

The girl who took the photograph must have phoned the press immediately, because things happened very quickly. I would have liked the chance to have explained the situation from my point of view to the papers, but, of course, I was never given that chance. These people don't believe in spoiling a good story with the facts. Having got the picture, obviously they decided they had better write a knocking piece to support it. My biggest crime in the whole sorry affair was, I think, to have been a bit naïve. I should have known better than to have allowed the photograph to be taken in the first place, but I didn't, so I just had to live with it. Even now, there remains in my mind an uncomfortable suspicion that I was set up. So much for your super-cool image, Sheringham.

Meanwhile, Barry was mounting a damage-limitation exercise at home. He got together with Martin John, our lawyer, and framed a statement in which they denied on my behalf that I had been drunk, and said that I disliked smoking so much that I certainly would not have lit a cigarette. Barry released the statement to the press, then rushed round straight round to my place in Buckhurst Hill to check whether there were any press men there. At that point there weren't, and neither was there anybody at the airfield where we were due to land – Barry checked that, too. My friends and I arrived in England in our private jet at about 2.30 on the Friday morning and Barry whisked me back to my flat.

At about 8.30 he returned, armed with the morning's newspapers. The *Sun* might have been the first to get the story, but it hadn't taken the rest long to catch up. Even the papers at the top end of the market, not usually purveyors of gossip and dirt, covered it. I could see how it was going to make me look in the eyes of a large section of the general public. Here I was, part of a squad that had been entrusted with the task of bringing the World Cup home to England, and now it appeared that I had let down myself, my team-mates, my son, my family, the England manager and the whole country.

There was a gaggle of photographers and reporters outside the gates to my apartment block when Barry arrived, and when we left to take Charlie to school there must have been thirty or more of them milling about. We enlisted the aid of the local police to help us to get away, but when we got to Charlie's mum's place there were more snappers loitering about. Thankfully, either they hadn't discovered which school Charlie went to or, if they had, they had had a sudden and uncharacteristic crisis of conscience, because they left the school alone.

From there we continued on to what proved to be a very emotional meeting with my mother and father, and yet again we had to run the gauntlet of the press before we could get into their house. My parents let me know exactly what they thought. My mum, in particular, said that what had appeared in the papers was disgraceful. She clearly felt deeply ashamed and was very disappointed in me. I was upset by the effect the affair had had on her, and did my best to explain to her and Dad what some of the papers were capable of doing to people. We talked about it all for a while, and after I had put my side of the incident to them they assured me that they would support me through thick and thin, just as they had all my life. But they reminded me again – as if I needed reminding – of the pressure it was going to put on me, especially in view of the fact that the papers were all clamouring for Michael Owen to take my place in the team.

We left my parents' home at about 10.30 and went back to my flat, somehow managing to wade through the platoons of newshounds outside the front gates. I had survived so far, but the moment I was dreading was getting ever closer; the moment when I would have to face the England manager.

Glenn Hoddle returned my call as I was packing my things to join the England squad. I told him my side of the story. He was not best pleased, to say the least, but he said he would talk to me properly when I got to the England hotel. Barry drove me to Burnham Beeches. I thought the journey would give me some respite but even that contributed to my anxiety. As we turned into the country lane leading to the hotel, we were nearly killed when we rounded a bend and found ourselves confronted by a rusty old Ford Sierra that must have been doing at least 90mph. Somehow we missed the car and, still shaken by our narrow escape, eventually got to the hotel, where dozens of photographers and TV news teams were milling about. Sheringham, the man whose place was supposedly under threat from an eighteen-year-old prodigy, was suddenly news for another reason.

Both Barry and I were quiet as we approached the hotel. We both knew the next few minutes might decide whether I went to France or not; whether my World Cup was going to end before it had even begun. Barry dropped me off, wished me luck and said goodbye. He was worried for me, but he could hardly have been more apprehensive than I was.

At least I did not have long to wait for Glenn's verdict. No sooner had I stepped out of the car than he called me in and told me pretty straight what he thought of me. I attempted to justify my actions to him. I told him the truth – that it hadn't been a drunken holiday, that I hadn't been boozing it up with some girl I'd met casually in a nightclub and that I could no more smoke a cigarette than fly. I said that I thought I had been careful and had looked after myself health-wise; that I had just been trying to be polite and jolly to people, and that all I was doing was taking it easy for a couple of days. Glenn heard me out, and I think he believed me. Nevertheless he made it crystal clear that he was still very cross with me. He reminded me again of what he expected from his players, and told me, as much in sorrow as in anger, I think, that I had let him down. He insisted that I went before the cameras to make a formal statement of apology to him, my family and the whole football-loving nation. He had put his trust in me, he said, and I had let him down badly.

The boss, David Davies, the FA's director of communications, and I prepared a statement, then we went straight outside and I read it to the assembled press corps. It was one of the most harrowing experiences of my life, and viewers who saw me on their television screens that evening couldn't have failed to notice how uncomfortable I was. In his turn, Glenn added that he accepted my version of what had happened, but made it clear that what I had done had not helped my prospects for France '98. His message was obvious – I was forgiven, but the incident would not be forgotten in a hurry. He was right, I was wrong. It was as simple as that.

It was a horrible time for me and everybody around me, and I wish with all my heart that it had never happened. I take my football very seriously. I respect the job I do, and I appreciate that I am in a very privileged position, a position that millions of people would give anything to be in. There were letters to the papers. In the broadsheets learned doctors speculated about how my actions might or might not affect my fitness for the job ahead. People have since told me to my face that I was a disgrace to England in Portugal, and I can understand why they feel that way. But they have no idea of the way I have looked after myself and prepared myself over a fifteen-year career in professional football. The Portugal incident was unfortunate, to say the least, but I do think that people overreacted. I don't know for certain, even now, if my explanation was believed by the public. Some of them will undoubtedly hate me for the rest of my career, and they're entitled to their opinions. All I can do is to ask them to accept that the situation was nothing like as black as it was painted. It was simply blown up out of all proportion.

The rest of the players, meanwhile, weighed in with their support. They all knew me and the way I led my life, and they couldn't believe how I'd allowed the tabloids to take me to the cleaners. They told me they knew I wouldn't have been silly, because there was too much at stake. It helped that they were behind me; I'm not sure what I would have done if they had turned on me as well. In spite of appearances on the field sometimes, professional footballers are a tightly knit clan, and if your fellow players condemn you, you know beyond all reasonable doubt that you have messed up big-time.

The incident was not forgotten, and probably never will be, but I had to push it as far as I could to the back of my mind. It was time for me and my twenty-one team-mates to buckle down and prepare for the biggest challenge of our careers. With the exception of Michael Owen, most of us were highly experienced footballers who had been through some big matches in our lives, but even so, we were all breaking new ground. Now that Gascoigne had been banished from the squad, there was nobody left in the England party who had ever before played in the final stages of a World Cup. Treading into the unknown is not always an unpleasant experience, of course, but having been somewhere before undoubtedly gives you an advantage.

Once my summit meeting with the British media had been disposed of, we trained hard during the rest of that Friday and continued with our preparations the following day. In the evening all the players' wives and girlfriends came over for a meal and we went on to a show in London together in the evening. I was one of about six single lads there – my long-time girlfriend, Nicola, and I had split up about a month before. We had been together for more than five years, and our split was a long and painful one, drawn out over six or seven increasingly fraught months.

During that miserable period I'd felt that for the first time ever my personal life had had an effect on me as a player. I'd had my problems in the past, of course, but before I had always managed to keep them separate from my football. Sometimes there had been the odd difficulty with Denise, Charlie's mum – but these were as nothing compared with the traumas Nicola and I went through.

The sadness of our split was heightened that evening as most of the other players made the most of their time with their wives and girlfriends before our departure. I felt a bit left out and wished Nicola was there with me.

The girls stayed on at the hotel for the rest of the weekend. Once they had left, we all turned our attention to the big move to our training camp at La Baule in northern France. The World Cup finals were going to be a new experience, but at least La Baule was familiar: we had stayed there when we played in Le Tournoi in 1997, so we immediately felt at home when we arrived. And it was a good place to prepare for the tournament. Our accommodation was in little chalets gathered in a horseshoe shape around the swimming pool. The management could not do enough for us. They had thoughtfully equipped our rooms with Sky TV as well as ITV and BBC to give us some idea of what was going on at home. We were allowed to read *The Times*, the *Daily Telegraph* and the *Guardian*, but the tabloids were strictly off limits, which was probably just as well. The rest of the hotel – the pool, the restaurant and a TV room where we could watch the early World Cup games together – was first class. There was a golf course surrounding the hotel and just down the road a football pitch which was in mint condition. All in all, everything was organised to perfection and nothing was left to chance.

We arrived just in time to see the opening ceremony and the Brazil–Scotland game that followed, in which I thought our neighbours from north of the border acquitted themselves well in narrow defeat. Alan Shearer and I ran a book for the duration, just to make things more interesting. By and large, Shearer and Sheringham got the odds about right, but we nearly came a cropper once or twice.

We also felt under pressure from the demands of the media. We would come in from training feeling relaxed and upbeat only to get keyed up again at the prospect of laying ourselves open to the scrutiny of the note-books, tape-recorders and television cameras. We knew that if we uttered one word out of place it would lead to screaming headlines. To relieve the tension a bit we held a competition to see who could get the most song titles into their responses to questions from the likes of Des Lynam and Jim Rosenthal. After one training session held in the pouring rain, Gareth Southgate declared that it 'was not exactly the "Bermuda Triangle"' out there, while Alan Shearer conceded that we were not 'Dancing on the Ceiling' after the Tunisia match. But I think the record went to Tony Adams, who was particularly good with the press. He managed to mention about eight song titles in the space of a couple of minutes. However, he came in for a lot of ribbing for that, because he didn't even attempt to answer the questions. Of course it didn't take long for the press to rumble that little game, but it was fun while it lasted and helped to lighten the atmosphere.

We were desperate to get cracking, but our group, Group G, was the last to start. As time went on, the atmosphere grew increasingly tense. It was a long week, but we knew the waiting would soon be over. There was the odd compensation for this period of limbo: for example, it was instructional to see how the referees were interpreting the laws – especially the one that was going to make the tackle from behind a sending-off offence.

We didn't really discuss our respective chances of getting into the team for the first game against Tunisia. I don't think anybody wanted to tempt fate. But I'm willing to bet that nearly every player in the squad, with the exception of the two reserve goalkeepers, Tim Flowers and Nigel Martyn, was hoping during that nerve-racking week that he would be in the side. Some of them, of course, needn't have wasted a second worrying – there was no way we were going into the competition without Glenn Hoddle's trusted 'spine' of David Seaman, Tony Adams, Paul Ince and Alan Shearer. I had a good week in training and was fairly confident that I would be in the starting line-up, although a lot of people in the press were already pushing for Owen to be included in my place.

During that week Alan Shearer went on television and assessed the relative attributes of Michael and myself. Owen, he said, was very talented and lightning fast – two yards faster than most, he thought – but my strength was that I could think two yards faster than anybody else. It was typically generous of the captain, a hugely respected figure in the squad, to say such kind things about me. I felt he had been very fair in recognising that young Owen had tremendous talent, but I also reckoned he had made it fairly clear that he wanted to go into the first game with me at his side.

Our four days of waiting and wondering ended when the manager announced the team to us on the Friday before the Monday match. The moment when he read out my name will stay with me for a long time. I was in. After all the hullabaloo over the Portugal incident, Glenn had kept faith with me. I had tried to stay confident and upbeat about my chances, but I'm not the sort ever to make assumptions about anything. I had found countless times during my career that the more you build up your hopes, the more disappointed you will be if they aren't realised, so I had tried to play everything low-key. The relief, though, was enormous, I must admit. I knew Michael was a very serious rival for my place, and I felt that I would have to perform at my best from the off if I was to remain in the team during what we hoped and believed would be a long run in the competition.

The biggest surprise was that David Beckham was left out. I'm told it caused a massive uproar at home. Becks had been seen as the man who had the craft and guile to set up chances for Alan and me, and his talent for scoring incredible goals from set pieces was another weapon in his armoury. Darren Anderton was the controversial choice to play instead of Beckham on the right side of midfield, and he became an increasingly important figure for England as the tournament went on. I'm glad for Shaggy that he made a success of his return to international duty. I've never made a secret of my admiration for him – he's a tremendous player who has had some terrible luck with injuries. When he's fit, I don't think there is a better right-sided midfield player in the country, given that Beckham's future, in my view, lies in central midfield, where I believe he can become as influential a player as Paul Gascoigne once was.

Gary Neville's omission was nearly as big a surprise as Beckham's, but for this first game, at least, Gareth Southgate was preferred as the right-sided member of the back three, which was completed by Adams and Sol Campbell. It was not a team that pleased everybody, but it was Glenn's choice, and – my own personal considerations apart – I admired him for sticking to what he felt was right.

Our first game was preceded by some awful scenes in Marseilles, where warring factions of English and Tunisian fans fought running battles in the streets of the tough southern sea port. Some of those who had the nerve to call themselves England supporters were anything but; their behaviour brought nothing but disgrace on the country they claimed to be rooting for. The hooligan element in English football had not been seen as much of late, but now, when the chips were down, they were crawling out of the woodwork in the same old disgusting way. There's no room in football for these yobs, and the sooner we rid ourselves of them, the better.

The game itself was a crucial one. We knew we were expected to win, we knew we had to win and we knew, too, that on established form and pedigree we should win. We were not disappointed. People complained that our 2–0 victory was not a glittering performance, but it didn't need to be. We had a job to do, and I thought we did it with great efficiency. From first to final whistle on the hottest day we'd had since we'd been in France, there was only ever going to be one winner in this encounter, and that was England.

I've always been my own worst critic, but I felt that my contribution vindicated Glenn's decision to pick me. I had a great first half and nearly scored with a dipping volley from 30 yards which el-Ouaer just managed to tip away. I was satisfied that I had worked hard and made openings for other players from comparatively deep positions. My performance perhaps dipped slightly in the second half, but even so, when I left the field with six minutes to go, to be replaced by Owen, I felt I had done my bit.

The victory might have been a routine one, but the goals we scored weren't. Graham Le Saux made the first for Shearer's glancing header just before half-time and Paul Scholes capped a marvellous, mature display ten minutes from the end with a magnificent, curling finish into the top right-hand corner of the net after a surging run by Paul Ince had set up the chance. I celebrated with the rest when the final whistle went. Then came a small irritation which took the wind out of my sails. Yet again I had been selected to take the random drugs test, and yet again my fellow guinea pig was Gareth Southgate. Memories of that significant night in Rome the previous autumn washed over Gareth and me as we sat in another little room waiting for the vital moment of inspiration to deliver the goods. Eventually a doctor came in and said we could have a beer if we wanted one, but we declined, mainly because of our diet and the vitamin tablets we took all through our campaign. We stuck to water until we were ready to perform, and then it was back to the coach to return to the airport for the flight back to La Baule.

As we sat in the coach, there was an air of contentment about the party, but I couldn't help glancing over at David

Beckham and Gary Neville and wishing for them that they had been part of the playing eleven. No matter how hard a manager tries to convince his reserve players that they are part of the side, it's never the same if you don't actually get on to the pitch. As good team men, they were as happy as the rest of us that we'd got off to a winning start. Their consolation was the awareness of the amazing speed with which things can change in football. And so it proved: by the end of our participation in the competition there was a different story to be told about both of them, although David was to find out that even when you think you're getting there, football has a way of cutting you down to size.

We had made a good, workmanlike start to France '98. One test faced, one overcome, two more to go in our group. Our next game was against Romania, which we knew wouldn't be an easy ride, but we left Marseilles that night optimistic about our prospects, and personally, I felt I had done my chances of a long run in the team no harm. A week later, I was to find out that I had been sadly mistaken.

Chapter Seventeen

The Rise and Fall of England United

The three England managers under whom I played before my recent recall to the squad under Kevin Keegan, who replaced Glenn Hoddle in 1999, were very different in their approach to the game, but all were alike in one important respect. Against the odds, they tried as hard as they could to instil into their squads the character of a club side. With Graham Taylor, you didn't always feel entirely comfortable in the company of players you spent most of your working life competing against, largely, I think, because, although I'm sure the manager knew what he wanted, he wasn't sure how to achieve it. Terry Venables, on the other hand, was notably successful in achieving this aim and Glenn Hoddle carried on where Terry left off.

Thus it was that England United returned to La Baule on the Sunday evening feeling good about our record to date. Of course, there were players on that short flight home who had not made it on to the pitch and so felt a little out of it, but it didn't alter the fact that, all in all, we were twenty-two very happy footballers.

It was important that we didn't forget the euphoria of that sticky night in Marseilles, but at the same time there could be no resting on our laurels. Yes, we had got over the first hurdle and done our jobs well, but it had not been a perfect performance. I suppose that would have been expecting too much, but there was no escaping the fact that in our next match we would be facing a much better side, a team against whom we could not afford the slight drop in standard of which we had been guilty in the second half against Tunisia. We had to be right on our game to stand a chance against Romania in Toulouse. They were the strongest opposition we would meet in the group games; if we slipped against them, the whole thing would be back in the melting pot again.

We worked hard in the week that separated the two games. We did about two hours' hard training and preparation each day, looking closely at a different aspect of our task in each session. We also examined the Romanians in detail on video, assessing their potential strengths and weaknesses, where we could attack them, which players were the likely threats. We knew that Adrian Ilie was lightning fast up front, while the other danger man, Gheorghe Hagi, had to be kept on his relatively weaker right foot as much as possible. Personally, I knew a bit about Popescu and Dumitrescu, my former Tottenham team-mates, so I was able to make a contribution to our discussions. Our preparation was nothing if not thorough. If we were beaten on the day, it would not be for the want of effort put in beforehand. All the players took the training sessions very seriously. It was hard work, but we were aiming for the biggest prize in football.

There were suggestions that a whole week's gap between

games was not ideal for us, but we felt it was just right. The heat in Marseilles in the Tunisia match had been strength-sapping, so the recovery time was useful, and most importantly, it gave the lads a further chance to bond together. We watched a lot of the games on the television, continuing to monitor how the referees were interpreting the laws and generally getting a feel for the way the competition was developing, and we had some leisure time around the swimming pool, although it was rarely warm enough for us to do that very often.

By the time match day came, we were raring to go. We were really up for the game; we felt that the work we had put in on our opponents had armed us brilliantly. That good feeling continued until the moment the referee blew the whistle for the start of the game. After that, there was nothing but disappointment. From the very first moments, Romania controlled the tempo and dictated the pattern. They played us, and me in particular, very well. They had obviously concentrated some of their tactical approach on how to play me. I suppose I should have been a bit flattered. Unfortunately, it worked perfectly. I didn't play well at all – I could not seem to get into the game at all. They drove me deeper than I would have liked, and apart from a decent volley after about a quarter of an hour, which I hooked narrowly wide of the far post as Tony Adams was advancing fast, a matter of inches from getting his boot to it, I wasn't really a factor. If that volley had gone in, perhaps what became a poor World Cup for me could have been very, very good. But it just wasn't to be.

Romania's neutralisation of me was just one element of what became a parade of Romanian pluses and English minuses. One of the biggest misfortunes we could have experienced came only half an hour into the game when

Paul Ince limped off with a bad ankle injury that was to put his participation in the rest of the tournament into question. Paul is an inspirational character who works from box to box and never knows when he is beaten. His departure was a signal moment for England.

Yet there was a silver lining even to this black cloud. David Beckham had been one of the two names on everybody's lips since his omission from the Tunisia game. The other was Michael Owen – and what a part he was to play in the fortunes of England in general and yours truly in particular. But for now, it was David's chance to prove to everybody that he could do a job for his country in this World Cup. He had been put in front of the television cameras a few days earlier to express his terrible disappointment at being left out of the first game. I felt he shouldn't have been forced into the spotlight at that moment to bare his soul to the assembled media. Everybody knew the torture the lad was going through; there was no need to put him in the hot seat. It would have been far better for him to have left him alone to come to terms with the shock quietly. He was potentially a great player, but for all that he spent every day of his life in the glare of publicity, what with his celebrity engagement to Victoria, aka Posh Spice, he was still, basically, just a kid, with all the insecurities of youth to handle. As it was, the publicity that came David's way then was as nothing compared to what he had to contend with later on.

We went in at half-time with no goals on the scoreboard and were, quite honestly, lucky to have held Romania. That situation did not last much longer. The goal they scored two minutes into the second half was created by a catalogue of defensive errors from us. First, from a

Romania throw-in, Hagi got the wrong side of Graham Le Saux, and Tony Adams got pulled out of position. Sol Campbell went to cover him, but only succeeded in leaving them both a yard off their opposite numbers. Hagi got his cross in and Moldovan, the Coventry striker, smashed a half-volley past the hopelessly exposed David Seaman.

As so often happens, we were shocked by the goal into producing a good little passage of play. Gary Neville, in the team for Gareth Southgate, who had been injured in training, got himself into a good position but chose to pass when a shot might have been better. Then Anderton's pass ran across the goalmouth with nobody on the end of it. Our third opportunity again stemmed from the boot of Anderton, whose cross was headed over the bar by Paul Scholes. Amid all these chances I was still struggling to get into the action. As the hour mark came and went we were still battering on Romania's door and the cries from the fans on the terraces were growing more and more agonised. It became increasingly obvious that we were going to have to turn things round if we were to get anything out of the game. It was also pretty clear that to achieve this there was only one person coming off (me), and one coming on (Owen).

And that was to be the end of my World Cup. It was a horrible moment. Nonetheless bringing Owen on for me was the right thing to do at the time, and I was realistic enough to accept it. Owen now had about seventeen minutes to impress the manager, and the only way he was going to do that was to score. He has a priceless ability to come up with the goods when they are most needed and he demonstrated this again now. The all-important move was started by Beckham, who released Shearer down the right. Our skipper pulled the ball back from the line. Scholes was in on the end of the pass, but he failed to control the ball, and Michael came in like a flash and thumped the loose ball into the roof of the net from the edge of the 6-yard box.

Although, understandably, I was feeling a bit sorry for myself, at that instant I was thrilled for the team and also for Michael. The little Liverpool striker had done his stuff before thousands of England fans in the stadium and millions watching on television. He had been offered his chance and he had grabbed it with both hands. I knew it was going to take an awful lot for me to dislodge him now.

Michael's goal gave us the lift we needed and we created several half-chances, the best of which fell to Beckham, who shot wide. Suddenly an England victory began to look possible. Was this, after all, to be our night? Michael almost did the trick for us when his 20-yard drive beat Stelea in the Romanian goal, but it bounced back off the base of a post and was cleared to safety. Even so, we looked to be heading for a draw, which would have been a satisfactory outcome from an unsatisfactory performance. Instead, in the dying seconds of the game, we were hit by the biggest sucker punch of a goal you're ever likely to see. We were asleep and all over the shop at the vital moment when Dan Petrescu, Chelsea's dangerous right wing, popped up on the left side of the box, cut past his club team-mate Le Saux, took the ball on his chest and virtually toe-poked it between David Seaman's legs.

Glenn said after the game that defensive displays like we had put up were unacceptable. 'If you defend like that at this level, that's what's going to happen to you.' He was right, too. The England squad that wended its way back to base was very different from the jubilant one that had left Marseilles a week earlier. We knew that the performance from the whole team had just not been there, especially in the first hour. We never flowed like we had at times against Tunisia. We deserved to have been beaten, and now we had to pick ourselves up from the floor and get ready to do a hell of a lot better against Colombia.

In the aftermath of the Romania game I felt I might still have a part to play when we met Colombia. However, it wasn't long before the manager pulled me aside and told me that although he hadn't finally made up his mind about the composition of the side, in training he was going to put Owen alongside Shearer and replace David Batty with Beckham to see how it went. This experiment obviously worked to his satisfaction, because when he named the team the next day I wasn't in it and Michael was. I had harboured some hopes that I might get the nod from the start with Michael waiting in the wings to come on if the pattern did not gel again, but I think, deep down, that Owen had to play. I wasn't bitter about it. It wasn't as if I had been denied my opportunity. I had been given the chance to shine and I hadn't. Owen, on the other hand, had come on with not very much time left on the clock against Romania and had done what he was paid for – put the ball into the back of the net.

Glenn Hoddle said later, in the controversial book he wrote about our World Cup campaign, that he felt Michael could open up the Colombians with his electric pace, and that he had always intended to play him against Colombia, regardless of whether I had played a blinder against Romania and scored a couple of goals. That may be so, but it wasn't the way he put it to me during training. Perhaps he was trying to let me down gently. If he was, he didn't have to: I've been in football for a long time and my shoulders are broad enough to take disappointments. I'm a big boy now.

We were expected to beat the Colombians, who, it was felt, were pretty much a one-man team. Their playmaker, Valderrama, was getting on a bit in years but still capable of turning a game with one perfectly weighted pass, one priceless interception in midfield, one advance on the opposition goal. Well, as it turned out, the South Americans did depend on one man – but it wasn't Valderrama. He was anonymous from start to finish, if you can use the word 'anonymous' of someone with a shock of bright ginger hair that looks as if it has had 25,000 volts launched through it. No, the player Colombia depended on more than any other was the goalkeeper, Mondragon. Time and time again he kept his side clinging on to the game by the skin of their teeth as he stood alone to repel wave upon wave of attacks by an England team which made it obvious from the first minute that they were in no mood to make a premature exit from this World Cup.

I thought we were brilliant that night. We got on top right from the start and Darren Anderton gave us a perfect launch-pad for our best performance of the competition to date with a terrific goal. This time Owen turned provider as he whipped in a cross from the right, which Bermudez headed away. But it went only as far as Anderton, who, without hesitation, thumped in a right-foot volley from 10 yards which gave Mondragon no chance whatsoever. I was delighted that Darren had vindicated Glenn's faith in him. I had believed, from the first time I had seen him and played with him at Tottenham when he came to us as a youngster from Portsmouth, that he was potentially an international-class performer. Having become such close friends with him in the four years we had known each other, I had felt for him as he battled against his long succession of injuries. He had by no means been the people's choice at the start of the World Cup and it was generally perceived that he and David Beckham were competing for the same spot in the side. But Shaggy improved dramatically during the tournament, and by the time we were eliminated he had marked himself down as a great success and had proved that there was a place for both him and Beckham in the same team.

Darren's goal came after about twenty minutes, and ten minutes later it was Beckham who scored, with one of those magnificent free kicks that he takes as well as anybody in the world. Paul Ince, fit for this game, was dragged down 30 yards out and Beckham sent a curling, dipping shot over the five-man Colombian wall and into the left-hand corner of the goal. This time the courageous Mondragon was nowhere to be seen.

Once we had scored that goal, we could have got five or six – and we would have done had Mondragon not defied us for the entire second half. Scholes brought a fingertip save from him, Shearer was denied three times and two Owen efforts were beaten away, once after Sol Campbell had brilliantly evaded five frantic Colombian tackles. Had he gone on to score it would have been the goal of the decade, never mind the World Cup. It was a terrific performance produced in front of a huge English contingent in the 41,000-strong crowd – Lens was the perfect venue for the game, and especially for our fans, as it was not that far for them to travel to.

So we were through. What a relief. I must admit I had been a bit depressed at times in the days before the game, especially when I realised that for me personally it was likely that the World Cup was over. But collectively we were still here, and the result against Colombia bucked me up as much as it did the other lads in the squad. And some of them had not managed to get on to the field at all in the group games. We had finished second in the group, which meant that we would be playing Argentina in the second phase. I was not to be involved again, except possibly as a substitute, and obviously I was disappointed. But it would have taken a brave – or foolhardy – manager to have changed a winning combination. For a while I clung to the hope that the manager might play me from the start against Argentina and then bring on Michael for the last half-hour to scare the living daylights out of them with his speed. But now I look back on it all I can see that I was being just a little bit optimistic. It was never really on.

I thought the Argentinians were outstanding on the night of a match that had everything: great football, great drama, great joy, great sadness. It was a killer blow when Diego Simeone hammed it up for the first time in the match and got a sixth-minute penalty out of referee Kim Milton Nielsen. Ortega chipped the ball into the penalty area and Batistuta flicked it on. Simeone trailed his foot deliberately as David Seaman came out to challenge him and then he crashed to the ground. I think Nielsen must be a theatregoer – he obviously took quite a liking to Simeone's cynical play-acting, which was to have an even more dramatic effect on our chances in the second half. Seaman didn't deserve to have a penalty given against him, and he certainly didn't deserve to get booked. He almost retrieved the situation when he got his hand to Batistuta's spot kick, but in the end there was too much power in the shot for him to prevent it from going in the net. From where I was sitting, I had no doubt that, for the first but not the last time in the game, Simeone had cheated and got away with it.

There is a good bit of sharp practice in modern football, so much so that it has become part and parcel of the game, but I think Simeone went way over the accepted limits in this match. I don't particularly blame him for trying it on – I suppose I have done, too, from time to time. The person at fault was the referee. It's up to the man in the middle to see through the stunts players pull. You can blame anybody you like for the result of this game, but in my opinion, the buck stopped with the referee.

Nielsen played a symphony on his whistle again four minutes later when Owen was tipped over by Ayala after a jet-propelled run through the Argentinian defence. Penalty. Of course, Alan Shearer scored, driving the ball high into the net. Nobody in the England camp expected anything else. One each, all to play for.

The match now developed into one of the best I've seen since I've been a member of the England squad. Beckham was brilliant, Anderton tormented the defence, Owen looked a threat every time he got the ball. For Argentina I thought Ariel Ortega was absolutely brilliant. I don't think I've ever seen one player pull so many nutmegs on so many different opponents – it must have been half a dozen.

From trailing 1–0 not long after the start we were soon one up, thanks to what was probably the goal of the tournament. Michael Owen got the ball just inside Argentina's half, controlled it brilliantly in one touch with the outside of his right boot, left Chamot for dead, side-stepped Ayala then scored with a perfect cross-shot from 20 yards, giving Roa in the Argentinian goal no chance at all.

It was just about the perfect striker's goal. It had everything – skill, pace, awareness and an immaculate finish. If there was a better one scored in the whole competition, I didn't see it. The whole ground was in uproar, and on the bench we were on our feet hugging each other before Roa had picked the ball out of the back of the net.

And if Paul Scholes had scored when he got on the back of their defence, it might have been all over. Sadly, Paul put his shot a foot wide of the post. A 3–1 deficit would have been a killing psychological blow to Argentina, and they may well not have been able to come back from it. As it was, they hit us instead on the stroke of half-time with a well-rehearsed free kick. Sol Campbell fouled Lopez outside the penalty area and, while everybody was expecting a Batistuta shot, instead Veron slipped a pass to the side of our wall and Zanetti peeled off, controlled the ball in a flash and drove it past David Seaman. Ironically, we knew about this free-kick tactic – we'd seen it on video – but we just weren't quite up to speed with the plot when they brought it into play. It was a major disappointment to us, but we reasoned at half-time that we were better off than we had been five minutes into the game, and there was no reason why we shouldn't go on from there and win.

The decisive moment came five minutes into the second half. It was the moment which effectively put England out of the World Cup. The initial culprit was, again, that man Simeone, who crashed into the back of David Beckham, splattering him all over the place. Simeone then compounded his dirty tricks by tapping David on the head as he lay on the ground, obviously in some pain. Becks reacted by just lifting his foot. He couldn't have known where Simeone was, because he was lying face down, but he just made contact with the back of Simeone's leg. From our vantage point on the bench we could hear Simeone let out a wail as though he had been shot or something, right in front of the referee. Nielsen was sucked in by the dramatics and immediately sent David off.

Ninety per cent of English referees would have said something along the lines of 'Who are you trying to kid, son?' and got on with the game, but for Mr Nielsen it was enough to prompt him to whip the red card out of his pocket. I'm convinced more than ever now, having seen the incident again and again on television, that the referee allowed himself to be conned, although I note that David Elleray, one of our own top officials, said later that Nielsen could not have done anything else. I must remember to mind my Ps and Qs whenever Mr Elleray is officiating a game I'm involved in.

I have to say that Becks was a bit silly, but that's all it was – just a bit of silliness. How that justified the press and the sickening public reaction to which he was subjected afterwards defeats me. I can't believe he was made the scapegoat for us not winning the World Cup. If Becks had done something like Dennis Bergkamp did, stamping on Sinisa Mihajlovic in the Holland–Yugoslavia game, I could understand it. As far as I'm concerned, Bergkamp should have been dismissed after that incident, then sent home in disgrace, and yet he didn't even get booked. If he had been given the treatment Beckham subsequently had to put up with, perhaps it would have been more understandable. Once again it just highlights the biggest single grouse that players have against referees: inconsistency.

Whatever the rights and wrongs of the issue, Beckham was sent off, and then we really had no alternative but to defend. It killed Argentina's game as well, because they now had a hell of a job to break down our two-banks-of-four defensive unit. After what I'd say were the best forty-five minutes of football in the entire competition, the game was dead in the water as a spectacle and so were any realistic chances we had of going through to the quarter-finals.

Defending in numbers didn't mean that we completely gave up trying to score goals, though, and indeed, some of our players, most of our fans and even, I'm told, the television commentators, thought Sol Campbell had done the trick for us when he headed home on the far post. However, the referee disallowed the goal because of a foul by Alan Shearer on Roa. I was as indignant as the rest at the time, but I've seen videos of the incident since and I must say that the referee was right to penalise Shearer. As for Sol, he just lost it when he thought he'd scored the winning goal. I'd never seen the Sol Man like that before. He was on cloud nine. He came haring over to the bench with his arms raised and a look of jubilation on his grinning face, only to be confronted by all of us telling him to get back on the field because they'd taken a quick free kick. I suppose the incident did have an element of farce about it, but all we could see was Argentina advancing on our penalty area while one of our three remaining centre backs was celebrating a non-existent goal.

I don't know how the other players felt as the game ran its ninety minutes and we went into golden-goal time, but for me it was purgatory. My stomach was twisted up in knots, I felt sick and I couldn't breathe as my mates on the pitch sweated and toiled their way through thirty minutes of extra time. The fact that I wasn't on the pitch only made it worse. I just felt impotent.

As the extra time wore on, the team inevitably began to wilt. The manager had to make changes and get some fresh legs on to the field. He replaced Graham Le Saux, who had cramps in his calf, with Gareth Southgate; then he pulled off Scholes and put Paul Merson on in his place. With penalties looming, I thought I might have been given the chance to take the field for the last few minutes, if only to take one of our spot kicks. I would have fancied taking one of those, even though I have missed a few in my time. The boss, however, thought otherwise, and instead he sent David Batty on for Anderton. In his book Glenn Hoddle said that he thought about putting me on in the last few minutes but decided that he 'couldn't take the risk'. It's an uncomfortable feeling, to say the least, to learn that my manager thought it would have been dangerous to trust me to help out for a few moments in the defensive system we were being forced to play. As it was, the changes left us a bit short of penalty-takers on the field.

But the die was now cast and I, together with the other lads who had not been put on to the field, would have to suffer the torture of watching our team-mates decide our fate. And inevitably our extra time ran out and, for the third time at a crucial stage of an important international competition, our success or failure would have to be determined by penalties. It may have made for great drama, but it also left us in indescribable tension. We went on the pitch to try to reassure the other lads that they could do it, they were equal to the task of taking England on to further glory.

That sequence of spot kicks will never be wiped from my memory. It's a toss-up whether it is worse to be a member of the penalty squad or to have to watch the scene being played out before you, but I know what I'd rather do: take a kick. I can tell you this – I have never in my whole career been in as much agony as I was during those few dreadful minutes in St Etienne. Berti, who had come on for Argentina in extra time, went first and scored, then Alan Shearer nervelessly slotted his second penalty of the night, again high into the net past the helpless Roa. We could hardly bear to look, but for a few brief moments we were glad we'd forced ourselves to watch as Crespo missed. Seconds later our yells of joy turned to groans as Paul Ince failed with his kick. Still 1–1. Veron made it 2–1 to them with a well-taken shot, then Merson showed immense character as Roa played for time, claiming that the ball wasn't properly on the spot. That little bit of gamesmanship didn't do him any good, because Paul coolly put away his shot. Gallardo put Argentina back into the lead, and then it was the turn of Michael Owen, who finished off a display in which he had shown a maturity far beyond his tender years by scoring easily.

We were still in it at 3–3. Crunch time was coming, though, especially after Ayala put Argentina 4–3 ahead. Before this there had been some leeway; now we simply had to score. David Batty was the man entrusted with the job of keeping England in the World Cup, and as the whole footballing world now knows, he missed. We were out. In a one awful second our dream had come to an end. It was dreadful for David, but he is an incredibly strong character. Deep inside, his heart was breaking – we all knew that – but he behaved with great dignity and fortitude as he walked back towards us. It wasn't until later that he revealed he'd never even taken a penalty before, much less scored from one.

David and Incey joined an exclusive club that night, a club that nobody wants to be in. It has only three other members: Gareth Southgate, who missed the vital penalty in Euro '96, and Stuart Pearce and Chris Waddle, who faltered in the World Cup in Italy in 1990.

Penalty shoot-outs are vicious things, and I wish there was a better way of deciding who wins and who loses, but I don't think there is. There have been alternative suggestions, such as to play on to a finish after the 120 minutes of normal time plus extra time are up, but I don't think that would work. You cannot just keep on playing when one side or the other will be faced with another important game very soon afterwards. You would be drained by the physical effort. Indeed, Argentina proved how debilitating even extra time and penalties can be in their next game, in which they were beaten by Holland, largely because they were still shattered after their exertions against us.

The whole squad was quiet after we had got back into the dressing room. Shearer, our inspirational captain, sat on the floor gazing into the distance, seeing nothing. Tony Adams was a bit more agitated, but most of us just sat there, stunned. We had come so far together and now it was all over. We couldn't believe that we were to take no further part in a tournament we honestly believed we could win. No matter what the critics say, there weren't many better sides than us in the whole competition. We had some outstanding players, players any nation on earth would like to have in their team, and they were supported by some very good footballers around them. I truly believe we had the potential to go all the way, but we did not get the rub of the green against Argentina, and now we had been beaten in the cruellest manner.

I might not have played against Argentina, but that didn't mean I was going to be spared by the press in the aftermath. One notoriously unscrupulous tabloid reporter did a knocking piece in which he said that I had been spotted on TV laughing when the ten-man England side were up against it in the second half. I had, indeed, been filmed sharing a small joke with Steve McManaman to relieve the tension in the second half. But why on earth allowing myself to smile should lead anyone to call into question my total commitment to the cause is beyond me. I see little reason to dignify this particular hack's disgraceful, dirt-digging story with an explanation. All I can say is that there are a hundred different ways to deal with pressure, just as there are a hundred different ways to twist facts to suit your pathetic need for a story. I could also point out that earlier in the match I had been shown on television to be the first to leap from my seat when Alan Shearer scored from the penalty spot, but that camera shot, of course, went unreported.

This sort of stuff doesn't affect me any more. I've become used to it. But I do worry sometimes about the hurt it causes my family and my girlfriend. They haven't had the chance to develop a protective shell against it as I have done. Being used to it doesn't mean you have to like it, but if you're going to do a job that puts you in the public eye, you have to learn to live with it.

When we came back from the World Cup we were told we had eleven days off before we needed to start pre-season training, so I took Charlie to Florida, where we two kids trooped round Disneyworld and spent some quality time together. We went on all the fast rides and saw all the sights, and I think I enjoyed it as much as he did. It was a great holiday, but I wanted to do something more to cheer

Charlie up after England were knocked out of the World Cup, so while we were away I did some telephoning round. When we got back to the airport in England we were met by a lady who presented Charlie with an envelope. Inside it, to his surprise, he found tickets for the World Cup final. We were going straight on to France. In spite of how tired he was – we had already travelled all through the night – he was beside himself with glee. We got to France, had a bit of sleep, then went to the Stade de France.

Charlie and I arrived for the match well before the start and watched all the people filing into the great stadium. I couldn't help myself having those 'if only' thoughts. It could so easily have been England they were coming to see, and I just couldn't get that out of my mind.

The final itself was a bit of a let-down, to be honest. There had been a lot of talk about Ronaldo. I had watched him play against Morocco, when he scored the first goal in a 3–0 win, and he looked plain uninterested. He looked just as uninterested in the final. But that's the way he plays, seeming bored with it all until he bursts through with that incredible power he has and blasts on to the scene.

Apart from their performance in the final, I thought that Brazil looked the most accomplished side in the competition. The Argentinians also impressed me, especially in that wonderful cut-and-thrust first half against us; the Dutch were very composed and made a formidable team. Finally, you couldn't take it away from France. They played very well in the final, and the brilliant Zinedine Zidane – for me, one of the players of the tournament – scored two wonderful goals in a thoroughly professional and committed performance by the whole side.

The atmosphere in the stadium was magnificent, but although the crowds blocked the Champs Elysées until the next morning, I gather, the mood just after the French victory was strangely subdued. If it had been us up there collecting the Jules Rimet Trophy, the whole of England would still have been singing five days later. But it wasn't, and there was no useful purpose to be served by thinking about what might have been. The World Cup was already behind us: now for the future.

Chapter Eighteen

Final Thoughts

All I've written so far concerns the past. My past, and the part that others have played in it, happiness, sorrow, ambitions achieved, good and bad memories of what has gone before. But what of the future?

I like to think I'm a pretty resilient character. My advice to would-be footballers is simple: when people are raving about you and praising you to the skies, remember you're just a good player, not a god. That way, when you're going through the rocky times, you have the sure and certain knowledge that you *are* a good footballer to fall back on. You are never, ever, as good or as bad as they tell you you are.

Just remember what happened to me. I returned home from France '98 a disappointed man, on the whole dissatisfied with what I had achieved in the most recent year of my career. I had gone to Manchester United, the greatest club in the country, to win honours, yet, apart from the essentially meaningless Charity Shield, that first season I had ended up with nothing. And I had had a tough time convincing the fans at Old Trafford that I was a fit person to pull the famous red jersey over my head. My second season with United, blighted as it was by injury, was hardly a bed of roses, either. But just look how it ended: not only did my club seize that glorious treble, but I could be well and truly satisfied that I had made my own contribution to our achievement. After scoring at Wembley in our FA Cup final victory and being made Man of the Match, my joy was sealed by that vital goal two minutes from the end of the European Cup final on that thrilling night in Barcelona.

So as to my future – well, I still have confidence in my ability to continue doing the business for Manchester United for a few years yet. The 2002 World Cup might not be a realistic ambition, bit I'm not prepared to accept that I have reached the end of my international days just yet, and I'd love to be involved in Euro 2000. I've had lulls in my career before, and every time I have turned them into something positive. The only difference between me today and me then is that now I'm thirty-three, but maybe that has its advantages too: perhaps my experience will come in even handier than it has before. I have never been a player who has relied on blistering pace – I've always preferred the subtle approach. I can say in all modesty that although I've scored just about as many goals as any current Premiership striker, I've made a few for other people, too, and that's an achievement not all my fellow goalscorers can claim. For the moment I'm certainly not ruling anything out as far as England is concerned. Once you stop believing in yourself, that's the time to stop. I haven't reached that stage by any stretch of the imagination.

For the moment I've no fixed plans about what I would like to do when my days as a footballer are over. It's been my whole life for fifteen years – almost half the time I've been on the planet – and since I'm not yet ready to stop, I'm not going to make any premature decisions. One thing I do know, and that is that I want to play at a decent level for as long as I can. Not for me the slide down the leagues until I end up in some forgotten backwater, no longer remembered as a player who was good enough to play for Tottenham Hotspur, Manchester United and England, but rather as a hopelessly optimistic has-been seeking to rekindle the glories of his lost youth – or even worse, not really caring as long as there's a few quid coming in at the end of the month. I know that some players have little choice but to follow this path, and I'm not criticising them for it. It's not for me, that's all.

There are things in my life I would like to do when it's time to hang up my boots; things I can't do while I'm still a professional footballer. I'd like to spend more time with my son and to play a bigger part in his life; I'd like to go skiing for the first time; I'd like to go to the Caribbean at Christmas – and a hundred other things.

Some people have been kind enough to describe me as the thinking man's footballer, and to say that I would be an ideal candidate for coaching or management. I wouldn't rule that out, either. I do have ideas about the game which I feel I could perhaps pass on to the younger generation. I think a lot about the tactics and strategy of the game and I like nothing better than to get involved in discussions about it with coaches and other players. At the moment, though, it's too early to tell whether that is the route for me. There are many roads I could choose when the time comes, but for now I don't want to think about any but trying to continue as one of the country's better players. The buzz is still there, and I firmly believe that it will be with me for a good while yet. I'm lucky that, by and large,

I seem to remain pretty free of injury, and as long as I stay that way, I still want to be a part of the game at the top.

On a personal level, like most people, I would like to achieve some stability in my life. In spite of what some of the newspapers would have you believe, I'm basically a home-loving individual who wants to settle down one day into family life. I'm lucky in that I have come from a happy family background, and my parents, my brother, and, of course, my son, are still the most important people to me. My long, sometimes stormy relationship with my girlfriend, Nicola, has been difficult at times but happily we got back together again after the split before the World Cup, and I hope that this time it will be for good.

I would be the first person to hold up my hand and admit that I've been blessed. From my earliest days I knew what I wanted to be when I grew up, and, unlike so many people who are forced to accept second-best when it comes to their dreams, I've achieved what I set out to do. I have come a long way in the last twenty-five years, and I've got a long way to travel yet. I never thought when I was banging in five goals in an 8–1 victory for Selwyn in the final of the Birmingham Cup in Walthamstow all those years ago that one day I would be scoring for England and playing in the World Cup finals. But I did it, and I did it my way, as the cliché goes. And I'm proud to say that I'm still as excited now about the wonderful game of football as I was when I was a boy of eight smashing a ball up an alleyway in Highams Park. I've had bad times and good, and the good times have outweighed the bad times by a long way. It's been a good life, and one that I wouldn't have swapped for anything. I've achieved a fair bit and met and worked with some remarkable people: Maurice Newman, who saw something in me as a kid; Bob Pearson, who gave me my first chance at Millwall; George Graham, John Docherty, Brian Clough, Terry Venables, Alex Ferguson, Glenn Hoddle. I thank them all, for I would not have become what I am today without them. I hope I haven't disappointed them and I hope, too, that I've given a few people some pleasure along the way.